CHEVRON

Patrick Stephens Limited, a member of the Haynes Publishing Group, has published authoritative, quality books for enthusiasts for more than twenty years. During that time the company has established a reputation as one of the world's leading publishers of books on aviation, maritime, military, model-making, motor cycling, motoring, motor racing, railway and railway modelling subjects. Readers or authors with suggestions for books they would like to see published are invited to write to The Editorial Director, Patrick Stephens Limited, Sparkford, Nr Yeovil, Somerset, BA22 7JJ.

CHEVRON
THE DEREK BENNETT STORY

DAVID GORDON
FOREWORD BY BRIAN REDMAN

PSL

Patrick Stephens Limited

© David Gordon 1991

All rights reserved. No part of this publication may be reproduced, stored in a retrieval system or transmitted, in any form or by any means, electronic, mechanical, photocopying, recording or otherwise, without prior permission in writing from Patrick Stephens Ltd.

British Library Cataloguing in Publication Data

Gordon, David
Chevron: the Derek Bennett story.
1. Racing cars
I. Title
629.228

ISBN 1-85260-318-6

Patrick Stephens Limited is part of the Haynes Publishing Group P.L.C., Sparkford, Nr Yeovil, Somerset BA22 7JJ.

Printed in Great Britain by J. H. Haynes & Co. Ltd.

10 9 8 7 6 5 4 3 2 1

Contents

Acknowledgements   **6**
Foreword, by Brian Redman   **7**
Introduction   **9**

Chapter	1	The dream that came true	**13**
Chapter	2	The competitive spirit takes off	**17**
Chapter	3	Little workshops, big ideas	**27**
Chapter	4	Straight out of the box – the first Chevrons	**45**
Chapter	5	Taking on the world	**62**
Chapter	6	They make single-seaters in Bolton too	**83**
Chapter	7	B16 – the ultimate Chevron?	**97**
Chapter	8	Classic sports cars and the path to Formula 2	**118**
Chapter	9	The fairy story continues	**136**
Chapter	10	Squaring up to real life	**151**
Chapter	11	Surviving the oil crisis	**167**
Chapter	12	Finding a successful formula	**180**
Chapter	13	Famous victories in Formula 2	**199**
Chapter	14	'It's no more dangerous than driving a racing car'	**215**
Chapter	15	Postponing the inevitable	**226**
Chapter	16	The Chevron tradition lives on	**245**

Appendix 1   Chevron Type Numbers   **253**
Appendix 2   Major Chevron Successes   **259**
Index   **268**

Acknowledgements

MY thanks go to everyone below for their help in making this book possible: Kent Abrahamsson, Derek Alderson, Roger Andreason, Peter Ashcroft, Robert Ashcroft, Neil Bailey, June Bennett, Rodney Bloor, John Bridges, Albert Brown, Bobby Brown, Tony Charnell, Brian Classick, Jim Crawford, Derek Daly, Nigel Dickson, Keith Duckworth, Neil Edwards, Bob Faulkner, Derek Faulkner, Graham Gauld, Peter Gethin, Robin Gordon, Colin Greenhalgh, Adrian Grundy, Brian Hart, Alan Henry, John Hine, Graham Hobson, Tommy Humphreys, John Lepp, Doug Linton, Vin Malkie, Digby Martland, Alan Minshaw, Stirling Moss, John O'Donnell, Fred Opert, Paul Owens, Riccardo Patrese, Brian Redman, Paul Rice, Keke Rosberg, Steve Sheldon, Doug Shierson, Peter Shorthouse, Geoff Smith, Robin Smith, Wendy Smith, George Walker, John Watson, Dave Willars, Reine Wisell.

The Chevron logo and Chevron name are the property of Chevron Cars Limited, Winchester, England, and are used with permission.

Foreword by Brian Redman

IT was a great pleasure to know that a book was to be written on the life and cars of that remarkable racing car designer, constructor, and driver, Derek Bennett. It was an additional pleasure to be asked to write a foreword to that book.

Although I was aware of his success with the Clubmans cars, I did not have any personal contact with Derek Bennett until David Bridges commissioned the building of the B5 with the BRM, 2-litre Tasman engine in 1967. Driving this led to outings in the 'factory' BMW-engined B8, including the full Springbok series in 1968. Looking back it seems incredible that Paul Owens and I would set off for Johannesburg, Cape Town, Bulawayo, Pietermaritzburg, and other African destinations of dubious distinction in a borrowed International estate car with 150,000 miles on the clock, towing an open trailer, and with almost no spares!

By this time, a close working relationship had developed between Derek, Paul and myself, and when it became time to test the exciting new B16 coupé in 1969, excellent progress was made. Derek was a first class driver and some of the fastest and most productive testing I was ever involved with took place with Chevron. I would drive the car — usually at Oulton Park — and make some comments, then Derek would drive and say, 'Yes, you're right, and I think it's because of so and so.' Then he and Paul would dash off back to Bolton, work half the night making modifications, and reappear at Oulton the following day for more of the same!

The performance of the B16 was everything that could be hoped for, but at Paul Ricard the following April we were shocked by the speed of Jo Bonnier's Lola T210, an open car, which was much lighter. Immediately an open version of the B16 was requested (begged for!) and, by July, Derek was hard at work forming aluminium panels for the new body of what was to become the B16-Spyder. Once again this 'new' Chevron was superb, and was responsible for Chevron Cars winning the 1970 2-litre Manufacturers' Championship. Even today the B19 stands out in historic racing and is truly one of the outstanding sports cars of its — or any other — era.

In 1972, having had a miserable Formula 5000 season in a McLaren M18, I asked Derek if he could build me a Formula 5000 car. Ten weeks later the B24 was rolled out and once again, out of the box, it was a winner, being under the lap record at Oulton Park the first day out and winning its first race there.

Since 1982 I have continued to drive a B19 in American historic races and am constantly amazed by just how good the car is, even in comparison with modern ground-effect cars — proof, if it were needed, of Derek's belief in structural integrity combined with light weight.

Derek's death in 1978 was a great loss to motor racing, to his many friends, to his employees, and to the town of Bolton. This quiet, unassuming man ranked at the very top of his chosen profession — he is sadly missed.

Brian Redman
Ponte Vedra Beach, Florida
July 1990

Introduction

WHEN I was 12 years old my voice broke and the church choir no longer had the need of my services on a Sunday morning. So I took to riding shotgun in the back of John Lepp's Triumph 2.5PI Estate car, as John and his mechanic — my stepfather Robin Gordon — travelled the country in pursuit of the *Motoring News* GT Championship, with Don Parker trailer and Chevron GT in tow. My job was to lunge over the back seat into the assembled tools and spare parts and quell the slightest squeak or rattle at its first occurrence — and to watch for the numerous police cars, which in those days lurked up every slip road, or hid in front of apparently innocent lorries. John was only ever stopped once, and that was accelerating down the slip road on to the M6 at Knutsford — strictly speaking before we moved into my jurisdiction.

I had fallen in love with John's car at the previous year's Oulton Park Gold Cup meeting, in September 1966, when he wheeled out this sleek new replacement for his Lotus Elan for the first time. When we got to those race meetings there would usually be at least two more Chevrons there, for Derek Bennett and Digby Martland, and there was an infectious feeling of all being part of a big team. As my father worked on John's car, Derek would often wander over, and if there was a problem he would stand there, quietly thinking for a while, his arms folded in front of him, his chin resting in one raised hand. Then he would suggest his cure for the problem.

As John's Chevron continued to win I grew increasingly impressed by the thought that this man actually made Chevrons himself. Never having felt the necessity of giving my support either to Manchester United or Manchester City, I became instead a Chevron supporter. I kept scrapbooks of *Motoring News* cuttings, filled notebooks with information about the cars, and willed them on to win everywhere they raced.

After practice for the two-day Spring Cup meeting at Oulton Park in April 1968, I went up to the factory in Bolton for the first time and savoured the atmosphere that characterised Chevrons. In amongst the new cars that were being built, the cars that had been brought back from Oulton were being prepared for the next day's race. Mechanics, drivers and Chevron's own staff worked into the night, straightening damaged cars, or solving mechanical problems with others. But the thing that most impressed me was when it came time to eat and Paul Owens took an old oil can with one side cut out of it, filled it with water, dropped in a can of tomato soup, and set to work on it with a blow torch. This was real excitement!

Whenever I saw Derek after that I would ask what cars he had in the factory, what colour they were, and who was going to buy them, and it all went down in the book. As Chevron's success grew and they built more and more cars, Derek would joke that I knew more about the cars he had built than he did. Then when Brian Redman tested the new B16 with its FVC engine for the first time, Derek gave me a photograph of it that he'd taken himself. It was given pride of place in Volume 11 of the scrapbook.

As my own Chevron archives grew I always had it firmly fixed in my mind that one day I would write a book about Chevrons. When they were a world-famous Formula 1 team, I would be the one who could tell the story of how it all started. In the meantime, my interest in racing broadened, I began to write race reports for *Motoring News* and *Autosport* and, after leaving university, I went to work for *Motoring News*. Called upon to write my first feature, in March 1975, I decided I would go up to Bolton and interview Derek about Chevron's first 10 years. By this time Derek had a high-powered publicity director to save him from the tiresome business of having to talk to the press and it seemed to mystify him that anyone should want to talk to him anyway. But he agreed to do the interview and we sat in his office and talked about the way he had achieved his success and where Chevron might go in the future.

By this time Chevron's successes throughout the world had become too numerous for my scrapbooks to cope with and they had been confined to a box somewhere. When Derek was killed hang gliding three years later, I assumed that was where they would stay. Later that year I moved out of motor racing into the mainstream of journalism and I didn't see another Chevron until 1985, when I went to a historic meeting and was amazed to see a race full of scrapping Chevron B8s. I dug out the old scrapbooks and the ownership records and started trying to fill in some of the gaps in the life stories of the cars. As I renewed old acquaintances, I was constantly asked if I was writing a book. Eventually, I came to think that that was what I should be doing.

When I started work on the book the first person I stuck my tape recorder in front of was John Lepp. 'I'm not doing

INTRODUCTION

this for you — I'm doing it for Derek,' he said with his usual caustic charm. I chose to take the comment as a joke not an insult, but it was a remark that kept coming back to me as I travelled thousands of miles, tracing the people who had known and worked with Derek through his life. Some of them I knew well, some remembered me only vaguely, while others had never met me before. But they all willingly gave their time to talk about Derek Bennett and his Chevron cars.

An old friend of Derek's told me that he felt privileged to have known him, and that feeling seemed to be echoed by everyone I spoke to. Over the years a few people came to know Derek very well, but to most people who met him or drove his cars he remained an enigma — a quiet, unassuming genius, who built racing cars that looked like racing cars were supposed to and that were almost guaranteed to win races.

Because Chevrons always remained so much Derek Bennett's personal creations, I felt that the only way to tell the story of Chevron was to tell the story of Derek Bennett. It is a modern fairy tale of a very ordinary man with a very extraordinary talent, who started out mending cars in a lock-up garage in the back streets of industrial Salford and became one of the world's leading racing car manufacturers. On the way the success of Chevron became entwined with the success of the drivers who raced the cars and the Chevron story contains some fascinating episodes from the careers of many top racing drivers — among them no fewer than six World Champions.

Trying to write the story of Derek Bennett was like trying to make a jigsaw when all the pieces are hidden and nobody can tell you how many pieces there should be. I still cannot be sure that there are not some pieces missing, but I hope I have made a picture that is recognisable.

In writing this book, I have tried to establish what happened and why it happened the way it did. Many people played a part in the success of Chevron. I have not set out in any way to place their contributions in some sort of order of importance, but I have merely tried to acknowledge everyone whose involvement in some way influenced the progress of Chevron Cars.

So many people have helped me in the research for this book that it would be impossible to detail their contributions individually. But I would like to thank Paul Owens especially for finding the time in his hectic schedule to be subjected to some gruelling interviews over many hours, as well as answering endless queries over the phone. I am also very grateful to Derek's sisters, Wendy and June, for being so open with me about their family life and Derek's childhood, as well as letting me use some of their family photographs. Doug Linton's help has been invaluable as well. I must also thank Brian

Redman — in so many ways the epitome of a Chevron driver — for agreeing to write the Foreword.

I respect the honesty with which everyone has spoken to me about their relationships with Derek Bennett and their own involvement with Chevron, and I have been moved by the tremendous admiration for him which they all felt. I hope this book does justice to his achievements and to his memory.

David Gordon
Stockport, England
August 1990

CHAPTER 1

The dream that came true

IT was turning into quite a satisfying weekend for Peter Gethin. Yesterday his new Chevron B24 had annihilated the opposition to win the opening round of the Rothmans European Formula 5000 Championship. Now here he was a day later, just 10 laps from the finish of the Brands Hatch Race of Champions Formula 1 race, holding down third place in that same Formula 5000 car.

It was barely 18 months since he had won the fastest Grand Prix in history, crossing the line first at Monza in his BRM P160 in one of the closest finishes ever seen. Some of the drivers he had beaten that day were in this race — Ronnie Peterson, Emerson Fittipaldi, Mike Hailwood, Howden Ganley ... It felt good to be racing against them again, even if he was back in a Formula 5000 car after his acrimonious parting with Louis Stanley's BRM team.

Those same P160 BRMs had started the Race of Champions from the first three places on the grid, but Niki Lauda and Vern Schuppan had both gone out, and Jean-Pierre Beltoise was behind him now after a pit stop for a tyre change. James Hunt had closed right up on him in the Surtees TS9, hired for him by Lord Hesketh. But it was his first Formula 1 race and Hunt was coming under pressure himself from Beltoise. Gethin was confident he could keep them both behind him for a few more laps. Finishing in the first three in this race was going to be sweet.

Then, with less than five laps to go, as he came up towards the fast, right-handed Hawthorn Bend, he was confronted with waved yellow flags and frantic activity. Up against the bank on the left of the track was the smouldering wreckage of Mike Hailwood's Surtees TS14 — the car that had been leading. A lower link had fractured on the suspension, sending Hailwood slewing out of control at around 150 mph. The car had hit the bank on the right and bounced back across the track before finally coming to a halt and catching fire.

Hailwood had jumped out, unhurt but cross, and as Gethin picked his way carefully through the débris, he knew he was now second, with just the McLaren M23 of Denny Hulme

CHEVRON

ahead of him. This race was getting harder to believe by the minute.

Then his pit signals started to show that he was catching Denny; and soon he could see for himself that he was. The McLaren had to be in trouble. A thrust bearing had broken on the clutch and Hulme was stuck in third gear. As they came into the long right-hander at Clearways for the penultimate time, Gethin's blue Chevron was right behind the white and orange Yardley McLaren. As Hulme laboured onto the pit straight, Gethin dived past and into the lead.

Less than two minutes later it was all over. In front of 44,500 people at the circuit and millions watching on BBC Television, the Chevron took the waved chequered flag — the first Formula 5000 car ever to win a Formula 1 race. Gethin's hand punched the air and everyone in the Chevron pit jumped up and down, sharing delight and disbelief in equal measure. The eight years since Derek Bennett built his very first Chevron had often seemed something of a fairytale. But this time the men from Bolton had really slain the giants. Tomorrow morning they would pinch themselves and discover it had all been a dream.

But the next morning, there was the face of Peter Gethin beaming out from the front page of the *Daily Mail* — the race's sponsor — as he received his trophy from Mrs Vere Harm-

Peter Gethin waves from the cockpit of his B24 after winning the Race of Champions.
(*Photo LAT.*)

THE DREAM THAT CAME TRUE

sworth, wife of the chairman of the newspaper's publishers, Associated Newspapers. And inside, there was his car, with the Chevron badge emblazoned along the side for all to see. Suddenly the fortunes of Bolton Wanderers football team wasn't the only Monday morning talking point in the Lancashire town. The world had heard of Chevron racing cars. Meanwhile the motoring press were asking, now that his cars had won their first Formula 1 race, when was Derek Bennett going to build his first Formula 1 car?

It was a question they were unable to ask him at Brands Hatch, for the simple reason that he was not there. The 1973 season seemed to have got off to a particularly hectic start for Chevron. Three of Derek Bennett's brand new B25 Formula 2 cars were already out in South Africa, where they had been racing in the national Formula 1 series. After the success of the prototype Formula 5000 car the previous year, there were a number of orders for the production version of the B24, and four of them were wanted for the Race of Champions weekend which began with practice for the Formula 5000 cars on Friday 16 March.

The car which Peter Gethin was to race was eventually destined for the United States, where Gethin would be driving it for Doug Shierson's Marathon Oil team. Shierson would be at Brands to see the car put through its paces before he took

Moment of triumph as Peter Gethin acknowledges the crowd from the winner's podium at Brands Hatch. (*Photo LAT.*)

it back to America. The car was finished with a couple of days to spare and Derek took it to Oulton Park on the Thursday, using his own formidable driving skills to give it a shake down.

Two more B24s, for Yorkshireman Tony Dean and his American team-mate, Bobby Brown, were finished at three o'clock on the Friday morning. They would have to compete at Brands in familiar Chevron fashion — 'straight out of the box'. Time caught up with the unceasing workers at Bolton before they could finish the fourth B24 — the car with which Belgian Teddy Pilette would win the European Championship for Count Rudi van der Straten's team.

It had been just as hectic one week earlier when the Formula 2 season kicked off at Mallory Park. Dave Morgan's customer B25 had been ready to take the grid, but Peter Gethin's works B25 had barely made it, and the second works car for Gerry Birrell was still in the factory.

With everyone away at Brands Hatch for three days, the Chevron factory in John Haslam's old mill in Bolton was how Derek Bennett liked it — quiet. Now he could get on with the business of building racing cars unmithered. Birrell's car needed to be ready for Hockenheim in three weeks' time when the European Formula 2 series would really get under way, and there were B23 sports cars to be finished in time for the opening round of the European 2-litre Sports Car Championship at Paul Ricard on the same day.

When there was work to be done, Derek Bennett got on and did it. So he wasn't at Brands Hatch on 18 March to see his greatest triumph unfold. Indeed he didn't even watch the Race of Champions on television. His girlfriend could tell him who had won when he went over for a meal after he had finished at the factory.

To those immersed in the egotistical world of international motor racing it might have seemed strange that 'Mr Chevron' was not in the thick of the celebrations at Brands Hatch, accepting the accolades and savouring the triumph. Just what kind of a man was this?

If you asked that question then, or now, to any of the people who counted themselves privileged to have known Derek Bennett, they would answer the same thing — Derek was . . . Derek.

CHAPTER 2

The competitive spirit takes off

ON the last day of 1933, at the church of St John in Cheetham, north Manchester, the Reverend Charles Burke baptised Antony Derek, the first child of Ethel May and Arthur Bennett. All had not gone well with the birth of the baby on 28 November. His neck was cricked over to one side, but doctors at the Flixton Cottage Hospital were confident that it could be operated on when he was older. So for now the worrying was over and the family could look forward to a happy New Year.

There was nothing to hint at the future that lay in store for Derek Bennett as his family went home to their rented bungalow in the growing Manchester suburb of Flixton, close to the Manchester Ship Canal, where his father worked as a clerk. The Bennetts had once been Derbyshire farriers, but Arthur Bennett's father had come to Manchester to join the army of men who were building the Manchester Ship Canal. When this great feat of engineering was opened in 1894 he had found more work with the Ship Canal Company where his son, too, now earned his living.

Arthur Bennett was one of only two children, but Ethel May Rider was used to a livelier household. Her mother had given birth to 11 children of which seven had survived. Her father was a bookmaker and did well enough for the family to be able to afford domestic servants. Ethel herself became a good seamstress and dressmaker and always encouraged the creative side in her own children.

When Derek was about four years old the Bennetts bought their first house – a new, three-bedroomed semi in Merton Road, Prestwich, a northern suburb of Manchester that was becoming increasingly popular. Ethel was keen to move into the area to be closer to her sister, Mabel, and it seemed a good time to move with Derek due to start school shortly. The house would also give them extra space when they were ready to add to their family. The operation to straighten Derek's neck was carried out successfully and he was able to start at St Margaret's Parish School. In the summer of 1940, June — the first of his two sisters — was born. But the country was now at war. Arthur Bennett had joined the Royal Air Force and been given a clerical position in Southampton.

The Ship Canal and the adjacent Trafford Park industrial complex were prime targets for German bombs, so Ethel rented out the house and took Derek and June 30 miles over the Pennines to the Yorkshire village of Cullingworth, close to Haworth and its 'wuthering' moors. Her eldest brother, George, and his wife lived in the village and had found them a cottage on a farm nearby. While they were there Derek gained a second sister, Wendy. At the age of eight he became seriously ill with pneumonia. Although he had recovered well from the recent operation on his neck, his general health had never been good and he suffered from asthma and eczema. As his mother nursed him through his pneumonia his life seemed more precious than ever. When he recovered, there was nothing she would not do for him.

Life in the country seemed to suit Derek, but from an early age he obviously found his two younger sisters something of an imposition, especially when he was supposed to be looking after them. He once left the two little girls upstairs in the cottage while he repaired to the outside toilet with his chemistry set. Demonstrating that his natural flair would lie in other branches of science, he managed to set fire to the building, creating a difficult task for the fire brigade who had to manoeuvre their fire engine down the narrow lane to bring his experiment to an end.

Derek at the age of seven with his baby sister June, and his mother, Ethel.

THE COMPETITIVE SPIRIT TAKES OFF

Baby sitting was never something Derek relished. When his sisters were a little older his solution to the problem was to lock them out of the house so he would not be interrupted, and June remembers kicking through the glass in the front door as she tried to get back in on one occasion. That was back at Merton Road, where they returned at the end of the war.

With the stay in Yorkshire and his illnesses, Derek's early education had been extremely patchy. Once back in Prestwich he returned briefly to St Margaret's Parish School before being sent on to Heys Road Secondary Modern, close to his home. Little was expected of the children who did not make it to either the grammar or the technical schools, but Derek had still made an impression on his headmistress at St Margaret's.

One day she asked Mrs Bennett to come into school and take a look at her son's desk. 'This is how he lives,' she exclaimed, opening the lid to reveal a mess of half-eaten cakes, crumbs and miscellaneous litter. But then she added, 'I hope I'll be alive to see the success this man's going to bring'.

Derek never let his poor health stop him doing what he wanted to do, indeed he seemed possessed of tremendous stamina and determination. The summer after the Bennetts had returned to Manchester, his aunt in Cullingworth looked out of her window one day as a group of local children played cricket in a field beyond. 'I'm sure that's our Derek there,' she mused as she looked more closely. And it was. At the age of 11 he had cycled 30 miles over the Pennine hills to play with his friends! His family wasn't on the telephone and eventually his aunt had to ring the shop across the road from his house with a message telling his parents where he was.

During the war the Government had fostered a widespread interest in aircraft, and in particular aircraft recognition. Every young boy had books or cards showing the silhouettes of 'ours' and 'theirs' so he could scan the sky ready to warn of enemy attack. After the war many kept their interest in aviation and the hobby of aeromodelling become enormously popular, first with static models, and then with powered gliders.

Derek was no exception, especially as his father had been in the RAF. He quickly got caught up in this craze and his remarkable instincts as an engineer began to show. The wide open spaces of Manchester's Heaton Park were within walking distance of Derek's house and he was soon taking his planes there to try them out. A friend of his Aunt Mabel had three sons, who all became interested in aeromodelling. John O'Donnell, the eldest son, was an avid enthusiast and introduced Derek to the Whitefield Model Aircraft Club. John, who was a year older than Derek, was already an established modeller in his own right, but Derek soon developed a following of his own, teenage boys who sensed that here was someone whose ideas were a step ahead of everyone else's.

Through his aeromodelling he made friends who would remain close to him for the rest of his life, and who would also have parts to play in the story of Chevron Cars. Brothers Derek and Bob Faulkner first met him flying planes in Heaton Park, and Dave Willars met him at the end of his garden in Prestwich on another popular flying field, long since displaced by the concrete of the M62 motorway. In years to come Bob Faulkner would undertake the technical drawings for some of the first Chevrons, Derek Faulkner would become Chevron's workshop foreman, and Dave Willars would become a founder shareholder in Derek Bennett Engineering, the company which made Chevron cars.

The driving force for the young aeromodellers was competition. From the age of 12 Derek would join other members of the flying club early on a Sunday morning to pile onto a coach bound for a flying competition somewhere in the country. Getting a competitive edge became Derek's preoccupation and his growing band of followers eagerly anticipated his latest developments. Building and preparing the planes for these competitions was soon an all-consuming occupation and the Bennetts' house in Merton Road became an extraordinary haven for the model-makers.

Every day after school a group of boys would be drawn to the house, which was always open to all. Often it seemed as if there was not a room in the house which did not contain a couple of boys making wings or modifying engines, even when Derek himself was not at home. But the focal point of activity was the dining room table, which truly suffered in the name of science. Before going home one modeller might think nothing of nailing his wing to the table, knowing it would still be there when he returned the next day to continue working on it. In urgent need of something on which to mount an engine, Derek once calmly sawed off half of one of the table legs.

In the winter the modellers turned their attention to indoor models and even the bathroom became a centre of activity. The planes were made from a flimsy wooden frame covered with a membrane of home-made cellophane. Cellulose dope and castor oil poured on luke-warm water spread out to form a cellophane film, and of course the Bennetts' bath was the obvious place to mix this cocktail.

Derek's father had no mechanical aptitude himself and opted out of this bizarre extended family life in favour of the local golf club. But his mother would happily sit sewing in the midst of the invasion, and indeed joined in the activity on occasions, becoming accepted as an aeromodeller in her own right. She seemed quite happy to sweep up the mess of sawdust and shav-

Derek's mother watches as he puts the finishing touches to one of his model aircraft at home in Merton Road.

ings left behind at the end of each evening, and during the day she would often be despatched to the model shop in Manchester with a list of parts and materials that Derek needed for his next session.

Derek's existence dominated the household. He always came first and nobody questioned it. Even his father accepted that nobody could open a fresh bottle of milk in the morning until Derek had poured the cream from the top onto his Corn Flakes.

Eventually his sister June grew to feel somewhat resentful of the hordes of Derek's friends occupying *her* house, of not being able to eat off the table because it was always covered in glue, and of the pervasive smell of dope. But Wendy always wanted to join in and Derek soon learned to make use of her, teaching her enough to make her a help instead of a hindrance. Her devotion to him made her the only one prepared to get up at six o'clock in the morning to go flying with him, holding his aircraft while he prepared them and joining in the chase to recover them after they had made their flight. She would do anything to earn the respect of her big brother.

Derek's younger sister Wendy took on the role of assistant when he took his planes flying.

Even Chico, the family Scottie dog, had a contribution to make. Dope brushes were often made of animal hair, but why waste money when you have your own natural supply? So when the dope needed applying Derek would call Chico, snip off some hair, tie it to a stick and carry on with the job.

Derek is remembered, even by his closest friends, as a scruffy kid, and as the aeromodellers travelled to competitions further afield, the scruffy little Northerner became the scourge of many who fancied themselves as flyers. At the age of 16 he mounted his boldest mission yet as he, John O'Donnell, Bob Faulkner, and another friend named Alan Wrigley, set off for the International Week held at a grass aerodrome at Eaton Bray, near Leighton Buzzard. The four friends camped there for the duration and took on the world. Derek came second in the glider competition and John O'Donnell picked up a fifth place. *Aeromodeller* magazine sponsored the event and 'Dekka' Bennett was now making regular appearances in its columns.

Gliders and rubber-powered aircraft were the mainstay of the aeromodelling scene and Derek carried on making them throughout his flying days. But it was the engine-powered machines that really caught his imagination. John O'Donnell was always somewhat bemused by Derek's 'fan club', who appeared to need his advice at every step. He had his own modelling room at home, so he had no need of the Bennetts' dining room table. The planes he designed and built himself were very successful and he believed he was a better modeller than Derek, but when it came to mechanics he had to concede that Derek was out on his own.

Derek's early development work on model aircraft involved modifying their little two-stroke engines, opening up the ports a bit, and generally trying to squeeze a little more power out of them. But he soon started tackling more fundamental problems associated with flying the models in competition and the developments he pioneered helped make the Whitefield Model Aircraft Club known throughout the land.

The object of the competitions was for the plane to climb under its own power for a maximum of 15 seconds, and then glide for at least four minutes. Landing before the four minutes was up incurred penalties and running the engine beyond 15 seconds brought exclusion. When Derek began modelling, the accepted way to obtain the 15-second engine run was by restricting the amount of fuel available, which was measured by crude calibrations on the fuel pipe. Because this was not a very accurate means of getting the optimum engine run, modellers had progressed to using clockwork camera timers to operate a valve which cut the fuel supply off.

But this too was unsatisfactory as the fuel supply was not

cut off cleanly and the engine could begin to splutter before the maximum time had been reached, and then still splutter on beyond the 15 seconds and into disqualification. So Derek filed three teeth off the wheel on the clockwork motor. Now the cog would come round with a sudden click, slam the push bar across and clamp the valve shut. No more disqualifications.

So now everyone with Derek's little modification could make their plane climb for the full 15 seconds. But, once the engine cut, the plane would stall and lose maybe 100 feet of its precious height before settling down into a glide path. Offsetting the engine slightly to try and make the plane spin out of its stall more quickly had been tried, but Derek took the idea a stage further. He kept the engine offset to the right, but counteracted its effect with a rudder, spring-loaded to the left with an elastic band to make the plane turn slightly to that side as it climbed. Also attached to the rudder was a piece of piano wire, joined at its other end to the push bar that operated the fuel cut-off valve. So when the timer cut off the fuel supply, the bar also pulled the wire, which snapped the rudder hard over to the right. The plane's momentum would still be carrying it to the left but the rudder, now working with the weight of the engine, would suddenly snap it to the right with the result that the plane turned straight into its glide path without stalling. To those on the ground this must have looked like magic!

This variable rudder technique is now completely commonplace, but John O'Donnell remembers Derek being 'streets ahead of his time' in discovering it. He certainly was not too proud to incorporate it into his own aircraft pretty smartly.

Derek was always quite happy to pass on his ideas to people who were genuinely interested to learn. If someone gave the impression that they knew everything there was to know, he was quite happy to let them go on believing it. But if they came to him to ask for his help he would always give it. The idea that he might be giving away a competitive advantage did not seem to concern him. He would be too busy trying to work out the next development.

For the older boys, an overlap developed between aeromodelling and an interest in cars. The better your plane flew the further you had to go to retrieve it, so a motley collection of motorised forms of transport would appear at many venues. A motor-driven bicycle might be your first step, then someone else would find an old motor bike rusting in a garden shed, or even a battered van in which the whole group of flyers could chase after their aircraft.

Wendy remembers Derek using his first Austin 7 for such a purpose. But although she was no more than 10 or 11 years old at the time, he insisted that she drive it down the runway so that he could stick his head out through the roof to try and keep track of his plane as it flew along. She was terrified, but would not let him know it. By this time Wendy was also flying her own planes and she caused quite an upset when she very nearly qualified for a place on the British team in 1952. That same year Derek came fourth in the British Nationals at Gosport, while John O'Donnell won in two other categories. Then at the Woodford Rally the Whitefield group took over. As Derek became Senior Champion, John O'Donnell and his brothers, Hugh and Michael, won six categories between them, and even Derek's mother got in on the act, winning the Women's Trophy.

By now, Derek's involvement with cars was beginning to draw him away from model aircraft, although he took with him a fascination for aerodynamics which would find an outlet in so much that he was to do later. He had not liked school and used to be 'off sick' whenever he could get away with it. He was never in trouble at school and worked well enough to be in the 'A' stream, although he could not wait to be out of Heys Road and he had left as soon as he was able at the age of 15.

Derek's father had wanted him to be called Tony, but when everyone else called him Derek he would always refer to him

Trophy winners at Woodford in 1952. Derek, aged 18, is the smallest in the group, in the centre. His mother is on the far left, next to Hugh O'Donnell and Alan Wrigley. (*Photo John O'Donnell.*)

THE COMPETITIVE SPIRIT TAKES OFF

as Dickie. If he had any aspirations for his son he had probably long since given up on them. He himself had been a keen sportsman — he had been a champion sprinter and played rugby for Higher Broughton. During a family holiday in North Wales he had once entered Derek for the annual gala races, rubbing the liniment into his son's legs and setting him off on the run, but Derek had struggled in at the back of the field. It seemed as though his asthma would always preclude Derek from sporting success and he showed no interest in any organised sport. Arthur Bennett went back to his golf clubs.

Derek's mother was content to encourage him in whatever he wanted to do, but when he left school he followed the path of most boys his age who were not going into further education, and looked for an apprenticeship. He found one at Metropolitan Vickers in Trafford Park. Although it was an engineering company, he was working with large and impersonal factory machinery. This and the restrictions imposed by such a big company did not suit his independent spirit at all and he left after three months.

His uncle, Mabel's husband Foster, was a manager at the Colmore Depot car salesrooms in Old Trafford and he arranged for Derek to take up an electrical engineering apprenticeship in the company's motorcycle department nearby. He stayed at Colmore's until he was 21 years old but, just as he had been at school, he was far more committed to his spare time pursuits than he was to his work.

Transport to work now presented a problem, so Derek came up with one of the earliest of his seemingly impossible ideas. With petrol in short supply, powered bicycles were popular, a little 25cc engine turning the wheel through a friction drive operating directly onto the tyre. Derek took the engine and made it rotary valve, much like the model aircraft engines. He then mounted it behind the seat and ran a chain drive through a Sturmey Archer gearchange on a pannier above the back wheel and on to a four-speed *dérailleur* gear system in the hub. Not only did it all work, but it got him to and from work with indecent haste.

When Derek reached the age of 17 he persuaded his Uncle Harold, a bus driving instructor, to teach him to drive. He learned in his uncle's Lanchester, but failed his first test. Apparently he was put off by the surprise of discovering that his examiner was a woman. When he did pass he got himself a $2\frac{1}{2}$-litre Jaguar, which was in need of a lot of attention, and commandeered an old shed at the back of someone's house to use as a workshop. Here he created a world of fearful contraptions, made from nothing but scrap and his own imagination. He modified an old belt-driven lathe, making it independently driven by powering it through a car gearbox and a motorcycle gearbox. There was also a compressor built from the engine out of an old Triumph motor bike. Bob Faulkner contributed materials and often helped Derek in the workshop. Dave Willars remembers gas leaks, a huge flywheel, and disquieting whomping noises which always made him want to leave as soon as possible before something went bang.

At Colmore's, Derek had moved away from a strict apprenticeship as an electrician and over to the mechanical side. He was also working on cars a lot and developed a much-envied knack of assembling driveshafts on Citroens. When his apprenticeship was over, he asked for a pay rise. When he did not get it he decided he would rather work for himself and left. Now his spare time activities could at last spread out to command all his attention. So, with high hopes of making a living repairing cars, he began to look for premises of his own.

Eventually he settled on a lock-up in Frederick Road, Salford, in the midst of the tightly packed streets which, until a few years earlier, L S Lowry had sketched while making his rounds as a rent collector. Some of the people that were to pass through Frederick Road would make up another group of Derek's close friends, and some of them would find themselves drawn into the Chevron story as well.

CHAPTER 3

Little workshops, big ideas

THE urge to compete which had spurred Derek on with his model aircraft had begun to turn his thoughts to trying some form of motor racing. Stock car racing was popular in the Manchester area and it had the essential advantage of costing virtually nothing to take part in, so while he had been on the look-out for his own workshop, Derek had joined a couple of people from Colmore's in a former church hall in nearby White City to build a stock car — a Model Y Ford with a V8 engine.

The impecunious stock car racers would tow their car to race meetings either on the end of a rope, or sometimes with its front wheels in an A-frame. For this to be legal someone had to be sitting in the car when it was being towed, and coming back across the Pennines from a meeting in Yorkshire one night it had fallen to Derek to be the passenger. Huddled low in the cold, windscreenless stock car in the dark Derek could see very little. Suddenly, a loud bang shook him out of his bored discomfort. Almost immediately the car rolled over sideways and then pitched itself end over end before coming to rest back on its wheels. The car's doors were welded up for strength and, more startled than hurt, Derek struggled to get out through a window. Once out he gazed into the empty darkness, seeing nothing but a sheer drop to one side of the road. He peered over, expecting to see a burning wreck at the foot of the hillside. But there was nothing there. The towing car had actually become unhitched and it was the A-frame digging into the road that had flipped the stock car over. His friends didn't even realise they had lost Derek until they got down off the pass and into the next town!

Towing eventually brought about the demise of Derek's first stock car. It had been towed on the end of a rope to a meeting in Liverpool, but an accident there rendered it incapable of being dragged home. He left it there until he could commandeer a trailer, but when he returned the next day it had gone.

He had bought another stock car, a Lincoln, but he had only raced it a few times when something new caught his eye

— Midget car racing. The bumping and banging of stock car racing hadn't appealed too much to Derek, but here was something which looked altogether more skilful, and with open-wheeled cars that looked like proper racing machines.

Midget racing had begun a couple of years before when Belle Vue's manager, Johnny Hoskins, was concerned at the way the crowds were starting to desert his motorcycle speedway meetings. He thought some kind of car racing might be the answer and when Bob Parker took his circuit racing Cooper for a few laps of the oval, he liked the look of it and asked if Parker could come up with something about half the size. Parker — whose family made the famous Eccles cakes in the nearby suburb of the same name — went away and produced the first car, and before long enough people had copied his idea for Midget races to be held.

The basic concept was really one of speedway on four wheels and some of the earliest drivers came over from motorcycle grass track racing. The speedway riders themselves did not want to know about the Midgets: they just saw them as a threat to their livelihoods and swore that they would not let them near the track. By the time Derek joined the scene, bookmaker Jimmy Abbott had come along and sorted the cars out. He had called his development of Parker's original design the Parker 500, and his were the cars to have. The cars took the 500cc JAP speedway motorcycle engine, mounted it behind the driver and used a chain to drive a single gear on the back wheel. Changing the engine sprocket or the wheel sprocket enabled the drivers to gear their cars for different tracks. The cars had no brakes and speed was scrubbed off by sliding sideways through the shale-covered bends in traditional speedway style. With six cars in each heat it made for close and exciting racing.

As ever, buying a car was not an option for Derek, so he set about building his own, which he decided to call the PRM — for Pendleton Racing Motors — after the district of Salford where his workshop was. Inevitably, Derek had his own ideas about how things should be done and his own car was immediately distinct from those around it. He kept away from the normal practice of running front wheels smaller than the back ones, and came up with his own suspension geometry. His cars were also higher off the ground than the Parkers and although this did not seem to present Derek with any problems, the first one he sold to a customer had a reputation for falling over frequently.

Although Derek's car was not immediately as fast as the other cars, it impressed everyone with how well-made it was. Its home-made aluminium body looked immaculate and Albert Brown, an established Midget driver, admits that their cars really looked thrown-together alongside Derek's. Midget racing

LITTLE WORKSHOPS, BIG IDEAS

Derek demonstrates the opposite-lock cornering technique required for Midget racing at the wheel of his own PRM special.

also gave Derek the opportunity to develop his skills as a driver and he was soon a regular winner himself. Albert Brown remembers him as being fast and safe, 'You get to trust certain people when you're racing, and one of those was Derek. Some of them you wouldn't go anywhere near, but he was very good.' Derek's showings in the PRM were also good enough to bring him his first customer, a former stock car driver rejoicing under the pseudonym of Bruce Blood.

Derek only shared the tiny workshop in Frederick Road and there was barely enough room for the repair work he was doing to scrape a living, so he still did much of the work on his own projects at home. The dining room table had not yet suffered enough! When Derek needed a test bed for the engine for his Midget he cut a hole in the middle of the table to mount it in. The rest of Merton Road must have become accustomed to some rather unconventional goings-on at the Bennett household. 'We had understanding neighbours,' said June. But when the 500cc JAP engine roared into life nestling in the dining room table, even the most understanding neighbours felt moved to express a little disapproval.

One of Derek's aeromodelling friends, Geoff Smith, later married his sister, Wendy. He remembers coming to the house to pick her up one night and hearing a roaring noise as he approached it. It turned out to be a compressor in the garden, from which an air line was running across the kitchen and into the fireplace, which was blanked off with sheet metal. Derek had created his own furnace and was melting down unwanted old pistons to recast as something more vital.

Midget racing also led to Derek meeting Paul Owens and the start of a working partnership that would last for the rest of his life. Not long out of school, Paul was 15 years old and used to cycle past Derek's workshop in Frederick Road every morning on his way to the corporation bus garage in Weaste where he was an apprentice fitter. The Midgets and stock cars that were often outside the workshop caught his attention as Paul had racing aspirations himself, although at that time he wanted to be a speedway rider and had a part-share in a bike. While trying out the machine at Belle Vue one day, he recognised one of the Midget cars being tested and introduced himself to its owner. Paul volunteered his help if Derek ever needed it at his garage, and Derek took up his offer. Paul was on his way to becoming Chevron's Racing Manager.

Derek's sisters were now into their early teens, and only two or three years younger than some of their brother's aeromodelling friends, who had become so familiar around the house. So the group of modellers became more of a social group and the nearby Cheetham Ice Palace became a popular haunt. His mind forever on other things, Derek was a reluctant participant in his friends' social life, when he could be persuaded to join in at all. He generally drew the line at ice skating, but was once persuaded to go bowling with them. Though his priorities may have been somewhat different to those of his contemporaries, he was not immune to Cupid's arrows. He had met the first love of his life by this point, the cousin of an old friend, and she was given the credit for getting him out to socialize. So he went bowling, although Geoff Smith still remembers him spending the time between turns drawing little sketches of cars on the backs of packets.

Being seven years younger than Derek, Paul Owens was the same age as his youngest sister, Wendy, and he eventually became involved in the social circle too. Somehow Derek was the common link in a growing social group, even though he was its most elusive member. Derek met his next girlfriend through Paul, and when Wendy married Geoff a few years later, she was her bridesmaid.

Meanwhile, back in the workshop, Derek had been getting

a lot of his early bread and butter work smartening up second-hand cars for Peter Shorthouse, a local dealer. But lack of space at Frederick Road soon became a serious problem and so Shorthouse suggested that he move round the corner to Broad Street and work from some premises he had there. Hidden behind a 30-foot high advertising hoarding on the main road into Salford was a 'lean-to' with a sloping, leaking roof. This was to be Derek's workshop, rent-free if he did all the repairs and maintenance Peter Shorthouse needed on his stock.

Shorthouse had bought Derek's Lincoln stock car off him, but when he crashed it beyond repair one night at Belle Vue he decided to join Derek in the Midgets. Derek was already building his third PRM, so when that was finished he sold his original car to Peter and they began going racing together, travelling further afield as the Midgets became more popular.

Derek's racing was always financed by what he could make repairing cars and he began to establish a reputation for creating roadworthy cars from write-offs. Peter Shorthouse would provide the wrecked cars, then Derek would restore them to life and take a share of the proceeds when they were sold. Nowadays the practice of welding one half of each of two different cars together to produce a new one has become rather discredited. But then it was a new idea. Police Constable Peter Ashcroft was the local bobby on the beat for Broad Street at the time and remembers the beginning of 'the cut and stick business'. As a motoring enthusiast he was trying to get the local police to take more of an interest in dangerous vehicles in those days before the compulsory Ministry of Transport test. He took a close interest in the local crash repair scene and set himself the task of separating the good from the dangerous, as well as trying to weed out the villains who used local workshop businesses as unwitting accomplices in the disposal of stolen cars.

PC Ashcroft would often find Derek working alone in Broad Street at nine or 10 o'clock at night when he came by on his rounds. He remembers 'a very quiet lad' who he had a job to drag into conversation. But he knew enough to be impressed by an ability which seemed to be beyond his age and says he would not have hesitated to buy one of Derek's rebuilds himself.

But the thing that most fascinated him was Derek's latest 'spare-time' project — a three-wheeler. The winter of 1956 saw the height of the Suez Crisis and the prospect of petrol rationing got Derek and Peter thinking about more fuel-efficient means of transport. They came up with a three-wheeled car, driven by a small motorcycle engine, with two wheels at the front and a fibreglass body. Throughout that winter the car slowly took shape in the back of the workshop.

The wooden framework for Derek's planned three-wheeler.

The basic framework was made up of dozens of strips of wood, scavenged in true Bennett style by cutting up floorboards from the house outside which Peter Shorthouse had his car lot. The frame was then covered with Plaster of Paris, which Derek spent most of every day and night for about three weeks rubbing down by hand to make it smooth enough to provide the buck for a fibreglass body. Parts of the body were made, but then the Suez Crisis came to an end and suddenly the three-wheeler did not seem like the money-spinning idea it had once appeared. The project was abandoned and Derek went back to rebuilding write-offs.

Ideas like the three-wheeler often had their genesis just across the road from Derek's garage in Broad Street, upstairs in Jim's Snack Bar. The café was a meeting point, a place to eat, take a break and thrash out ideas. Sometimes you would go there for practical advice from a regular like Derek, other times you would wile away the hours in search of that elusive get-rich-quick idea that really was going to deliver the goods. Doug Linton, who was to become Chevron's Company Secretary, got to know Derek at Jim's Snack Bar. A friend of Peter Shorthouse, he was a professional drummer and the nature of his job meant he would often be free during the daytime, so the café was a good place to go and share his enthusiasm for motor racing with Derek.

Another regular at the café was Derek Alderson, a conspicuous personality and local entrepreneur who had a business building caravans around the corner from Derek's workshop in Frederick Road. He had first met Derek when he had come round to borrow some paint for a car he was doing up, and since then he had used the young mechanic whenever one of his cars needed attention. Up in Jim's Snack Bar, the ideas would come out of Alderson like a slot machine delivering a jackpot, and Derek was to find himself caught up in more than one of them before too long.

Jimmy Horrocks ran the snack bar and soon came to regard Derek as more than just another customer. He learned to spot the uneasy manner that meant Derek was short of a few pounds for some vital part without which he could not finish a job. 'How much do you need, Bennett?' he would ask, before diving into the till or emptying his pockets. He did not mind helping someone who was always so quick to pay him back, and years later he was to put up the money that enabled Derek to set up his own company building Chevrons.

He also remembered Derek as a very hard man — never aggressive, but always very tough — and would tell the story of the day he smashed his thumb with a hammer and came into the café for a cup of coffee before they took him off to hospital. Derek seemed equally nonchalant about his first serious accident when he crashed his Midget while he and Albert Brown were giving a demonstration at Odsal Stadium in Bradford. He said little about the accident when he returned to Salford, but under the heavy bandages his fingers were recovering from being badly split open. The story went that the hospital had left half the cinders and shale from the track still in there when they had sewn them up.

Much of that apparent toughness must have come from his fight against asthma. It had persisted right through his teens, and his sisters remember him gasping for breath so badly that he would have to go to bed. But he had sat down with his doctor at the age of about 18 to learn all he could about his condition and how he could try and control it. From then on brown medicine and determination had enabled him to hold his asthma at bay for much of the time and he refused to let his discomfort show. His asthma also prevented him being diverted into National Service as he failed his Army medical.

While he was racing Midgets he was also moving towards his first stab at circuit racing. He had helped Joe Fray to build an Austin 7-based Special for the 750 Formula, which had sent him off to the rule book and given him some ideas of his own. Derek decided that he could incorporate the obligatory bits of Austin 7 into a fully enveloping monocoque and he began working away on a streamlined creation that might have come out looking something like a small D-Type Jaguar, had it ever been completed. In the end the project was abandoned and,

CHEVRON

along with Bob Faulkner, Derek bought the original 750 from Joe Fray. The idea was for Derek to race it and Bob to use it as his road car.

Derek first took the 750 Special to Oulton Park in 1957 and over the next three seasons it developed from a road car to a racing car as Derek tried out an endless stream of ideas on it. For 1958 he replaced the Austin 7 engine with a Ford 100E side-valve engine to move up into the 1172 class. The car was never going to be fully competitive with the purpose-built 1172 chassis, but in those days most of Derek's thoughts were directed at engine performance and he used his mechanical ingenuity to improve the car's speed. The superior engine performance meant that Derek could usually tear away into the lead at the start of a race, but he would be swamped by the pack as the better handling of the newer cars told in the corners.

Paul Owens remembers the way Derek would always begin with whatever standard parts were readily — and cheaply — available, and then adapt them to his own purposes. The big problem with the side-valve engine was getting the gas flowing properly between the side chamber and the combustion

Racing in shirtsleeves. Derek on the grid in the 750, still at this point in road-going trim.

LITTLE WORKSHOPS, BIG IDEAS

Doug Linton, Paul Owens, and Derek Bennett pose proudly with the 1172 Special at Brands Hatch in 1959.

chamber, especially if you were trying to run a high compression ratio, which restricted the throat between the side-valves and the cylinder head. So Derek made the piston come out above the top of the cylinder itself and up into the cylinder head. Now the high compression ratio was there, and so was the throat for the mixture to flow efficiently. Others may have been working towards similar solutions, but Derek's ideas were always his own and were certainly new to everyone around him, just as they had been in his model aircraft days.

On 11 July 1959, at Oulton Park, Derek had a freak accident in the 1172 which was to spark off a lifelong superstition about the number 11. The Mid-Cheshire Motor Club meeting was one of those fraught occasions that seem to happen sometimes in motor racing. Heavy rain had brought a heatwave to an end that morning and practice had already seen one car disappear upside down into the smaller of Oulton's lakes, and another embed itself in a tree. Derek was due to race in the 1172 event, but first came a chance of a few extra laps in a race for sports cars.

As the proper sports cars — the Lolas and Lotus XIs — went away in front, Derek found himself in the thick of a following bunch. Coming into the banked Esso hairpin he found a slower car on the line and ran wide. But the outside of the track was still damp and very greasy and he lost all grip and slithered helplessly up the banking and through the Esso hoarding. A piece of the wooden framework hit him hard in the chest, penetrating the skin and breaking his collar bone as it pushed up into his shoulder. Fortuitously, he was wearing a new terylene shirt which didn't tear in the impact. Instead it wrapped itself round the piece of wood, stopping it from splintering, thereby preventing infection and potentially more serious injuries.

Car number 11 was taken away in a sorry state and Derek was removed to Ward 11 of Chester Royal Infirmary to spend the night of the 11th and the next 11 days. Other 11s and multiples of 11 also came into the story, some remembered, some forgotten, and others imaginary, but still now passed into myth — like the accident happening on the 11th lap of the race, which was actually only run over seven laps. But the string of coincidence was long enough that it affected Derek con-

LITTLE WORKSHOPS, BIG IDEAS

siderably and from then on he refused to have anything to do with the number 11. The superstition stayed with him throughout his life. There was never a Chevron with the type number 11, or any multiple of it, and the same gaps were left when it came to numbering individual chassis.

Meanwhile, the 1172 race went ahead without Derek Bennett's Ford Special, and was won by the Len Terry-designed Terrier of a certain Brian Hart, who continued his domination of the category with his ninth win in a row.

While Derek was in hospital, Derek Alderson took his father there to visit him. It was the only time Alderson ever met Arthur Bennett, and he remembers him thinking that Derek was a fool to be involved in something where he could get himself hurt like that. But Derek was undeterred and the phone was soon ringing at Jim's Snack Bar as he called from his bedside with instructions for Paul Owens about how to rebuild the car.

Derek in the 1172, Brands Hatch, 28 June 1959. He was outpaced in the race, which Arthur Mallock's Austin won after Brian Hart spun away the lead in his Terrier.

Paul got the car rebuilt and Derek raced it again soon after. The following year Brian Hart had moved on to bigger things and Derek stormed off to win the first three races while the new boys were still getting to grips with their cars. But it remained obvious that the Bennett-Ford, with its Austin 7 base, was never going to be fully competitive, so he sold it to Doug Linton and began building his own Formula Junior car.

By this point he had also moved premises again, across Salford to School Street in Lower Broughton. Despite his and Paul's efforts concreting the old dirt floor and rebuilding the leaking roof, the Broad Street workshop was still a pretty appalling environment, and Derek was becoming unhappy with his arrangement with Peter Shorthouse. Shorthouse was losing interest in the motor trade anyway and with Broad Street coming up for development and the adjacent Salford Technical College looking for land to expand onto, he decided to sell up. So the two went their separate ways, Shorthouse into the property business and Derek to School Street. Helping him pay the bills at the new workshop was Tommy Humphreys, a cellulose spray painter who Derek had first met during his apprenticeship at Colmore Depot, and who had undertaken work for him at Broad Street. He was as much a perfectionist with his paint jobs as Derek was with his repairs, so they made a good partnership for the bread and butter work of rebuilding write-offs.

At this point Derek's association with Derek Alderson became much closer. Alderson had a passion for big American cars, which he only partly justified by their suitability for towing caravans. He had run a Buick, which he had brought round for Derek to 'soup up', which in those days seemed to entail no more than fitting a somewhat noisy motorcycle silencer. Then he replaced the Buick with a glamorous new Packard which — 'in a moment of exuberance' — he cut in half by wrapping it round a lamp post in Blackpool. The car was only covered by third party insurance, so he took the two halves to Derek Bennett, hoping for some kind of miracle. The garage was so small that Alderson had to bring in a builder to widen the doorway just to get the Packard inside. But Derek got to work and performed the impossible, rebuilding the Packard so that even Alderson himself could not detect that it had so much as suffered a scratch. He became a fully paid-up member of the Derek Bennett fan club on the spot.

The growing success of his caravan business had enabled Alderson to take up circuit racing himself, first with a road-going Volvo which Derek had prepared for him, and then with an Elva Climax, which Derek had built up from a wreck. Rebuilding written-off road cars continued to be the mainstay of Derek Bennett's precarious existence and Alderson took over the role of procurer, buying the wrecks and taking a share of the eventual profit, much as Shorthouse had done. With the money he was earning Derek began that first 'from scratch' circuit racing car, the Bennett Formula Junior. From scribbled sketches drawn on the back of paper serviettes in cafés, the project progressed to a full-scale drawing on the back of a roll of wallpaper, and soon Derek and Paul were off on a never-ending round of workshops and storerooms, tracking down the components with which to do the job.

Austin parts proved particularly suitable within the budget and Paul was soon set to work to make an Austin A30 rear axle independent. The A30 also contributed the brakes, although they cast the drums themselves, as they did a number of smaller components which Derek designed himself. Triumph Herald uprights were also part of the package, joining the Ford 105E engine and gearbox in a multi-tubular, spaceframe chassis. Derek also added Watts linkage suspension for good measure, very much as an experiment on the grounds that nobody had tried it before.

Formula Junior, which had originated in Italy, was still only in its first full season in Britain in 1960. Derek's car was front-engined, but the success of the rear-engined Lotus 18 soon proved that this was the way to go. Derek Bennett, then 26, was six years younger than Colin Chapman and still had some catching up to do before his cars would beat Lotuses. But he persevered with the project, as ever using ingenuity in place of cash. A major contribution to the success of Jim Clark's works Lotus was its Ford 105E engine, built by a fledgling company by the name of Cosworth. Derek could not afford to follow the other leading runners in beating a path to Keith Duckworth's door, but he did send Doug Linton down to his little workshop in Friern Barnet to buy one of Cosworth's A2 camshafts. The rest would be down to Derek.

Unable to afford the stronger, replacement A3 cams which appeared later in the year, Derek continued with his own development, adapting his knowledge of aerodynamics from model aircraft to gas flows in engines, thinking his way through each problem in turn, and producing innovations like offset valve guides. Lack of financial resources did not seem to frustrate Derek. It merely sharpened his mind to alternative possibilities. The car was reasonably successful in local races, but at national level it was not in the same league as the Lotuses of Clark, Trevor Taylor and Peter Arundell, or Ken Tyrrell's Coopers, driven amongst others by John Surtees. The end of the season came and he put the car up for sale. It was bought by a local car auctioneer and aspiring racing driver, Robert Ashcroft, who was also destined to be a key figure in the formation of Chevron.

CHEVRON

The spaceframe of the Bennett-Ford Formula Junior car sits on the pavement outside the School Street workshop where Derek would later build the first Chevrons.

Over that winter the irrepressible Derek Alderson came up with the hottest money-making scheme yet. It was a child's push chair which would pull up into a high chair, or fold away to be carried. Proving that his engineering mind did not need the glamour of motor sport to stimulate it into tackling problems, Derek set about putting Alderson's designs into practice, helped by Paul Owens who remembers the time spent perfecting trays for the baby to eat from, which would clip onto the chair without clipping off the baby's fingers.

Eventually they produced one that worked, and Alderson had great fun taking his youngest son to restaurants in it, wheeling him up to the table and watching the onlookers' jaws drop as he magically transformed the device into a high-chair. A second prototype went to the woman across the road from the workshop in School Street, who had become the official purveyor of tea and sandwiches in the absence of Jim's Snack Bar. With two models in active service, Alderson took out a patent application and offered the idea to Valor. When their initial enthusiasm vanished, along with the prototype they had been sent, Alderson commissioned a feasibility study on producing the High-Low Chairs themselves. But the costs of mass-production were going to be way beyond their means. Another one bit the dust . . .

Derek's personal life began to put him under pressure now. He had been going out with the same girl for four or five years. He was 27 years old, she was approaching the magic age of 21. It was accepted that they were engaged, so when was that going to be translated into a wedding? It was a question Derek could not answer. He was not ambitious and he had no great plans, but his inventive mind and the need to make a living meant that he was almost always physically and mentally occupied. He did not feel ready for the commitment, and he did not feel financially secure enough to take it on.

Throughout his life Derek obviously had a vulnerable personality and an apparent innocence that made women want to look after him. The appeal was the same to the mothers of his friends — who would feed him when he called round — as it was to his girlfriends. His sisters felt much the same way and so, in later years, did the wives of many of his friends. Some part of Derek Bennett always remained the tussle-haired kid that needed looking after, and there was never a shortage of volunteers.

The problem was finding one person who could meet all his needs. Someone practical enough to be able to do the mothering, attractive enough for him to want to marry, and loyal enough to cope with the impossible lifestyle. On top of this he also needed someone who was an intellectual equal, who knew how his mind worked and could understand enough to be involved in what he was doing and the ideas he was working through. It was an impossible brief, but for four years someone had been prepared to try and carry it out. She had a scientific background and became directly involved in a lot of Derek's early engineering work. She was popular with Derek's friends and they were widely thought of as well matched. But ultimately, she was still unable to break through the preoccupations. When he forgot about her 21st birthday and failed to turn up at the party until someone telephoned to remind him, she finally decided she was wasting her time trying to get Derek to marry her.

For months, Derek Alderson's baby chair had been another constant reminder of the lures of a domestic life, so Derek was probably relieved to get back to working on racing cars in 1961. Alderson had an Elva Climax, which he had bought as a wreck the year before after a crash in which its driver had been seriously injured. Derek had rebuilt it and raced it a few times, but it was always difficult to drive and he had ended up in the lake at Mallory Park. After the car had been rebuilt again, Derek Alderson crashed it and they decided that it was too ill-fated to be repaired once more.

Alderson was attracted by the locally-built Rochdale Olympic and he decided to get Derek Bennett to build one using a lightweight shell and as much of the Elva as he could. Creating the Olympic took most of that year and Alderson remembers it as the most immaculate car he ever saw. When it was finished, they took it to Oulton Park. The two Dereks drove it for a couple of laps each and were agreed that it needed

CHEVRON

With his Formula Junior in the foreground, Derek prepares to try Derek Alderson's Elva Climax at Oulton Park as Alderson looks on.

a lot of work to cure its severe understeer and instability at high speeds. Before they packed up, Paul Owens, who had also put many hours of his own time into building the car, was given a go in it. Paul found the handling frightening, but he still entertained hopes of being a racing driver and decided to try to make the best of it. Unfortunately the Olympic got away from him as he turned through the left-hand kink at the top of Clay Hill. The back went onto the grass and the car immediately rolled end over end.

Hearing 'a God-awful bang' the Dereks ran to the scene to find Paul sitting on the grass, bruised, shaken, and lucky to be alive after being thrown out of the car. The Olympic had not been so lucky, going on to hit a steel hawser supporting a telegraph pole, which sliced it in two before it finally hit a wall, which promptly fell on it.

Recollections of Derek Bennett's reaction are varied, but Paul insists that he did not berate him for destroying his handiwork, even though Paul felt so guilty that he almost wished he had done. Relieved that Paul was not badly hurt and accepting that events could not be undone, Derek was able to be philosophical about the accident, but he was obviously far from pleased as he shovelled the wreckage onto a trailer and took it off to be scrapped. 'Derek was pig sick about that,' recalls Bob Faulkner.

With no car of his own to race that season, Derek had made

the occasional outing in Doug Linton's 1172 Terrier, which he had prepared for him. But with the demise of the Olympic, Derek Alderson decided to get serious for 1962. He went to the Motor Show and did a deal with Colin Chapman to buy two Series 2 Lotus Elites. Derek Bennett built the cars up from kits and drove his on the road. The idea was that he would pay Alderson in kind for his car, working to cover its cost. But he soon became uncomfortable with the commitment and was so short of cash that he could not afford to run the car anyway. On top of this he felt his was a 'rogue' car and was never happy with the way it handled, so when he damaged it by running hard into a kerb, he decided to sell it and bought instead a second-hand Series 1 Elite.

He set to work preparing this and Alderson's car for the coming season, and the two Dereks drove them under the Ecurie RCS banner, mixing the fashionable racing epithet of the time with the initials of the latest incarnation of Alderson's business, Rochdale Caravan Services. Alderson spared no expense and for the first time Derek Bennett was given his head to prepare — and race — a fully competitive car. The result was first and second in the Clubmans GT Championship, against the works Team Elite cars. Alderson won the championship, but he is under no illusions that he was ever the better driver. He believes Derek just built him a quicker car, anxious not to beat the hand that fed him. Alderson has always had tremendous respect for the fact that Derek never tried to take advantage of him, 'He hadn't got a bent thought in his mind. I could never believe that a fellow could be so honest,' he recalls.

When Alderson went on holiday to Jersey that year, Derek asked if he could borrow his car for the weekend to race at Brands Hatch. Presumably he wanted to see just what he could do in the faster car, but it all went wrong and he ended up bouncing off a bank in an enormous accident. With his skill and his prodigious work rate he might well have had the car back in one piece before Alderson returned from holiday, leaving him none the wiser. Unfortunately a photograph of the spectacular crash made the front page of the *Daily Mirror,* which the unsuspecting Alderson was perusing over breakfast the next morning. Drawn to the picture he started to read the caption below it. When he read the name Derek Bennett, the awful truth dawned on him! 'My bloody car!' was all he could say for some time afterwards.

Derek's ideas about preparing and setting up racing cars continued to progress with the Elites and his ability to come up with short-term 'fixes' on the day also raised a few eyebrows. One of the most widely remembered is a trick with a lever-action Wesco oil can which was pressed into service when the brake master cylinder on Alderson's car developed a leak. Derek filled the oil can with brake fluid and wedged it inside the driver's door. He then commandeered the piping from the windscreen washers, jammed it over the oil can spout and ran it to the master cylinder. Now all Alderson had to do to get round the corners was to remember to pump the oil can in the door with his thumb while he was going down the straights!

Aerodynamics kept cropping up as well, When they could not get enough downforce on the back wheels, Derek tried taking the boot lid out. This worked marvellously, but was not going to prove too popular with the scrutineers. So Derek put a piece of metal in to lift the back edge of the lid up, adding a bungee to hold it in place — he had turned the boot lid into a crude wing, and it did the trick.

The year had been a tremendous success, but the cost was not something Alderson could sustain any longer. He calculates the season cost him around £10,000 and all but wrecked his business, partly through the sheer cost, and partly because of the amount of time he spent in Salford when he should have been in Rochdale. So the cars had to be sold and Alderson took a lower profile. He dabbled with a Shapecraft Elan the following season and then dropped out of racing altogether.

Derek meanwhile had scraped together the money to buy a damaged Series 2 Elite shell from Rodney Bloor's Sports Motors garage in Manchester, which had a Lotus dealership, and where Robert Ashcroft was now working as sales manager. The car he built from this soon became unbeatable in the North, adding to his growing reputation as a driver. Robert Ashcroft had kept in close contact, initially because the Bennett Formula Junior he had bought from Derek had barely left School Street before it was back there being rebuilt.

Derek and Paul had gone with him to Oulton Park when he first went to race it and they were all standing round the car in the pits during practice when a multiple pile-up sent a car hurtling in their direction. In those days before armco barriers there was only a white line on the track to keep cars out of the pit lane, and on this occasion it did not prove very effective. The other car hit the back of Ashcroft's Formula Junior, damaging it quite badly, and despatching Paul to hospital, fortunately with only minor injuries.

Derek had the car rebuilt by the end of the summer, but Ashcroft soon sold it and bought a TVR, which he raced under the Ecurie RCS banner on occasions the following year, travelling to meetings with Derek and his Elite. He became convinced that Derek's talents as a driver needed pushing, and as Derek was far too modest and retiring to contemplate selling himself, Ashcroft decided that he would start looking around for some deals.

CHAPTER 4

Straight out of the box – the first Chevrons

THE first thing Robert Ashcroft came up with was a Gemini Mk4, which he found in Ireland while Sports Motors were trawling for suitable Formula Junior cars to use at their new racing car school at Oulton Park. The car was offered to Derek and brought up to the new Formula 3 specification. Meanwhile, Derek also continued racing his own Elite at the beginning of 1964. At Oulton Park in March he won the GT race in the Elite, and then jumped straight into the Gemini to finish second in the Formula 3 race.

He had helped Dave Willars to build up a shoestring, club racing Ford Anglia and he would also race that from time to time. The car was lethal in the wet on its cheap, near-bald, tyres. But Derek found racing it in bad conditions amusing and enjoyed throwing it around. To Derek driving in the rain was only a problem if he was physically getting wet, something he hated. Willars remembers him racing at Oulton Park

Derek Bennett raced an enormous variety of cars during his career as a driver. Here he takes Dave Willars' Ford Anglia round Shaws Hairpin at Mallory Park.

in a single-seater in the pouring rain, wearing a bright yellow, cyclist's oilskin cape, which was draped over his head and taped all round the edge of the cockpit. To many the action would appear to be that of an extrovert — or maybe an eccentric — personality, but Derek would consider himself neither. It was just another practical solution to a problem. Dave Willars' mother even contributed some special double cuffs, which she made to stop the water running up Derek's sleeves in wet races.

As well as his dislike of getting wet, Derek was also fastidious about keeping clean, or 'not being messed' as Mrs Willars put it. Since his childhood eczema, Derek had always had problems with his skin. Dermatitis was a particular problem on his hands, where the skin was very sensitive and would flake easily if irritated by too much grease or dirt.

But if these things annoyed Derek, it did not show in his approach to racing. They seemed merely to strengthen his ability to put up with discomfort, and even pain, of any kind. The Gemini had a fundamental problem with inboard front brakes which used to lock up. The brake pads welded to the discs, and the wheels suddenly stopped going round. When this happened at Aintree he crashed heavily into the straw bales at Tatts Corner. He was due to race Dave Willars' Anglia in the next race and Dave was concerned that he might have hurt himself in the crash. 'He came back very quiet and said he was all right. But his legs were bleeding through his overalls during the saloon race.'

The Gemini was rebuilt with the brakes suitably modified to outboard form, and the car became increasingly competitive as Derek dragged more power out of the engine. Unfortunately more performance meant less reliability. Keeping the oil in the sump became a problem and the engine was forever breaking big ends. Rodney Bloor had been going well in a Brabham and Derek decided that was the way to go. The Elite was still winning locally, even though with its 1220cc engine it was up against the new 1600cc twin-cam Lotus Elans. But at national level the car was now outclassed and Derek had had to settle for fourth place at Oulton Park as Jim Clark's Ian Walker Elan beat the Chequered Flag/Team Lotus Elan of Graham Warner to win. So he decided to sell the Elite and buy a Brabham BT9 in kit form.

Derek built up the car, which came with a somewhat suspect Hillman Imp gearbox, preparing the engine himself as usual. It was soon running competitively and so Robert Ashcroft Racing decided to make its first trip abroad. Derek provided the tow car, a Hillman Minx Estate which he had made for himself from the leftovers of a number of crash repair jobs. Something about that Hillman seemed to put it on a par with any car he ever built and he never parted with it. Ashcroft had discovered that there was fantastic prize money to be had at the Monza Lottery, so they hitched a double-decker trailer behind the Hillman, loaded it up with the Brabham for Derek and the Gemini for young Scottish hope, Adam Wylie, and set off for Italy. Wylie failed to finish because the Gemini kept blowing engines faster than Paul Owens could repair them. But Derek made it into the final amongst some fairly exalted company.

Derek had now established a serious national reputation for himself as a racing driver, but he was already 30 years old and needed a serious commitment if his career was going to go any further. Robert Ashcroft decided that the car with which to do that was a 1500cc, twin-cam Brabham BT14, which he had bought with sponsorship obtained from VIP Petrol, a local brand belonging to car dealers, Isherwoods. The idea was for Derek to run the car in *Formule Libre,* a prestigious category in those days. But, to his surprise, Derek turned the drive down initially as he had become preoccupied with another project.

The Formula 3 Brabham had been a big disappointment to Derek. He had struggled to get it to handle even as well as the Gemini and the more time he spent working out what was wrong with the design and how he could improve it the more he realised that there was no magic to a chassis just because it had a famous name on it. He knew he had no resources to build a competitive Formula 3 car himself, but he thought he might have a chance of doing something for the new Clubmans Formula, which had just been announced. 'I figured Clubmans was the only thing with my money', said Derek when he came to look back on the success of his company 10 years later. 'I'd always been at the wrong end of the scale without the right gear. I chose it so that we could be at the right end of the scale and have a proper sporting chance. I'd endeavoured to study the theory of it all and we just figured we could do it.'

One of the people who was particularly interested in Derek's thoughts about Clubmans racing was Brian Classick. A young, articled, accountant's clerk, he had been racing a Daimler SP250, but he had picked up a written-off Lotus Elite very cheaply, intending to do some serious motor racing. Some time after he had bought his 'bargain' he realised that the task of making it raceworthy was way beyond his capabilities. 'You want to go and see Derek Bennett,' he was told. So he did. While Derek and Paul Owens worked on the Elite, Brian carried on racing the Daimler until a test day at Oulton Park when he entrusted it to a friend, who promptly rolled it at Lodge Corner. It was pointed straight at Salford and Dave Willars drove it back with considerable difficulty to join the

Elite awaiting repair at School Street.

In a convoluted deal, the completed Elite passed to Brian's friend and Brian ended up with an MG TD and the rebuilt Daimler. Brian was now visiting the workshop whenever he could get away from his father's chartered accountancy practice in Manchester, and he would move on later to the inevitable 'talking shop' session in a café. There he got drawn into the discussions about the new Clubmans Formula, which he thought might provide a good way for his racing to progress.

He discussed what he ought to buy with Derek and, for a while, Derek reckoned that a modified Terrier would be the way to go. But when the regulations came out, Derek felt it would be possible to build a car which was far more sophisticated than anything that was currently available. So Brian asked if he would build one for him, and Derek said yes.

The main intention of the formula was to separate out the growing numbers of Lotus 7s which were threatening to take over sports car racing grids and give them a category of their own. So the brief was to beat a Lotus 7. Derek's aim was to provide a strong, rigid chassis, with good weight distribution, and effective aerodynamics — a set of basic parameters which continued to guide his thinking as a designer throughout his career. A stressed propshaft tunnel contributed to the rigidity, he went for independent suspension all round, worked on getting the engine as low as possible with the driver alongside it, and designed a far more streamlined body than the rather stubby Lotus 7 had.

The Clubmans car also set the style for Derek's idiosyncratic method of designing and building a car. He was not an engineer or draughtsman, so he had no need of a drawing board. Apart from the odd sketch on a piece of scrap paper, everything was worked out in his head. 'If you gave him a pile of metal and a welding torch and a hacksaw he'd make you anything,' said Bob Faulkner. And that is pretty much how it was.

Dave Willars had been to university and was now a qualified civil engineer, but Derek Bennett's workshops still held the same fascination as they always had and he shared Derek's enthusiasm for the Clubmans project. He had a week's holiday coming up over Easter, so he went out and bought a pile of square section steel tubing and some aluminium sheeting. Derek finished a write-off he was working on and cleared the decks. For a while they just sat on the floor and drew round each other with chalk to get an idea of the basic shape and dimensions. Then out came the hacksaw and the welding torch and off Derek went.

The first frame was soon completed, but in his quest to get the cockpit size down to the dimensions permitted in the regulations, Derek had made the frame too small. Because of Brian Classick's very slight build the car could still be made to suit him, but Derek wanted to have a second attempt to get it exactly right. There was still enough tubing left over to get a second car underway, and Derek was keen to have one that he could race himself, but he couldn't afford to finance the building of two cars at once. So he went back to Classick and convinced him that his car would end up costing less if they built two together. As Derek's own resources could not run to this, Brian agreed to pay for parts and materials for his car as they went along. The bills trickled in on the backs of envelopes and Brian reckons he ended up paying £470 for his car.

Paul Owens was now working for Gresham and Cravens building automatic gearboxes for the likes of the Borgward Isabella. But he was only a few miles down the road from School Street and he continued to come along after work to help out, as he had been doing for the best part of 10 years. As Derek's involvement with racing had grown, Paul had slotted happily into race preparation, helping Derek maintain whichever cars he was driving and turning up at race meetings to be the mechanic on the day. In this role, he dived enthusiastically into helping Derek build the Clubmans cars. Brian Classick had put some entries in for July, so they were working hard to get both cars ready for then.

In the meantime, they had also come up with a name for their cars. Brian had wanted to know what he should call the car on his entry forms, and Paul and Doug Linton had convinced Derek that calling them Bennett Specials was not going to confer a sufficiently professional image on his creations. For weeks it seemed as if everyone had chipped in with a suggestion round the table in the café. Then one day Derek was waiting at a stores counter, idly gazing at a poster of Highway Code symbols. One of them was a line of alternate black and white arrows. The description underneath included the word

Derek Bennett and Paul Owens — their partnership was at the heart of Chevron and they shared each other's aspirations for 22 years.

Derek in Robert Ashcroft's Repco-Brabham BT14 on his way to victory in a Libre race at Oulton Park on 12 June 1965. (*Photo Frank Hall.*)

'chevrons'. It jumped straight out at Derek. 'That's it,' he thought. 'We'll call them Chevrons.'

With Derek busy with the Clubmans cars, Ashcroft had run John Cardwell and George Pitt in his Brabham, but he still wanted Derek to race it. When he ran into problems with the car's rear suspension he took it to Derek to sort out, and persuaded him to take over the driving when it was finished. Straight away the Brabham started winning. Then Ashcroft came up with another of his deals. With backing from Shell, they were going to take the Brabham over to Ireland for three races, and there was money for the Clubmans car as well if it could be finished in time.

Brian's car should have been finished first, but Derek and Paul turned their full attention to getting Derek's car ready to go to Ireland. Getting the sheet aluminium panels for the bodywork rolled and welded together proved to be the most time-consuming exercise. Derek had painstakingly put together a wire buck of the body on the frame and this was taken to a company in Manchester called Agnew and Clarke for the panels to be made. Dave Willars recalls 'a little Polish bloke' there who followed Derek's suggestions meticulously. Paul Owens was equally impressed: 'He was an old chap, who was very, very skilled, and it took a long time to get those done. He was having to do two sets of panels at a time and he had to have a chassis to do it on, so it was quiet a difficult job. It was a credit to the old chap, an absolutely fantastic job.' Derek came up with a Cortina GT engine to put into his car, but he had little time to tune it other than putting in some big, old, cut-down Jaguar valves.

The first of the three races was at Kirkistown on 3 July, a shakedown for the two big races in Eire that followed. But a week before, Derek was racing the Brabham in the Bob Gerard *Formule Libre* Championship round at Mallory Park where he won the race and took fastest lap, adding to his win at Oulton Park a fortnight earlier. He would be going to Ireland very much as a man to beat. Committed though he was to building the Clubmans car, it was almost a distraction he could do without at that point.

He was under pressure again to 'settle down'. The second of his sisters, June, had got married a couple of years before and, once again, Derek's girlfriend of the time had been the bridesmaid. She too wanted to know when it would be her turn. In the meantime Derek was having his most successful year as a racing driver and getting plenty of offers of drives, but none of them was worth any money. Something inside him wanted the security of a family life and a permanent relationship, but he still had neither the time nor the money to take that responsibility — the Clubmans car had seen to that, eating up all his funds and creating more late–night sessions than anything he had ever done before.

He had got the Brabham all ready for Kirkistown, but with the cars due at Liverpool to catch the ferry the following day and the Clubmans car nothing like finished, the pressure became too much and Derek performed the rare — but characteristic — disappearing act that was his response to such situations. He always kept his problems to himself, but those who were close to him knew things were serious when he performed

CHEVRON

his disappearing act. 'He'd been throwing a few wobblies all afternoon,' remembers Paul Owens, 'saying "Oh, this is crazy. This is stupid. We'll never get it finished." But I was working away at it merrily and Derek was working away, and I turned round and I thought I was talking to Derek — and he'd gone.'

Paul was not prepared to admit defeat yet, though, and he carried on working throughout the night. The next morning, when Derek walked in an hour before they were due to leave, the Clubmans car was sufficiently intact to be loaded onto the trailer with the Brabham. The bits that were not yet attached were thrown back into the back of the van and they set off for Ireland and Gerry Kinnane's garage off the Falls Road in Belfast, which was to be their base for the next couple of weeks. Kinnane was a friend of Ashcroft's and he had fixed them up with a Morris Minor as additional transport, and rooms at Mrs O'Brien's guest house. But while they finished building the car they snatched what sleep they could in the garage and the Chevron turned a wheel for the first time when they got to Kirkistown.

This view of the prototype Clubmans car shows how the 1500cc Ford engine was tilted and positioned alongside the driver to improve weight distribution and keep the centre of gravity low. (*Photo Brian Foley.*)

Paul was the first to drive the car, running with the shock absorbers slackened off to let the suspension settle in on the bumpy circuit. Then Ashcroft, who would be racing the car in Eire, took the wheel. Unfortunately, in the rush to prepare it, they had failed to lubricate the rose joints enough and during one of those sessions one seized up and broke. The car lost a wheel, but the damage was slight and they were able to repair it in time for Derek to give the first Chevron its début. It won the race and broke the lap record.

Full of renewed enthusiasm, the team moved over the border into Eire for the Leinster Trophy meeting on the closed public roads at Dunboyne two weeks later. Taking a particular interest in their progress was a 19-year-old Belfast lad with aspirations as a racing driver. His name was John Watson and he had taken a liking to Derek Bennett as soon as he met him at Gerry Kinnane's Grace Hill Motor Works. After a season racing an Austin Healey Sprite, John now had his first proper racing car, a Crosslé sports car with an 1100cc Formula Junior engine, and he was due to come up against the Chevron in a *Libre* handicap at Dunboyne. This time Robert Ashcroft drove the car and Watson had to settle for second place as it won again.

Driving Ashcroft's Brabham in the main Leinster Trophy scratch *Libre* race, Derek was beaten into second place by the Lotus 24-Chevrolet of his old adversary on the mainland, Chris Summers. But he still won his class and impressed all by beating Alan Rollinson's Formula 2 Brabham and Tommy Reid's Lotus 22. Sadly, the celebrations were muted because of the death of Adam Wylie in a practice accident at the wheel of his Formula 2 Brabham.

The last of the three Irish races was a week later at Phoenix Park where Robert Ashcroft again drove the Chevron in the *Libre* handicap event. Derek's Brabham was second in the scratch event, this time to Malcolm Templeton's Formula 2 Brabham, despite being hit by Gerry Kinnane's GRM in the early stages. The Irish trip had been just the boost Derek needed. It had underlined both his own ability as a driver and his potential as a racing car designer, and he returned with a new enthusiasm — and Brian Classick's car to get ready for its first race.

With a chance of winning the Mallory Park-based Bob Gerard *Libre* Championship, Derek's own driving efforts were still concentrated on the Brabham and a win on August Bank Holiday Monday brought him within two points of Alan Rollinson's Formula 2 Brabham. Rodney Bloor was only another point behind in another BT 14 twin-cam, with which he had beaten Derek earlier in the year at Oulton Park. But after an accident at Goodwood, Rodney had decided to await the imminent arrival of his first child in safer surroundings and had retired. The championship was not resolved until the Christmas meeting, on 27 December. Rollinson went into the race one point in front, but Derek won the race, equalling his points score and snatching the championship with the greatest number of wins.

In between races with the Brabham, Derek had driven the Chevron with considerable success. He and Brian Classick would frequently take the first two places and only David Wragg's U2 proved a match for Derek. Over a few months the cars created quite an impression and even before the year was over, a Manchester solicitor named John Carden was down at School Street asking Derek to build him a replica. With the cramped facilities there and the effort going into racing the Brabham, Derek had neither the time nor the space to make another car right away, so he agreed to Carden's suggestion that he supply the car on a do-it-yourself basis for him to have built himself.

So Derek produced a bare spaceframe and Carden's mechanic, Robin Gordon, set about building the car. Although it was subsequently designated the first of the 1966 production B2s, it was in fact a halfway–house between those first two prototypes and the first production Chevrons. Carden was not the only one to express an interest in buying a Chevron and Derek soon realised that he would be able to find customers if he had enough workshop space to produce more than one car at a time.

In the meantime, Robert Ashcroft had parted company with Sports Motors and was running a second-hand car business from a showroom in Chorley Old Road, close to the centre of Bolton. He needed somewhere to service cars and he knew how cramped Derek was in Salford, so when he came across an old mill just down the road, which was available very cheaply, he suggested to Derek that they share the premises. Ashcroft would have the front for his stock and Derek could have whatever he needed of the rest in which to set up his equipment.

If Derek was going to set out seriously to produce some replicas of the Clubmans cars he was also going to need something resembling some staff. Paul Owens had been spending more time working for Derek than he had at his own job for some years and he was an obvious choice to join the new enterprise, although initially he was employed by Ashcroft, who carried on entering Derek's racing cars, and remained heavily involved in race preparation. Paul also recruited two of the first Chevron employees, Roy Rogerson and Colin Greenhalgh, who had worked on the experimental side of the gearbox division at Gresham and Cravens while he was there, and were looking for a move after the company had been taken over by Westinghouse Hobbs. They were employed as fabricators and welders, brazing the chassis and building suspensions, and a third member of staff — a sheet metal worker called Bill Robinson — was recruited through an advertisement. Also part of the move was Tommy Humphreys, who was glad to be able to get his spray painting operation out of the cramped surroundings of School Street.

Friends joined in to help out however they could: brother-in-law Geoff Smith wired up all the power in the mill, while Dave Willars helped them set up the workshop. Derek had carried on preparing Dave's Anglia, racing it occasionally through 1965, and Dave was happy that much of the money he had spent contributing materials for the first Clubmans car had already been repaid in kind. But Derek came over to his house one night and brought with him a share certificate in David's name. The shares were in Derek Bennett Engineering Limited, the company which was being formed to build Chevrons — the Chevron name itself was already well tied up by a number of companies, including Chevrolet and Chevron Oil. Surprised — but touched — by the gesture, Dave accepted the shares as a 'thank-you' from Derek for helping him start the prototype, and assured Derek that his five per cent would always be behind Derek if he ever needed the support.

The share certificates were drawn up by Doug Linton, who was to be Company Secretary, and who also received 50 shares (five per cent) as did Paul Owens. Derek Bennett himself had a controlling 550 of the 1,000 shares and the remaining 30 per

Doug Linton drew up the share certificates when Derek Bennett Engineering Limited was formed in 1966. This is the certificate for his own 50 shares.

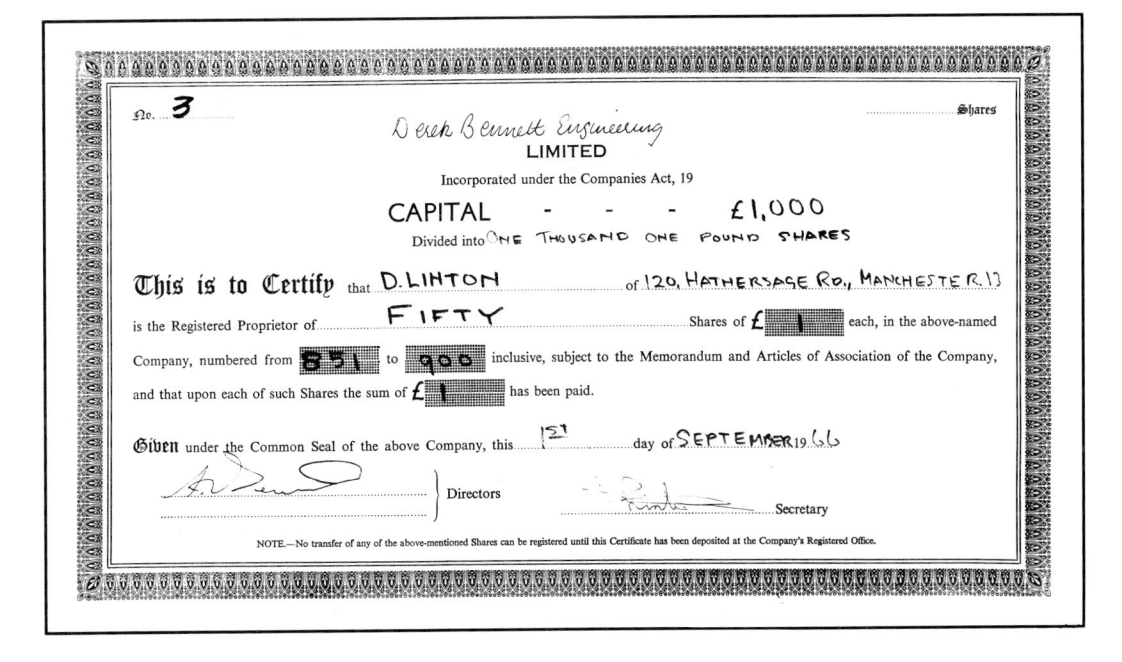

cent went to Jimmy Horrocks, who had moved on from his snack bar and was now dealing in gaming machines. Horrocks was the only one who put a financial stake into the company, helping Derek fund the move to Bolton. In recognition of this he became a director, along with Derek himself.

Derek set a price of £1,250 for the Clubmans cars and his new workforce was soon working on orders for three of them, 1500cc Ford-engined versions for Don Hill and Howard Heerey, and a 1-litre BMC-powered example for Andrew Smith. Derek's own car was sold to Jim Charnock, Brian Classick continued racing his, and John Carden finished building his, so when the 1966 season got under way there were half-a-dozen Chevrons ready to win races.

With the Clubmans cars creating quite an impression, a number of people approached Derek to ask if he could put a roof on one and make it eligible for GT racing. That idea did not particularly appeal to him, but Derek was interested in building a GT car from scratch. He liked the category and he had plenty of experience of it from his years racing Elites. Now the Lotus Elan was the dominant car and Derek firmly believed he could build something to beat it.

He had been tossing ideas around for a GT car for some time, mainly with his old friend Bob Faulkner, who was now working for the aero-engineers, A. V. Roe — later to become part of Hawker Siddeley. Bob was invaluable to Derek for talking through ideas on design and aerodynamics, and as a mechanical engineer he had a useful familiarity with stress testing. But most importantly, they had an instinctive understanding of each other, rooted in the early aeromodelling projects of their school days. The idea for the car's basic shape emerged from doodles that developed into a freehand drawing. Then Bob put the drawing onto graph paper, cut out some cardboard formers and stuck them together to make a model. Bob used this as the basis for a 12-inch long balsa wood model, which sat on Derek's desk at the new factory in Bolton as a reminder of what he would like to do next.

It did not take long for the local motor racing fraternity to find out where Derek Bennett had moved to and people were soon dropping in to the Chevron Works in much the same way as they used to visit his earlier workshops. When Derek had taken the Clubmans car to Oulton Park for the first time in July 1965, he had won his class and finished second overall, beaten only by Brian Redman in the Red Rose lightweight Jaguar E-Type. Behind Derek in third place had been Alan Minshaw, driving a Lotus 23. Minshaw would eventually establish his own successful motor sport accessory business, Demon Tweeks, but at that time he was a salesman for Fram Filters and as Bolton was part of his territory, he would drop in at

Chevrons whenever he was passing. The Clubmans cars did not appeal to him, but when Derek showed him the model of the GT car, he liked the look of it. Derek told him he was about to start building them and that he could be the first customer if he put down a deposit of £100.

Minshaw duly put his money down, but when he got a phone call to say that the car might cost £300 more than the £1,700 they had discussed he began to get cold feet. Seeing Elan racer Digby Martland at a party, he asked whether he had heard about the new Chevron GT that Derek Bennett was planning. Martland hadn't, but he knew of Derek and he remembered seeing the Clubmans car at Aintree and being tremendously impressed by them. Minshaw told him he could take over his order for the car if he wanted it, so the next morning Martland went straight over to Bolton, took a close look at the Clubmans cars that were being built and saw the wooden model of the GT car. Meeting Derek Bennett convinced him that the new car was going to be good. He decided on the spot that he had to have one and repaid the deposit to Alan Minshaw, who unwittingly became the motor racing equivalent of the record company man who turned down The Beatles.

Digby was only 23-years-old, but he had been racing since leaving school in 1960 and had been getting some good results in a lightweight Elan. His family was reputed to own half of Lancashire — including a lucrative stake in Southport Pleasure Beach — and this affluent young man who drove a white E-Type Jaguar was regarded with curiosity by the workers at Haslam's Mill. But Digby's enthusiasm soon made him a popular — if unlikely — member of the team, and he could not keep away from the factory while the car was being built.

With little more than the image of the wooden model to go from, Derek Bennett started building the GT car, equipped with his pile of tubes, his hacksaw, and his welding torch. It seemed he never fully knew how he was going to make something until he had started doing it. Then it would all fit into place as he went along. It was very rare indeed that he would have to backtrack and do something again. Once the spaceframe chassis was finished, Derek continued with his policy of using readily available equipment wherever possible, and the GT cars had standard Marcos windscreens and Triumph Herald front uprights. The rear uprights were made from their own castings, as were the wishbones.

Derek had not intentionally set himself up as a racing car manufacturer, but he was beginning to see the potential that was there and he decided he wanted to build a second car, not just so he could race it himself, but so the company would have a development car. Although Digby's car was being built

The prototype Chevron GT posed on the moors above Bolton in 1966.

with a 1600cc Lotus twin-cam engine — the obvious choice to put it in direct competition with the Lotus Elans — Derek was on the look-out for something that would eventually give the car a bit more power. He was impressed by the way Chris Williams' Lotus-Brabham ran with its BMW 2002 engine and thought that would be a route worth trying for his own development car. So Robert Ashcroft bought a second-hand Nerus-tuned BMW engine that had seen service in an Elva, and Derek's own car was built around that.

The two GT cars were built up side-by-side, much as the first two Clubmans cars had been a year earlier, but there was more of a sense of importance about these. They were destined for a more prestigious category of racing and it was important to Derek that they should win. So it seemed a good idea to try and sell a third car as well. Lotus Elan drivers were obvious potential customers as it was their cars he was intending to make obsolete, so he approached Cheshire jeweller John

Lepp, who had been extremely successful in an ex-Chequered Flag lightweight Elan.

Lepp had heard the rumours about Derek Bennett's new GT car, but he was sceptical about its chances. 'I couldn't see how somebody in a shed in wherever it was could produce a car that was going to be a match for something that Chapman was producing at the time,' he recalls. Although he was consistently the quickest Elan driver in the north, at national level Lepp was unable to beat the Willment Elan of John Miles. Anything that might enable him to put that situation to rights was worth taking at least half seriously, and the Chevron was being offered to him virtually at cost, so he said he was interested, but he would not commit himself until he saw the car run. So Derek agreed that he could have an option on the car until the first test day, and if he did not like what he saw, they would sell it to someone else.

In mid-July the call came to go to Oulton Park where Peter

CHEVRON

Digby Martland gave the Chevron GT its winning début at Oulton Park on 23 July 1966. He was beaten away from the grid by John Carden's Clubmans Chevron B2 (46) and Peter Deal's Lotus 7 (45). Peter Crossley's Chevron B2 can also be seen on the second row. (*Photo Frank Hall.*)

Gethin would be giving Digby Martland's car its first run. Gethin was driving a Formula 3 Brabham for Rodney Bloor's Sports Motors team at the time, so he was the most readily available 'ace' to demonstrate the car. Gethin was not too sure what to expect either, especially when he got to Oulton Park to find the Chevron had no doors and no rear bodywork. But any doubts he had were rapidly dispelled. 'The car was fantastic, straight out of the box,' he recalls, bringing up the phrase that would virtually become Chevron's trademark over the years. 'Eventually I spun it and they said, "Right, that's enough!" It was unbelievable, it was a winner from the word go, easy to drive, and very fast.'

The stop-watches gave Gethin a best time of 1 minute 47.5 seconds — an incredible six seconds inside John Miles' lap record. To the watching John Lepp this was just too good to be true. 'I went straight from not being sure to "How the hell can I live without this?" So I wrote a cheque there and then!'

The following Saturday (23 July) the sleek, dark blue Chevron returned to Oulton Park, this time complete with all its body panels, ready to race. Practice was the first time Digby had sat in his new car, but he put it on the front row for the opening event of the day, a combined Sports and GT race. Alongside him was John Carden's Clubmans Chevron, which went into the lead at the start before being passed by Peter Deal's Lotus 7. Digby sat behind the Elan of John Harris and the two Clubmans cars while he got the feel of the Chevron. By lap two he was second and on the third circuit he moved into the lead. As his confidence in the car grew he pulled out a comfortable lead, taking two seconds off Miles' lap record on the way to victory. The Chevron had won its first race — 'straight out of the box'.

Spurred on by this success, Derek threw everything into getting his own car ready for a trip to the lion's den in a fortnight's time. A weekend at Crystal Palace and Brands Hatch would be a good time to introduce the south of England to the new racing cars from the north. The Crystal Palace race was on the Saturday (6 August) and the BMW-engined car barely made it to south-east London in time as it was not finished until three o'clock that morning. Unfortunately there had not been time to equip the car with certain luxury items, like windscreen wipers that worked, and of course it rained. Derek hung on gamely in fourth place overall for as long as he could, but by the end of the race he had slipped back a couple of places as he struggled round the last lap peering out of the door to see where he was going! He was still rewarded with a class win.

Digby Martland fared better, chasing the winning Ferrari 250LM of David Piper through the spray to finish second overall, and meting out the promised defeat of John Miles' Elan in the 1600cc class. At Brands Hatch the following day, Digby went out with what became a recurring engine problem that was eventually traced to a blocked fuel filter. Derek meanwhile led the race comfortably and broke the lap record before the BMW engine lost its oil pressure, putting him out of the race.

Nevertheless the cars from Bolton had acquitted themselves well and Colin Chapman had certainly been given a shock. The Elan had indeed been rendered obsolete overnight and a radical, and hasty, new approach was going to be needed to put these upstarts in their place.

Derek Bennett's next visit to Brands Hatch was rather less auspicious. Watched by a 30,000-strong August Bank Holiday Monday crowd he lost control on a very greasy track and went straight into the marshals' post at South Bank bend. The car was quite badly damaged, but it was repaired in plenty of time for the next big occasion, Oulton Park's Formula 1 Gold Cup meeting on September 17. John Lepp's car was finished in time for that meeting and the presence of three of the locally built cars on the grid for the *Autosport* Championship race caused quite a stir, surrounded as they were by cars bearing the rather more glamorous names of Ferrari, Porsche and Lotus. David Piper's new Ferrari 275LM took its expected win, but Derek Bennett held a clear second place ahead of the 2-litre class runners until overheating problems caused him to drop back to fourth. Martland's car finished sixth and would have won the 1600cc class had there been one, while Lepp went out losing oil — his revenge on John Miles would have to wait a little longer.

CHAPTER 5

Taking on the world

CHEVRON'S new GT cars were already starting to attract customers for 1967, but Robert Ashcroft was very keen that the company should push ahead right away and avoid getting too caught up in British club racing. If they were truly going to establish Chevron alongside Porsche and Ferrari — and to capitalise on the sales potential which that could bring — they had to establish an international reputation.

Although Ashcroft had no financial stake in the company, he was entering Derek and Digby's cars under his Robert Ashcroft Racing banner and he had been taking on the role of front man for the company, compensating for Derek's characteristically low profile. So, with an international sales drive in mind, Ashcroft had tried to enter the two cars for the 1,000km at Montlhéry, near Paris, in October 1966. He had nominated

Derek's B4 is wheeled on to its trailer at the factory. Paul Owens is at the driver's door. (*Photo Bolton Evening News.*)

Brian Redman as one of his drivers, but the French had never heard of Redman and were unimpressed. So he had come up with the idea of taking the cars to a smaller meeting at Montlhéry earlier in the year to show willing. Derek and Digby had squeezed the race in, despite it coming only a week after Derek had crashed his car at Brands Hatch, but the organisers still refused to give them an entry for their first World Championship race.

Undeterred, Ashcroft came up with an even more ambitious plan — the Daytona 24-Hours, which was coming up in February 1967. American racing car dealer, team manager and racing driver Fred Opert had already been to have a look round the Chevron factory at the invitation of Ashcroft, from whom he had bought some second-hand racing cars in the past. Ashcroft introduced him to Derek Bennett and took him along to Oulton Park to see the prototype GT car in action. He was very impressed with it and liked Ashcroft's idea of taking a Chevron to America to get some worldwide exposure. Next to Le Mans, the Daytona 24-Hours was probably the most prestigious sports car race in the world, so a deal was struck to take Derek's BMW-engined development car to America in February where Opert would run it at Daytona with backing from his sponsor, Valvoline.

Derek was far too busy to get involved with the trip himself, so Peter Gethin was suggested as a driver. Gethin was keen to have the opportunity to race in the States and it was decided to team him up with fellow Formula 3 driver Roy Pike, who was an American and could combine the race with a trip home to his family in California. Opert himself would join the team as the third driver.

The car was shipped over to New York where Fred Opert, who was based in New Jersey, was going to arrange transport to take it down to Florida by road. To keep the costs down they used Opert's mechanics, Ashcroft went along as Bolton's representative, and Digby Martland went along for the ride. As it turned out, they were being a little over ambitious, although the main problem at this point was with the Chevron's second-hand BMW engine. Keeping the oil in it proved a difficult task and during practice they had the engine stripped down as they desperately tried to produce a solution to the problem. When they got it running there was some kind of vibration in the car, which they did not have time to pinpoint, and the car began to look like a doubtful starter. Pike went and bought himself a plane ticket to California for first thing Sunday morning, even though the race was not due to finish until Sunday afternoon, and Gethin was also becoming very doubtful about their chances.

Meanwhile Opert was loving it, spurred on by his own

natural enthusiasm and the need to get the car into the race to make sure of the team's starting money. 'To me it was a very exciting thing,' Opert remembers. 'It was the fastest car I'd ever driven at the time, but . . . well it wasn't perfect next to a Carrera 6 or something like that, and they were down on the project the whole weekend, which to me was very depressing.'

The oil leak turned out to be a self-inflicted problem caused by Opert's mechanics' unfamiliarity with the engine's dry sump system and, with that solved, the car ran for six hours in the race before a rear wishbone broke and it crashed — not too heavily — with Roy Pike at the wheel. Obviously the fledgling racing car manufacturer had a little more to learn before it was ready for World Championship long-distance races. But no-one was too discouraged, particularly Opert, who had been impressed enough with the car to want to keep in close touch with Chevron for the future.

Back at the ranch, Derek Bennett was working away on the production cars for the start of the 1967 season. They had several firm orders for GT cars and a number of things needed sorting out before they could move easily into production. The original bodies, for instance, had been made from sheet aluminium. They had used those to make the moulds for fibreglass body panels and a couple of local companies had done some work for them, but they were not particularly happy with the quality of the end result. Eventually, Derek tried Specialised Mouldings, a specialist fibreglass company formed by brothers Peter and David Jackson, based not in Lancashire, but on a trading estate in Huntingdon. They took over production of the bodies, beginning an association which would last right through Chevron's existence.

The other problem to be cracked was the engine. With a 1600cc twin-cam the Chevron had performed its original task of beating Lotus Elans with almost embarrassing ease. But if their sights were to be set on Porsche and Ferrari they needed a full 2-litre engine and a lot more power. Derek still believed in the potential of the BMW engine, but the reliability problem needed to be overcome. The engine had been designed to run inclined at an angle of 30 degrees in the BMW 2002 saloon and the oil would not drain if it was run vertically. Derek reduced the angle by as much as he could, compensating for this by incorporating his own dry sump system with a scavenge pump. In keeping with Bennett tradition, the scavenge pump came from an MG, and joined a water pump off a Ford Transit van, which could be operated from the side of the engine rather then projecting from the front of the block as the standard one did. The distributor also had to be moved so that it would not foul the body panel.

Other work doubtless could be done to improve the actual performance of the engine, but if they were going to be able to offer the BMW engine as an option for their customers, the next step was to find a source of supply. So Derek sent Paul off to Munich to go and see the men at the Bayerische Motoren Werke. Digby chauffeured Paul to Germany in his E-Type and they knocked on the door of the Competitions Department and introduced themselves to one of its bosses. After discussing their project with them he explained that BMW could not supply them with any parts direct, but he arranged for the main agent in Munich to supply them with everything they needed, and offered a discount. So, armed with all the components they needed to build their first new engine, and some useful information on tuning, they headed back to Bolton.

Although Chevron had orders for four GTs with BMW engines, David Bridges decided to go a different route and had a car built with a 2-litre Tasman-BRM V8 engine. David was the middle one of the three Bridges brothers, and ran a Formula 2 team. His driver, John Taylor, had died after being badly burned at the Nürburgring the year before and for 1967 he had asked Brian Redman to drive for him. Redman, whose family name was to be found above the grocer's shop in most Lancashire towns, had been discovered by the eldest of the Bridges brothers, Charles, in 1965. After a successful season driving Charles' ex-Graham Hill, John Coombs lightweight E-Type, Brian had driven a 6-litre Chevrolet-engined Lola T70 Mk2 for him in 1966, making his presence felt enough to pick up the third Grovewood Award.

But Charles was pulling out of racing and David needed a driver, so Brian moved over to make not only his Formula 2 début, but his single-seater début, in David's Brabham. Rodney Bloor promised he could get them a new Brabham and an FVA engine from Cosworth, but Brian had an ultimatum to contend with. 'You really need to decide whether you are going to be a grocer or a racing driver,' his father had told him. With such a good drive lined up, Brian decided against being a grocer. Then, a week after he left the family business, he found out that neither Brabham nor Cosworth considered him well-enough known to merit their latest equipment. So they had to make do with an older chassis and a Cosworth SCB engine. The season turned out to be an inevitable disappointment and Brian found the chance to drive the Chevron GT was a welcome one.

The Chevron-BRM won first time out at Oulton Park in April, and then at Crystal Palace on Whit Monday Brian drove a race that put Chevron firmly on the map. Watched by a television audience he fought an epic battle with Mike De Udy's

Brian Redman keeps the B5-BRM ahead of Mike De Udy's Lola T70 on his way to victory at Crystal Palace on 29 May 1967. (Photo LAT.)

Lola T70 — and won. Digby Martland backed up Redman's effort by finishing fourth in his new Chevron-BMW.

The race rounded off a tremendous weekend for Chevron as Digby had come straight to Crystal Palace from the Nürburgring where he and Nigel Moores (racing under the pseudonym 'Paul Kelly') had taken Chevron's first World Championship finish, coming in ninth overall and fourth in class in the 1,000km. Digby had slept curled up in the back of his E-Type while Paul Owens drove back to catch the overnight ferry, so he had not been at his best at Crystal Palace. Then for good measure, Derek Bennett had won at Brands Hatch on the Sunday in his works BMW-engined car.

Chevron was coming to mean something further away from Bolton than Oulton Park and three cars were granted entries for the BOAC 500 at Brands Hatch in July. Derek Bennett's own car was one of them, but it was crashed heavily by co-driver John Cardwell during the race. Brian Redman fared no better in the BRM car, which broke its differential on the first lap, but Digby Martland and Brian Muir completed the distance in 15th place, finishing third in their class.

With the cars beginning to make progress in the international arena, Chevron were also adding to their reputation at home, thanks in particular to the efforts of John Lepp, whose original 1966 twin-cam car was dominating the *Motoring News* GT Championship. On the day of the BOAC 500 Lepp was at Silverstone where his 1600cc car won the race outright, heading the newer 2-litre BMW-engined cars of John Bridges and Arthur Moore in a Chevron 1-2-3.

After his handful of races at the end of 1966, Lepp had had the winter to get the car into top shape. His mechanic, Robin

TAKING ON THE WORLD

Gordon, fitted a brand new twin-cam with the latest Tecalemit Jackson fuel injection, but when the season opened with two races over the Easter weekend, it had been plagued by an incurable misfire. Nevertheless, John had won outright at Oulton Park and Mallory Park and he found himself leading the *Motoring News* Championship. They made the decision to go for the title, but agreed the fuel injection had to go. To replace it they took two Weber carburettors off the highly-modified engine of John's 2.5-litre Triumph Estate tow car and the engine ran faultlessly, notching up a string of class wins, until engine-tuner Chris Steele came along and said he could build them a Cosworth Mk XIIIC twin-cam that would be even quicker, which duly he did.

Lepp consistently embarrassed drivers of the BMW-engined Chevrons with his speed, although one such giant-killing attempt cost him a race at Mallory Park. Leading his class comfortably and chasing Digby Martland's Chevron-BMW for the outright lead, he crashed heavily approaching Devil's Elbow. Ironically, Martland had a one-minute penalty for jumping the start, so the race had been Lepp's for the taking anyway.

John Lepp won the 1967 *Motoring News* GT Championship in his 1600cc twin-cam B3, seen here at Silverstone on 30 July when it beat the 2-litre BMW-engined Chevrons of John Bridges and Arthur Moore to win overall. (*Photo LAT.*)

CHEVRON

As the season wore on Lepp did not have everything his own way though. Lotus had brought out the twin-cam, rear-engined Lotus 47 as a response to the Chevron at the end of 1966. John Miles had given it its début at the Brands Hatch Boxing Day meeting, where Peter Gethin had lined up against him in Lepp's car. But when Gethin lost all his gears on the warming up lap, Miles had been left with an easy win, which had served to divert a few orders away from Bolton.

Ginetta also found a substantial number of customers for their latest G12 and so Lepp was frequently the sole Chevron driver in the 1600cc class. But nobody gave him any problems until his old rival, John Miles, appeared in Lotus Components' development version of the 47.

Early in the season the 47 was unreliable and Miles became increasingly despondent as he had to return to Lotus after each weekend with news of another Chevron victory. Chapman must have found it hard to comprehend what was going on — the might of Lotus ranged against a prototype built in an old Lancashire cotton mill, driven by a jeweller, and prepared by a part-time mechanic in a lock-up garage.

But Miles' time came in a chaotic race at Mallory Park. Struggling in torrential rain on a near-flooded track Derek Bennett spun away the lead, leaving Miles in front. Lepp gave

Derek Bennett (148) and Digby Martland (146) come through Lodge Corner at Oulton Park side by side in their B6s. On this occasion, 26 August 1967, Digby eventually got the best of the encounter. (*Photo Frank Hall.*)

chase until his Chevron aquaplaned passing the pits and spun its way along the main straight. He and Derek both got going again, only to slither into each other, leaving Miles with an unchallenged run to the flag. The following week at Brands Hatch Miles beat Lepp again in a straight race, although Derek's class-winning BMW-engined car deprived the Lotus of overall victory. Miles had proved the point, but his Formula 3 commitments for Lotus prevented him from taking in many more *Motoring News* rounds and Lepp's Chevron continued to dispose of all the customer Lotus 47s with impunity, ending the year outright winner of the championship. Digby Martland's appearances in the series, which included some very close races with Derek Bennett, were successful enough to make him the 2500cc class winner.

John Lepp was not Chevron's only champion in 1967 though. The Clubmans cars were far from forgotten and the formula was having its best season yet, now well established as a providing ground for hungry young drivers and with Formula Ford still only in a fledgling state. Howard Heerey was one such driver. Still only 22 years-old, he had raced a Mini before buying Derek Bennett's unloved Formula 3 Brabham from him. For 1966 Howard had ordered a new Brabham, but when it failed to turn up he went back to Derek and bought a Clubmans Chevron. Much of that season was spent develop-

Howard Heerey on his way to one of the many wins that brought him the 1967 Clubmans Championship title with his B2. (*Photo Frank Hall.*)

ing the car and, in particular, perfecting the use of the Holbay downdraught engine. When 1967 came round the car was a winner from the very first race.

Heerey's tally of 21 wins that year hides how closely contested the races were, especially between his Chevron and the U2 of Max Mosley. Their rivalry occasionally became too close and they collided with each other while fighting for the lead at Croft, but on the whole it was a season of close but clean racing and Heerey was a deserving winner of the National Clubmans' Championship at the end of it.

As well as the year's championship successes there were plenty of individual performances which contributed to Chevron's rapidly growing reputation. Tony Dean's Porsche Carrera 6 was the only car that could consistently beat the works Chevron GTs in the 2500cc class, but even the Porsche could be beaten, as Digby Martland proved with a memorable win at Crystal Palace in August 1967. Towards the end of the year Alan Harvey showed that southerners could win races in Chevrons as well when he took his BMW-engined car to victory in Silverstone's Colibri Trophy and followed that up with a series of wins at Brands Hatch.

In between his Formula 2 commitments, Brian Redman also continued to put in some appearances in Chevrons and was always guaranteed to astound everyone with both his and the car's ability. At Crystal Palace in September he tried Derek Bennett's BMW-engined car and stayed right in among the $5\frac{1}{2}$-litre Lola T70s to beat Bill Bradley's Carrera 6 easily in his class. Redman was only beaten overall by the T70s of Frank Gardner and Mike De Udy and took more than $1\frac{1}{2}$ seconds off Tony Dean's lap record.

A month earlier Redman had driven David Bridges' BRM-engined car at Croft and it had taken almost three laps for Denny Hulme to wrestle the lead from him in Sid Taylor's Lola T70. Brian hung on gamely in second place until the throttle cable broke. Towards the end of the season he also drove Derek Bennett's car again at Oulton Park, winning the GT race comfortably and bringing the lap record down to 1 minute 42.0 seconds — almost 10 seconds faster than Digby Martland's original lap record set on the debut of the twin-cam engined car little more than a year previously. Such was the rate of progress of the cars.

But there was still one more important event for Chevron in 1967 — the début of their first Formula 3 car. To everyone who was just getting used to the idea of Chevron as a serious manufacturer of GT cars, this was a totally unexpected development, but one which caused Derek Bennett to be considered in an altogether more serious light. Derek had always earned his living by doing whatever the paying customer asked him to do, and the progress of Chevron tended to be guided in much the same way — as a response to what the customers wanted rather than the result of any master plan of Derek's. So when Rodney Bloor asked Derek if he thought he could build him a Formula 3 car, off he went and did it.

The Brabham BT21 was the only customer car being produced in any quantity and easily outnumbered everything else on the grid put together in Formula 3 that year. Peter Gethin had been driving one for Bloor's Sports Motors team all season, but Rodney was curious to see whether Derek could build a car to match the Brabham. Gethin was enthusiastic about the idea after his earlier experiences with the GT car and visited the factory at Bolton regularly to check on the progress of the Formula 3.

Derek was also enthusiastic about the project as it let him develop many of the ideas he had formed in his own Formula 3 racing days. But this time, instead of endlessly modifying someone else's design, he could start from scratch with his own. He kept the car simple, small, and very light and barely three months after Rodney Bloor had commissioned it the car was ready to race at Brands Hatch on 8 October.

Gethin liked the car straight away, finding it comfortable and with a good feel to it. 'I remember it being a smashing

Derek Bennett's first single-seater Chevron, the Formula 3 B7, made an impressive début at Brands Hatch in October 1967 with Peter Gethin at the wheel. (*Photo LAT.*)

little car,' he recalls. 'A bit more sprightly than a Brabham, although it was a little less forgiving.' The car's début was far from smooth. Testing on the day before the race it blew an engine, which meant an overnight session to change it and a few problems to be sorted out on the replacement engine during official practice. Consequently, Gethin started the race from the third row. With everything to do he made a tremendous start, but the organisers decided it was too good and gave him a one minute penalty. Effectively Gethin's race was over, but there was still chance to demonstrate the eye-catching little Chevron's potential.

Out in front, John Miles was leading in the works Lotus 41C with Roy Pike's Titan challenging hard. Gethin brought the Chevron past Tetsu Ikuzawa's Brabham to move up behind the leading pair, and when Pike dropped out, he mounted an attack on Miles, who must have been developing something of a persecution complex — not content with haunting him in GT races, these Chevron people were trying to stop him winning Formula 3 races as well now! The two drivers thrilled the crowd right to the finish line, but Miles refused to be harried into leaving Gethin enough space to get past him and the Lotus flashed across the line just in front of the Chevron. With the addition of his penalty Gethin was unplaced, but he went away with the lap record and the name Chevron suddenly found its way onto the shopping lists of drivers looking to go Formula 3 in 1968.

Gethin raced the car a couple more times in 1967, but a win in Formula 3 was going to take a little longer to come by than it had in GT or Clubmans racing. At Oulton Park he went out in a start-line pile-up, and then at the Brands Hatch Motor Show International meeting he was lying fourth when the final was stopped as torrential rain reduced the race to chaos.

Chevron's progress in 1967 had been remarkable and Derek had to decided what he was going to do next. His original ideas had been based loosely around building a car to race himself and making the odd replica for a customer to help pay for it. But in the two years since he had left his workshop in Salford the enterprise had obviously ballooned far beyond that. As Company Secretary, Doug Linton had been coping with the rapidly increasing amount of administrative work that was linked to Chevron's expansion, and he sensed Derek's outlook beginning to change during 1967. They travelled round the country a lot together, buying parts from suppliers and approaching companies that they wanted to deal with, and it became obvious to Doug that Derek was beginning to see the potential to make a reasonable amount of money for the first time in his life if he could sell enough cars.

Chevron had already built up a good customer base for their

GT cars and they decided that getting the car homologated into Group 4 for international competition was the key to selling larger quantities. They had fallen out with Robert Ashcroft during the year, but they were really following the logic of his early ideas by looking to an international market. The original intention had been that Ashcroft would act as Sales Manager on a commission basis and he had even booked Chevron a stand at the 1967 Racing Car Show. But with customers walking through the doors at Bolton ordering cars as fast as the four-man crew could build them, Ashcroft had very little selling to do and there was a certain amount of resentment at him taking a cut. Derek was happy to let his cars sell themselves. As long as they could produce cars that would win races the customers would keep coming.

Nevertheless, going for homologation was a huge gamble as it meant producing more cars in six months than they had built in total before. His career as a musician all but forgotten, Doug Linton set about masterminding the homologation plans. To get the car into Group 4 they needed to build 50, which was plainly impossible — but all rules are open to interpretation . . .

Even if they could get away with not building 50 complete cars, they were still going to have to produce a large number, so the first thing they did was take on 10 more staff. Some they advertised for, but many were people who were already working for Derek in their spare time. Chevron was very much an extension of Derek's earlier workshops and operated along much the same lines with friends and other interested parties congregating there in the evenings after they had finished their day jobs, either to talk motor racing and see what Bennett

Over the winter of 1967/68 the production run of B8s began to take shape, ready for homologation. Derek Bennett is pictured here in the midst of some of his GT cars in December 1967. (*Photo Frank Hall.*)

was up to now, or increasingly to help him build his creations.

One of these helpers was Derek Faulkner, who had got into the habit of leaving work at Hawker Siddeley at four o'clock, going home for his tea, and then putting in another half–day's work in Bolton. Often he would not get home until after midnight, and the routine would begin all over again first thing the next morning, so it seemed like a good idea when Derek suggested that he come and work for Chevron full time. But he soon found that his working days did not get any shorter. 'The only difference it made was that I was not coming home for my tea! I was there all the time.' He looks back on the hours they all worked with horror, but recalls the way everyone was so involved in their work that it became more of a way of life than a job.

Everyone who worked at Chevron, whether they arrived as friends of Derek Bennett's or in response to an advertisement in the local paper, seemed to share the same sense of involvement and pride in their work, and at the heart of that involvement was a universal respect for Derek himself. Many were recruited solely for their job skills and had no previous interest in motor racing at all, but Derek's talent and attitude commanded their complete loyalty. Many of the people taken on at the start of 1968 were there until the day the company closed its doors in 1980, and they will still tell you they never had a better job.

In down to earth Bolton, Derek was respected as someone who never stood on ceremony but got on and did the job. He was always on the shop floor, ready with help and advice when it was needed, but otherwise stuck into the task of building racing cars just like everyone else. Indeed, Derek's anonymity was a constant source of amusement to his workforce who enjoyed seeing baffled customers trying to pick him out from amongst his staff. The more important the visitor was, the more likely Derek was to disappear as soon as they arrived, leaving the embarrassing business of talking to them to someone else. If he was the last to leave — as he frequently was — Derek would sweep up before he went home, and stories are told of someone walking through the door to find Derek, dressed in his overalls, brush in hand, sweeping the floor. 'Is Derek Bennett in?', they would say. 'No,' he would reply, and they would go home.

The people who worked with Derek in Bolton talk about it with the same enthusiasm that his teenage friends talk about their days aeromodelling with him. Derek Bennett was the focus of everyone's activity and enthusiasm. It was as if the Chevron factory was a giant version of the Bennett family's dining room table in Merton Road. Workers and customers alike all have their favourite stories, but the over-riding impression they all give is of how much fun everyone involved had.

With homologation of the GT car as a target, a system had to be worked out to keep the newly enlarged workforce working as efficiently as possible. The work of building the initial tubular spaceframe had been contracted out to Arch Motors in Huntingdon, who operated from the same trading estate as Specialised Mouldings, who were now producing a modified version of the car's body with a deeper, three-section opening in the nose for better airflow.

Paul Owens had also made a few more trips to Munich to get supply lines for the BMW engines and additional components sorted out. Special pistons were eventually supplied by Mahle, but only after Paul had driven down to Stuttgart and camped on their doorstep for a day and-a-half to convince them that Chevron meant business. Things had got considerably easier after Digby Martland's strong showing in the Nürburgring 1,000km in 1967. BMW had taken a great interest in the car there and invited Digby to take it back to the factory for them to go over. Digby raced a couple more times in Germany that summer and after one race his car was taken to Munich and deposited in the Competitions Department while Digby took himself off to Italy for a holiday. When he got back they had completely rebuilt the engine and Digby reckoned his car was quicker than Derek's own for the rest of the season.

BMW continued to help out with Digby's car during its regular European outings that year and Robert Ashcroft remembers them being called in one day to be informed, in serious tones, that the time had come to present them with the bill. Somewhat apprehensive that the terms of BMW's aid might have been misunderstood, Digby opened the piece of paper: it demanded the equivalent of £15 — 'For the books, you understand. We must keep the accountants happy.'

The first batch of engines was driven from Munich to Bolton by Paul Owens in the back of a van, but once the 1968 production run got under way all the parts were being flown to Manchester to be assembled in Chevron's new engine shop, which Paul had taken charge of. All Derek's modifications to the

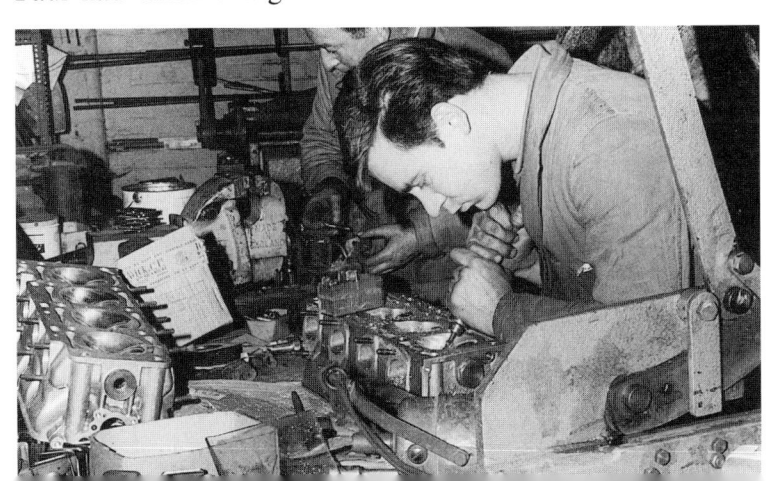

Paul Owens at work on a BMW engine. (*Photo Frank Hall.*)

CHEVRON

Shortly after Chevron took on extra staff at the beginning of 1968 this group photograph was taken outside Haslam's Mill. Digby Martland (front left) and Brian Classick, who were about to set off for Daytona, are pictured on either side of Paul Owens. Many such group shots were taken through the years, but this one is unusual in that it includes Derek Bennett (standing, second left).

earlier engines were carried out on each customer unit. Chevron's own dry sump would be fitted, the cylinder heads reworked, the pistons machined, their own inlet valves fitted, and so on. Some of the early engines had problems with valve springs, which were eventually replaced with stronger ones, but otherwise the BMW units were fast and reliable from the start.

They decided that the rules for homologation were all about having the intention and the capability of building 50 cars and that the wording was sufficiently ambiguous that they only needed to convince the authorities that 50 cars were on the way, rather than producing them in a line outside the factory to be counted. All the previous year's cars were brought in to be included in the count, and when these were added to the completed new cars, those in various stages of production on the shop floor, and those for which parts were on order, or customers' names were in the book, somehow the whole thing seemed to add up to 50 cars. The RAC and the FIA were happy that Chevron was indeed a volume producer of racing cars and the FIA's Homologation Committee announced that the Chevron-BMW GT was duly homologated into Group 4 from 1 May 1968.

A few weeks earlier the car had put in its most impressive international performance to date when Digby Martland and Brian Classick finished eighth overall in the BOAC 500 World Championship sports car race at Brands Hatch. After selling his Clubmans car, Brian had moved into Formula 3, racing a Brabham BT21 in Europe. He was already beginning to realise that he might not be destined for Formula 1 when he put himself in hospital by crashing spectacularly out of the Monza Lottery race. When he recovered from his injuries he decided he preferred the safety of a closed car and he and Digby went halves on a new Chevron to take in a full season of long-distance racing. They had taken Digby's old car to Daytona in February, where they had gone out with a blown head gasket. But the new, white, car was ready in time for Brands Hatch and impressed spectators all weekend. As the John Wyer Gulf Ford GT40 of Brian Redman and Jacky Ickx won the race, Martland and Classick's eighth place saw them only narrowly beaten for the 2-litre Group 6 class by the Porsche 910 of Rico Steinemann and Dieter Spoerry. The press described it as 'a coming of age for the Chevron team'.

The glory for that particular car was somewhat short-lived though. Just five days later Digby was practising for the sports car race at the Oulton Park Good Friday meeting when a slower Porsche moved over on him as he was overtaking under braking for the fast right-hander at Knicker Brook. 'He'd never seen me and he just smacked me one and I went over the top of him. It was just a motor racing accident, but that was the end of that car!' At least it meant another car to add to the homologation list.

The replacement car was ready in time for the Nürburgring 1,000km a month later, and this time it was Brian Classick's turn to do his bit for the Chevron order books. In a high-speed practice crash he fell foul of the notorious Nürburgring weather, aquaplaning off the suddenly wet track and hurtling into the trees, writing off the car and breaking his leg very badly. With Brian out of action — he was unable to walk for some time and still limps as a consequence of the accident — Digby shelved his international plans, had the car rebuilt (it was effectively another new car), and confined himself to the major British sports car races.

Nürburgring had been the first World Championship race for the newly-homologated Chevron and seven of them had made the journey. Fastest of these in practice was the Tech Speed car of Chris Craft and Chris Meek, which qualified in 14th place overall. But Meek crashed the car heavily on lap six, breaking his arm. The second of Gil Baird's Tech Speed cars was driven to third place in its class by Alan Rollinson and Mo Nunn. The Midlands pair beat the British-based Porsche 906s of Bill Bradley/Chris Lambert and Martin Hone/John Morris, but they were not yet a match for the German Porsches of Bitter/Jöst and Von Wendt/Kaussen.

With everyone at Bolton busy building cars, it was left to the customers to fly the flag for Chevron during 1968. Although the cars were now present in much greater numbers, and obviously very competitive, most of the quicker drivers only raced in Britain when international long-distance events did not clash, so there were no major British championship successes. Interest in Europe seemed to wane during the year, but John Bridges persevered with a Group 6 version of the car powered by a 1600cc Cosworth-FVA Formula 2 engine. John Lepp shared the car with him in long-distance events and was mixing it confidently with the works Fiat Abarths in the Nürburgring 500km in September. Third place looked assured until they lost a lap in the pits when the car jammed in third gear, but they still completed the race in sixth place.

Another fine international performance was put in by Barrie Smith, who put an indecently quick Vegantune twin-cam engine into his new GT and won the Ford Grand Prix at Denmark's Jyllandsring in August. Smith won two of the series of five races held over a weekend, which was enough to give him victory on aggregate over Terry Hunter's Porsche Carrera 6 and a trio of Chevrons.

A week earlier, Chris Craft had had his best result of the year, coming home first of the 2-litres as he took one of Tech Speed's cars to fifth place overall in the RAC British Sports Car Championship round supporting Oulton Park's Formula 1 Gold Cup. The meeting was also memorable for the performance of Chris Skeaping, who had been giving the Snetterton lap record a regular battering since buying Alan Harvey's car from him at the end of May. Fast but wild was the unanimous opinion of Skeaping, whose appearance loping round the paddock in Wild West-style boots and fringed suede jacket seemed to confirm the assessment. So when a Chevron appeared across the start line travelling along on its roof, it seemed reasonable that its occupant should be Chris Skeaping. It was his second big accident in a fortnight and his ability to emerge unscathed was adding greatly to Chevron's growing reputation for building very strong, very safe cars. Nevertheless, Skeaping did win half-a-dozen British club races in half a season and finished the year second in his class in the *Motoring News* GT Championship.

During 1968 Derek Bennett's own racing got pushed well into the background by his work as a constructor, but once all the customer cars were finished he did turn up at Croft one Saturday with a brand new car, which he had apparently built himself during the previous week. As Frank Gardner's Lola T70 was left on the line, a pack of Chevrons disappeared into the distance and Derek was obviously enjoying himself as he completed the first lap in the midst of a gaggle of his own creations, with Chris Craft leading him and John Lepp and Chris Skeaping behind. Eventually Gardner fought his way to the front to beat the impudent horde of Chevrons and Derek finished fourth overall, behind Lepp and Craft's class-winning car. With Skeaping fifth, Jack Oliver had to settle for sixth in his works Gold Leaf Lotus Europa.

A month later Derek found time for a busy weekend behind the wheel, taking on Tony Dean's Ferrari Dino at Crystal Palace on Saturday and at Lincolnshire's Cadwell Park on the way home on Sunday. Dean beat him at Crystal Palace, although Derek claimed fastest lap, but the Ferrari broke a front upright at Cadwell and a Chevron win was assured. It went not to Derek but to John Lepp, though, with Derek coming in fourth behind the FVA-engined Chevrons of John Bridges and John Blades.

Once the hectic months of building new cars had died down Derek was also able to look to the future. With a bigger order book and a larger workforce, cashflow was becoming something of a problem. He could not go on paying this week's wages from the proceeds of the car that had been sold last week, especially over the winter when they were going to have to buy in large stocks to enable them to start on the 1969 production run. The company was going to need an injection of cash to enable it to continue expanding, so Derek turned to John Bridges who had become one of Chevron's most loyal customers. John had first come into contact with Derek when he wrote off at Croft, the Lotus-Brabham-BMW which he had bought from Chris Williams, and responded to the usual message that Derek Bennett was the man to put it back together. John soon replaced the car with one of the first production Chevron-BMWs and began to race it under the banner of Red Rose Motors, his brother Charles' garage business at Chester where he had the car prepared. When Derek came to him John was in the process of buying Charles out, and investing in Chevron seemed to fit in well with the higher profile he would have in racing as the owner of Red Rose Motors. Jimmy Horrocks was looking to sell his shares, so John agreed to buy him out and take over as a director of Derek Bennett Engineering. He was also happy to put some more funds into the company, reasoning that he would eventually get much of his investment back by being able to buy his cars and parts at cost price.

While this reorganisation was going on, the idea of giving his cars type numbers was also suggested to Derek. Doug Linton had already had to put chassis numbers to that year's production to satisfy the homologation requirements, so it seemed like a good opportunity to add type numbers as well. Derek decided to give the type numbers a 'B' prefix, apparently out of deference to Bridges — but also being the first letter of his own surname it was inevitable it would be assumed to stand for Bennett.

A complete breakdown of Chevron type numbers is included in the appendices at the end of this book, but initially the numbers from B1 to B8 were allocated retrospectively late in 1968.

B1 was given to the first two Clubmans cars built in Salford in 1965. The customer Clubmans cars built at Bolton in 1966 were called B2s, and B3 was allocated to the prototype GT car built for Digby Martland and its sister twin-cam engined car built for John Lepp. Derek's own BMW-engined prototype was designated the B4. David Bridges' BRM-engined car was given another unique type number, B5. It was also the first car to be given an official chassis number, CH-DBE-1. The 1967 production GT cars were to be known as B6s, whatever their engines; B7 went to the Formula 3 prototype, and that left B8 for the current sports car.

Chevron sports cars seemed destined to become regular aids to recuperation during the hectic career of Brian Redman and in October 1968 he found himself at Montlhéry starting a race for the first time since his horrific accident in a Formula 1 Cooper at Spa in June. Lying 10th in the Belgian Grand Prix he had lost control at Les Combes when the front suspension on his Cooper-BRM broke. The car left the road, turned over, hit a parked car and caught fire. Brian escaped but his right forearm was badly smashed.

Once he felt able to drive again he had tried out a Chevron at one of the infamous Tuesday night practice sessions at Aintree after which he was offered John Lepp's B8-BMW to race in the non-championship 1,000km race at Montlhéry, co-driving with Chris Williams as Lepp himself would be sharing John Bridges FVA-engined car. Redman went out early on with no oil pressure, but his arm was holding up well so he took over the Lepp/Bridges car, which had been running sixth before its gearbox overheated, losing it two hours in the pits while a new one was fitted. With Redman at the wheel the car climbed back to 19th at the finish!

Eager to continue his rehabilitation programme, Redman agreed to join the Chevron team on their first trip to South Africa for the winter Springbok Series, which opened with the Kyalami 9-Hours. Derek Bennett shared Digby Martland's car, while Redman was teamed up with latest Formula 3 discovery — Tim Schenken — in the newer works car, and finished an impressive fourth overall. The next round was the three-hour race at Lourenço Marques four weeks later, which Redman drove on his own. He led the bigger cars during the early stages, but had to settle for third place behind the 5.7-litre Mirage of Mike Hailwood and Malcolm Guthrie, and the Ferrari P4 of Paul Hawkins, after losing time when the Chevron's rear body section started to break up.

While he was in Johannesburg waiting for the next race, Brian had a call from Porsche who asked him if he would drive for them for 1969. He said yes, but as he was still experiencing a burning sensation across the break in his arm, he decided to go to a leading orthopaedic surgeon in Johannesburg to have it checked. The surgeon made a thorough X-ray examination and announced that the broken bones had not joined back together. Brian told him that whatever was done, he had to be at Daytona in six weeks' time, so the doctor volunteered to delay his Christmas holiday and operate the next morning.

Brian recalls, 'He opened my arm right up again and cleaned off the bone ends that hadn't healed, and grafted bone out of my hip and into my arm. Then he sewed it all up again and didn't put it in plaster. And I went to Daytona really only able to use one arm to drive, but of course I couldn't tell Porsche this — I was praying for the cars to break down.' Fortunately for Brian, the cars did break down and he was out of the race before his disability was discovered!

In the meantime, Chevron's Springbok venture had been stopped short by Brian's indisposition and the works car was sold to South African Denis Joubert.

During 1968 Derek Bennett also became heavily involved in an unusual sports car project, building a special version of

John Woolfe's Repco-engined B12 leading a gaggle of Chevrons through the chicane at Croft on 5 May 1968. Giving chase are Trevor Twaites (B8-BMW), Peter Crossley (B8-Climax), and the B8 FVAs of John Blades and John Bridges. (*Photo Miles Linley.*)

the B8 around a 3-litre Repco 640 V8 engine which had come from one of Jack Brabham's Formula 1 cars. John Woolfe commissioned the car and Derek lengthened the B8 chassis by $2\frac{1}{2}$ inches to incorporate the bigger engine. A special 6-inch-longer rear body section completed the car's streamlined appearance. Designated the B12, it made its début at a Silverstone club meeting where Woolfe won the race and broke the outright lap record for the club circuit. A string of wins in British club races demonstrated the car's tremendous speed, but Woolfe's intention was always to race it at Le Mans and once they started trying to run the car over longer distances it began blowing head gaskets. They had been unable to solve the problem by the time Le Mans came up at the end of September and Woolfe went out just over two hours into the race — with a blown head gasket.

Digby Martland was his co-driver for Le Mans and he believes that a bad engine ruined a project with plenty of potential. They eventually discovered that the cylinder head was blowing between two cylinders. 'There was nothing wrong with the car,' he recalls. 'It was fantastic — better than a GT40. Derek really put a lot of time into it and if it had had a new engine, it would have been a winning car.'

Although Derek Bennett spent much of 1968 concentrating on developing his sports cars and producing them for an ever increasing number of customers, the greatest success of the year actually came from Formula 3, thanks in no small measure to the appearance in the Chevron camp of the young Australian, Tim Schenken. It was his performances in 1968 that set the course for Chevron's next area of expansion, the single-seater market.

CHAPTER 6

They make single-seaters in Bolton too

PETER GETHIN'S showings in the prototype Formula 3 Chevron at the end of 1967 attracted plenty of interest and a number of orders were taken for the B9 production version in 1968. Sports Motors took delivery of a new car, which was driven at first by Peter Gethin. But Gethin was committed to a Formula 2 season for Frank Lythgoe and so Rodney Bloor cast around for another driver. He found a 24-year-old Australian called Tim Schenken, who was already making his mark in the recently introduced Formula Ford.

Schenken was given a test session in the Chevron at Silverstone before being thrown in at the deep end in a Formula 3 international, supporting Silverstone's Formula 1 International Trophy at the end of April. Not many people noticed him as he qualified in midfield and finished 15th. At that point it was the more experienced Alan Rollinson and Chris Williams who drew attention to Chevron as they finished sixth and seventh in the pair of distinctive black, white and gold B9s which were being run from Williams' garage in Shere under John Bridges' Red Rose Motors banner. After buying Williams' Lotus-Brabham sports car from him, Bridges had sponsored Chris in a Formula 3 Brabham in 1967. He wanted to continue the involvement for 1968 and, as a satisfied Chevron customer himself, he thought they should try Derek Bennett's new Formula 3 car.

The Red Rose drivers were intent on doing an international season, but Schenken planned to cut his teeth on the British Lombank Championship. By the Oulton Park round a fortnight later he was showing more confidence with the car and he finished second to Cyd Williams' Brabham BT21, despite finding the steering heavy after damaging the steering rack in a practice accident. He was also helped somewhat by Silverstone winner John Miles dropping out when his experimental Lotus 41X suffered a fuel blockage, and by the early retirement of Peter Gethin, having a one-off race in one of Frank Lythgoe's Chevron B9s. This car was to have been raced by Digby Martland, but after making his F3 début from the back of the grid at Silverstone Digby had decided that single-seaters were not for him and had gone back to concentrate on sports cars.

Rodney Bloor was already very impressed with Schenken's commitment and his professionalism, and the way he was settling down as a test driver. The Chevron made rapid progress and on 2 June Schenken gave himself and Chevron their first Formula 3 win in a close-fought race at Brands Hatch. Leading away from the outside of the front row he held off challenges from the Brabhams of Tony Lanfranchi and Harry Stiller. Stiller finally snatched the lead by outbraking Schenken into Paddock, but a lap later he missed a gear and Schenken was back in front, where he stayed despite everything his more experienced pursuers could throw at him.

Two weeks later Schenken did it again at Oulton Park, but this time he made it look easy as he started from pole and left the Brabhams of Cyd Williams and Mike Beuttler well behind in the race. Now he was being talked about as the 'Australian Wonderboy'. The Oulton Park meeting that June was characteristic of Chevron's hold on racing at their local circuit. It was always satisfying to win in front of a home crowd and Chevrons always seemed to have a peculiar affinity for Oulton Park. That Saturday Chevrons were eligible for five of the seven races, and Derek Bennett looked on as his cars won all of them. Schenken added a second victory in the *Libre* race, John Bridges won twice in his B8-FVA, and Dave Rees won the Clubmans race in his B2. Days like that seemed as much of a fairy tale come true as some of the more prestigious successes in far away corners of the motor racing world.

Schenken's next race was another international — at Mallory Park — and this time he was right up with the leading lights. Racing in the second heat, he joined Alan Rollinson's B9 in a five-way scrap for the lead with the Titans of Roy Pike and Peter Gaydon, and Reine Wisell's Tecno. It all ended in tears when Wisell and Gaydon touched at the hairpin, but Schenken stayed clear of trouble to qualify in fourth place. He eventually finished the dizzying 50-lap final in third place, close behind Pike and Mo Nunn's Lotus 41.

With the British Grand Prix supporting race coming up at Brands Hatch, Sports Motors decided to try out a Titan. Schenken won with it at Oulton Park but elected to stick with the Chevron for Brands. Roy Pike's Titan qualified on pole position, but Schenken equalled the time to take the middle of the front row, with Alan Rollinson's Chevron alongside him. Pike led away, but despite lowering Piers Courage's lap record twice he could not shake off the blue Chevron. Then, watched by 50,000 spectators — including 19-year-old Prince Charles who was there with his uncle, the Earl Mountbatten

THEY MAKE SINGLE-SEATERS IN BOLTON TOO

— Schenken took the lead round the outside at Paddock, breaking Pike's new lap record on the same lap for good measure. Pike regained the lead, but the battle was cut short when Schenken's engine went onto three cylinders. As John Miles fought his way through to win in the Lotus, Schenken dropped back to a disappointing seventh place, but he had proved his tremendous skill beyond doubt.

For the rest of the season, Schenken never finished out of the first three and a string of wins at the end of the year confirmed him as the winner of the Lombank Championship. Despite his hectic F3 schedule, Schenken also carried on racing his Merlyn Mk 11A, adding the Guards Formula Ford Championship title to his Formula 3 crown.

While Schenken was taking the glory and the premier Grovewood Award in Britain, the Red Rose team were building Chevron's international reputation in Formula 3 abroad. Early in the season, Alan Rollinson, the winner of the previous year's top Grovewood Award, had taken a fine second place at Montlhéry, sandwiched between the winning Tecno of François Cevert and the Alpine of Patrick Depailler. He had gone on to finish a strong seventh at Monaco,

Tim Schenken rounds Esso Bend at Oulton Park on 28 September 1968, holding off John Miles' Lotus 41X in his Chevron B9. Miles was trying a Formula 1-style rear wing for the first time, but he was still unable to beat Schenken, who repeated the feat at Brands Hatch the next day. (*Photo Frank Hall.*)

85

and had finally given Chevron their first international Formula 3 win on 11 August in the rather obscure setting of Schleizer-Dreieck in East Germany, where he had led from start to finish. Chris Williams had also been impressive in the second Red Rose B9, taking pole position at Montlhéry and leading at Mallory Park, but being unable to translate that form into results.

If the East German race was regarded as something of a soft victory, Peter Gethin left everyone in no doubt that the Chevron could win against top international competition when he performed another of Chevron's 'straight out of the box' wins at Brands Hatch three weeks later. With Chris Williams ill, Gethin took over his entry in a brand new chassis — known as the B9B — which Chevron had built up as a test-bed for the following year's Formula 3 car. It was of semi-monocoque construction with sheet steel spot-welded to the spaceframe around the cockpit area. This technique was already standard on the B8 and stiffened the chassis considerably as well as providing a protective structure for the new bag fuel tank.

Gethin dominated his heat in the rain, but in the final he was beaten away from the start by Reine Wisell's Tecno. Five laps into the 25-lap race Gethin claimed the lead and the new car pulled away to win by more than two seconds. It was Gethin's first international Formula 3 win and it laid down the gauntlet for the 1969 season as Wisell's Tecno and the fancied Titans of Charles Lucas and Roy Pike trailed home in its wake.

The race had been less happy for Rollinson and Schenken whose Chevrons had disputed the lead of the first heat until they collided coming out of Druids side by side, putting themselves out of the race. But Schenken made amends in the last major race of the season, at the Brands Hatch Motor Show 200 meeting, when he too scored his first international victory. Schenken won his heat and Wisell's Tecno won the other. But when the Tecno broke a driveshaft accelerating away from the start of the final, it was left to Tony Lanfranchi's Merlyn to try and hold the Chevron. Lanfranchi swapped places with Schenken for a few laps, but the Chevron pulled away to win. With four Chevrons in the first six, Derek Bennett's ability to build single-seaters as well as sports cars could no longer be questioned, even by the hardest southern cynics. Rollinson and Williams had come in third and fourth, while Harry Stiller was sixth in the Chevron he had bought off Howard Heerey during practice!

Just how serious Chevron were about Formula 3 was made clear a month later when they announced that they had signed Reine Wisell to be their works driver for 1969. The decision to employ a full-time works driver for the first time came about as part of the reorganisation which was going on at Bolton following John Bridges' arrival as a director. He suggested that they bring in Dave Wilson to a new post of Workshop Manager. Dave had been Chris Williams' mechanic and had run the Red Rose Formula 3 team. There was a general belief among everyone who worked at Chevron that Wilson had been brought in by Bridges as a condition of his involvement — someone on the inside to protect his investment while he carried on running his own business. John Bridges himself says he never saw it that way. His trust in, and his admiration for, Derek Bennett was the only protection he needed, but when it was felt that the workshop needed someone to organise it, he suggested Dave Wilson as the obvious candidate.

Nevertheless, Wilson's arrival sparked a certain amount of resentment amongst the workforce, who saw him as an unwanted new layer of middle-management, restricting their direct access to Derek and trying to introduce his own ideas into the way things were done. Being a southerner also made him a natural target of suspicion. They already knew him through the Red Rose Formula 3 team, but they also remembered that he would never bring the Red Rose cars into the workshop until he had tidied up and swept the floor — some said he even cleaned the toilets before he would unload his cars! So Dave had to work hard to be taken seriously.

Signing up Reine Wisell was one of his first suggestions. The young Swede had been one of the top stars of the European scene that year and the Red Rose team had spent much of their time trying to beat him. So when Dave heard from his friend, Jürg Dubler, that Reine had not got a deal for 1969, he put the idea to Chevron. This was all a little bit much for the locals to take in. Not only was this person not a northerner, he was not even British. But the idea appealed to Derek. With Sports Motors having signed a lucrative sponsorship deal to run a works-supported Brabham for Tim Schenken, he knew he could not rely purely on customers to produce the results this time, and he accepted that putting an internationally known 'ace' into his car would strengthen Chevron's reputation as a serious racing car manufacturer. And as for him being Swedish, it seemed to appeal to Derek's sense of humour that people should be caught out by him doing something apparently so unexpected. However, the acceptance did not quite run to learning how to pronounce fancy foreign names, and Chevron's new works driver would always be known in Bolton as 'Rainy Whistle'.

Dave Wilson was given the go-ahead to approach Reine, who was now living in Britain, and had been testing a new

Brabham for Ron Tauranac. Reasonably happy with the car, Reine was considering signing with Brabham when Wilson called him to suggest a meeting with Derek and John Bridges if he was interested in driving for them for the coming year. There was no car to try, but Reine liked Derek's ideas and he had seen the prototype for the new B15 at pretty close quarters when Peter Gethin had beaten him in at Brands Hatch in September. So when they offered him £1,000 to be Chevron's works driver, he accepted. 'They offered me a good deal and I just decided to go for it.'

The deal also included driving a works B8 in sports car racing where it was hoped that a successful works car would stimulate sales, and Reine soon realised that Chevron intended to get their money's worth out of him. His first drive for Chevron was in a new works B8 at Silverstone where a Group 4 race supported the International Trophy. The 1969 car had various changes, aimed at making it safer and stronger still, and at giving it more power. There were better brakes, wider wheels, new shock absorbers and an adjustable front roll bar. Development work on the BMW engine, including the fitting of bigger valves, had increased its power, but the Chevron was still reckoned to be at a disadvantage of about 45 bhp against a Porsche 910. The disadvantage was pronounced on the high-speed Silverstone track and Wisell was beaten into second place in the 2-litre class by Charles Lucas's Porsche.

The following weekend was Easter and Reine was due to race the Formula 3 car for the first time at Snetterton on Good Friday. But with an RAC Championship Group 4 race at the same meeting he was going to be kept busy racing the B8 as well. Switching between cars in practice the day before, he failed to adjust his driving style quickly enough and the result was a huge accident in the sports car. 'After trying the Formula 3, I jumped into the B8 and I was going the same — trying to do a quick lap, but I was too quick for the car. So I just came out a little bit on the grass and there was a big earth bank and I went straight into that. I was just lucky not to hurt myself more.'

Reine was taken to hospital, in need of some stitches and treatment for cracked ribs and a suspected broken nose. But, bravely, he returned the next day to race the B15 for the first time. The race provided a foretaste of the frantic action that Formula 3 would provide that year as first Wisell, then Rollinson, then Schenken held the lead. Schenken's Brabham was back in front with only two of the 15 laps to go, but Wisell put the Chevron ahead again going into the last lap and held on to win by 0.4 seconds, with Rollinson's Brabham third. All he remembers about the race is how difficult it was to climb out of the car afterwards in his battered state. Without

THEY MAKE SINGLE-SEATERS IN BOLTON TOO

Wisell's works B8 to contend with, Charles Lucas had another easy ride in the sports car race, winning the 2-litre class from John Burton in the best of the Chevrons.

On Easter Monday the RAC Sports Car Championship moved to Thruxton where Tim Schenken was a welcome addition to the Chevron ranks at the wheel of Paul Vestey's new B8. With Lucas's Porsche delayed by a spin, Schenken had a clear run to victory in the 2-litre class, and John Burton's Chevron followed him home. Schenken's race was a shakedown for the following weekend's BOAC 500 at Brands Hatch where he was due to share the car with John Fenning. But during practice at Brands a track-rod link came apart as he came out of Clearways bend and the car flew off the track, hitting the bank and rolling over three times. Fortunately Schenken emerged from the wreckage unscathed, having joined the list of drivers with cause to be grateful for the inherent strength of Derek Bennett's racing cars.

Wisell had an altogether better weekend, sharing the works B8 with John Hine. Early in the race they were involved in a close contest for the 2-litre Group 4 class with the Team VDS Alfa Romeo T33 of Teddy Pilette and Rob Slotemaker, but the Chevron eventually pulled away to win the class by two laps as it finished in an impressive seventh place overall, a mere six seconds behind the 3-litre works Porsche 908 Spyder of Rolf Stommelen and Hans Herrmann. The other three 908s occupied the first three places overall, led by Jo Siffert and Brian Redman.

Reine Wisell and John Hine took their works B8-BMW to a class win in the BOAC 500 World Sports Car Championship race at Brands Hatch on 13 April 1969. Here Wisell holds off the Alfa Romeo T33 of Teddy Pilette. (*Photo LAT.*)

With the international Formula 3 season getting into full swing it became obvious that Wisell was not going to be able to race the GT car as often as Chevron might have liked. So the weekend after the BOAC 500 meeting saw Derek Bennett at the wheel of the works car, joining nine other Chevrons in a race at Croft. He led the race for a lap and-a-half before John Lepp — now racing his third Chevron — went past him in his latest B8. Lepp went on to win, but Derek was only two seconds behind at the finish.

Meanwhile Wisell had taken the B15 to Pau, where a Formula 3 race was supporting the European Championship Formula 2 round. He led from start to finish, leaving Schenken's Sports Motors Brabham BT28 trailing by more than 20 seconds as he won the race. A week later, at Jarama, he looked set to do it again, but lost the lead when he came into the pits for the first of a series of stops to replace a detached plug lead. Reine still managed to finish sixth as Schenken won the race. Next the international Formula 3 circus moved on to Montjuich Park in Barcelona, where they were supporting the Spanish Grand Prix. Again it was Wisell and Schenken who attracted all the attention as, for more than an hour, they swapped the lead on virtually every lap. But with one lap to go, Wisell tried a desperate attempt to squeeze by and clipped an armco barrier. The delay cost him barely a second, but it was enough to let Schenken get away and win.

Although he was snatching the limelight at the moment, Reine Wisell was not the only Swede racing in Formula 3. A certain Ronnie Peterson had been dominating the category in his home country at the wheel of a Tecno and everyone was waiting for the showdown between the two Swedish drivers. It came in May at Monaco, the most important Formula 3 race of the year. Tecnos heavily outnumbered Chevrons, with no fewer than 22 entered. But Wisell's works Chevron had strong support from the B15s of Peter Hanson and the promising young New Zealander, Howden Ganley, having his first race in a brand new car.

True to form, Wisell and Peterson each won their heats, so the confrontation was on as planned for the final. No-one was disappointed as the two drivers staged the best race of the year so far. It took Peterson eight laps to find a way past Wisell, then a lap later the cars touched as Wisell forced the Chevron back into the lead round the outside at St Devote. Peterson's next challenge failed, but with only four laps to go, Wisell slid wide at Mirabeau and Peterson pounced. Wisell tried desperately to regain the place but, a lap later, he slid straight on at the chicane 'Ronnie was charging very hard and we had done some battling so the brakes

THEY MAKE SINGLE-SEATERS IN BOLTON TOO

were fading. They were not the same brakes as I expected them to be so I had to decide to turn in or not, and I was going a little bit too quick, so I went straight off.' Peterson had beaten him this time, but the Chevron recovered to take second place ahead of Jean-Pierre Jabouille's Alpine, Schenken's Brabham, and Patrick Depailler in another Alpine.

Britain got a look at the international Formula 3 scene at Crystal Palace on Whit Monday, by which time the journalists were beginning to run out of superlatives to describe the racing, which was moving out of the realms of 'the best race this year' to 'one of the most exciting races ever'. After 25 laps of Crystal Palace and 13 lead changes the first six cars crossed the line covered by less than three seconds. The last lap sort-out left Wisell in fourth place as Schenken won from Peterson and Alan Rollinson.

Reine was becoming unhappy with his engine. He had started out with a Felday and tried a Pygmee and a Lucas at Monaco, but what he was really pushing for was one of the new, Italian Novamotor engines — like Peterson had. At £1,000 a time these were regarded as hideously expensive, but Reine convinced Chevron that he had to have one and it was duly installed when the red works car arrived at Montlhéry at the beginning of June. Wisell was right back on terms with

Reine Wisell's battles with Ronnie Peterson were a feature of the 1969 Formula 3 season. Here Wisell's works B15 (right) fights to stay ahead of Peterson's Tecno at Monaco.
(*Photo LAT.*)

Schenken again and the two staged another typically intense duel, with Schenken leading into the final lap. But as they came out of the pits chicane for the last time, the Chevron popped out of the Brabham's slipstream and pulled alongside as the cars crossed the finish line in a dead-heat.

And so the season went on, producing — week in and week out — the classic, wheel-to-wheel slipstreaming battles, the memory of which still sends those who saw them into raptures, much to the irritation of those not old enough to have seen them who, numbed by the tedium of most modern racing, refuse to believe that such excitement could possibly exist.

When Reine and Ronnie lined up at Anderstorp, the huge Swedish crowd — loyalties evenly divided — was treated to 'the best race ever seen in Sweden' as they swapped the lead constantly, with Peterson's Tecno eventually beating the Chevron by two feet and clinching the Swedish Formula 3 Championship. This winning margin was twice as big as the one Wisell managed to defeat Tim Schenken by at Brands Hatch a few weeks later in a thrilling race which was reported in *The Times* newspaper the following morning under the legendary headline 'Guards Trophy Won by A. Foot'.

With Reine and Ronnie bigger than football stars in Sweden, race organisers there were prepared to go to ever increasing lengths to get them to race against each other on home soil. A meeting at the new Falkenberg circuit clashed with a race at Crystal Palace, but the organisers agreed that Wisell could miss the qualifying heats while he raced in England on the Saturday and that they would then pay for the Chevron to be flown to Copenhagen where a transporter would pick it up in time for Reine to race in the Sunday final. At Crystal Palace, Wisell took revenge for his May defeat by Tim Schenken when he beat the Australian in a stunning last lap manoeuvre. Schenken had led into the last lap, but Wisell pulled out of the slipstream as they came off the main straight and amazed everyone by driving round the outside of the Brabham at Ramp Bend. Demonstrating the tremendous respect for each other's abilities that had grown up between the two rivals, they went right round the bend with their wheels interlocked before Wisell snatched the advantage for the last few hundred yards of the race.

When Reine met up with his car again at Falkenberg the next day he was due to start the final from the back row of the grid, having not actually qualified to race. With their fans in mind, Ronnie told the organisers that if Reine had to start from the back, then he would too! But the organisers felt this was too dangerous a prospect and came up with the novel idea of putting Wisell on an extra row of his own — at the front of the grid! So the crowd got their race and, once again,

Peterson just managed to come out on top.

Reine looks back on his rivalry with Peterson as one of the highlights of a very competitive year. 'We were very good friends, but he was a very hard racer. We were very, very near each other, but sometimes I had to lift off, otherwise he would climb over the top of you, I think. Someone had to give up, and most of the races I lost, I lost by just about a metre.'

Towards the end of 1969 the rivalry between the two Swedes took an unexpected twist when Peterson arrived at Cadwell Park to give the new March 693 a surprise début on the eve of the official announcement of the new company. As Peterson got to grips with the new car, Schenken and Wisell set the pace, winning a heat each and then battling for the lead in the final. But with four laps to go, Wisell spun out of the lead on some dirt thrown onto the track at the foot of the Mountain and Schenken went on to win, chased hard by Howden Ganley's Chevron. Peterson brought the March in third, getting the best of a close contest with recent Formula Ford graduate, James Hunt, in a Brabham BT21, while Wisell recovered to take fifth place.

A week later at Montlhéry another Formula Ford driver gave the established Formula 3 drivers an even greater shock. The young Brazilian Emerson Fittipaldi took his Lotus 59 to a sensational win as both Swedes' luck deserted them. Wisell went out with a broken gearbox, while lying second to Fittipaldi, and Peterson put himself in hospital after a frightening accident in which he hit a straw bale and flipped the March, which slid off down the track upside down and caught fire. Ronnie was fortunate to escape with only minor burns. But the March challenge had been signalled and their rivalry with Chevron would become a dominant feature of the next decade.

When the international Formula 3 season drew to a close at Brands Hatch in October, it was not March but Lotus who provided the threat. The efforts of Emerson Fittipaldi seemed to have galvanised the works team into action and Wisell had Gold Leaf Lotus 59s for Bev Bond, Mo Nunn and Roy Pike to contend with. He beat Bond and Nunn in his heat, but the final was wide open until the last bend when Wisell snatched the lead from Nunn to win as the first six flashed over the line covered by 1.4 seconds. Howden Ganley was fifth in his B15 and put himself in the record books by setting the first 100 mph Formula 3 racing lap on the Grand Prix circuit.

With six international victories and six second places among his successes, Wisell had been Chevron's star turn through the year. However, other Chevron drivers also had their high spots, notably the Yorkshireman Peter Hanson, who took his B15 to victory over Tim Schenken's Brabham in a two-part

CHEVRON

Barrie Maskell leads a trio of B15s over Deer Leap at Oulton Park on 4 October 1969. Cyd Williams (79) eventually snatched victory from Maskell and Richard Scott. (*Photo Frank Hall.*)

race at Hockenheim in July, and Alan Rollinson who won a slipstreaming epic at the Silverstone British Grand Prix meeting on a one-off drive in a new Goodwin Racing B15. At national level, Cyd Williams took his Goodwin Racing B15 to a win at Oulton Park in October as a Chevron trio fought all the way to the finish line. Barrie Maskell crossed the line virtually alongside him in the B15 which Rollinson had won with at Silverstone. He had bought the car to replace the ex-Schenken B9 that he had been racing for the first half of the season, and it finally gave him a win at Mallory Park a week after Oulton. Third at Oulton Park was Aberdonian Richard Scott, who switched from a Brabham BT21 to a new B15 midway through the year and picked up enough points to finish fifth in the Lombank Championship, the highest placed Chevron runner.

The rivalry between Reine Wisell and Tim Schenken had a postscript at the end of 1969 when both drivers went to America to race at Sebring on 27 December. Fred Opert had kept up his association with Chevron, buying the original B7 prototype Formula 3 car at the beginning of 1968 and then ordering three B14 Formula B cars towards the end of the season in his role as Chevron's first overseas agent. One of the cars was sold to comedian Dick Smothers, who was at the airport to be photographed taking delivery of his new Chevron. For 1969 Chevron produced a Formula B version of the B15 Formula 3 car, suitably modified to take the 1600cc twin-cam engine, and Opert ordered six of them.

At the time he was also importing Brabhams and racing one himself, although his sales manager maintained the balance by racing a Chevron. Opert invited Schenken over to drive the new Brabham BT29 at Sebring, but Dave Wilson got to hear of the plan and did not like the idea that the local Chevrons were going to be blown off by a Brabham. So he offered Reine and a new Chevron to even the odds. Everyone recovered from Opert's Christmas party in time to get to Sebring and Wisell beat Schenken comfortably, much to Wilson's relief and to the benefit of Chevron's order books.

On the sports car front, Chevron's international effort rather petered out as Wisell concentrated on Formula 3. Chevron had scored their first point in the international Championship of Makes at Daytona in February when Miami drivers John Gunn, Hugh Kleinpeter and Bob Beatty had finished sixth in the 24-Hours, winning the 2-litre Group 4 class. After their class win at Brands Hatch in April, Reine Wisell and John Hine had teamed up again for the Nürburgring 1,000km at the beginning of June. They were leading their class when Wisell was caught out by a sudden hailstorm at Aremberg and put the B8 into a ditch. 'Paul Owens was not very happy with that,' Reine recalls.

A number of privately owned Chevrons continued to take part in long-distance events, but there were no more major successes. Barrie Smith did repeat his previous year's success in Denmark, however, when he won the Ford Grand Prix at the Jyllandsring for the second time. Driving a new B8-FVA he won two of the weekend's three races to beat the B8-BMW of Guy Edwards on aggregate.

Back in Britain Chevrons continued to have a strong presence on the national sports car scene. As the season progressed John Lepp began to get the measure of the Porsche 910 and he beat Charles Lucas's car to win the 2-litre Group 4 class at the Oulton Park Tourist Trophy in May, which was run as a round of the RAC British Sports Car Championship. Sadly, Lepp's fine fourth place overall was totally overshadowed by the fatal accident of the popular Australian Paul Hawkins, whose Lola T70 crashed in flames, curtailing the race as blazing wreckage blocked the track.

Lepp won again at Mallory Park, and moved into equal second place in the championship with another fine 2-litre class win in a two-day, two-part international at Croft, where he was only beaten overall by the Lola T70s of Chris Craft and Trevor Taylor. The championship would be decided at the final round, at Thruxton on 10 August. Charles Lucas arrived with a two-point lead, but he had taken another Porsche in part-exchange for his own and he scratched from the race after failing to get the unfamiliar car handling properly in practice. That left Lepp's championship hopes dependant on the fortunes of Chris Craft's Lola T70 in the big class as they started the two-part race equal on points.

When the gearbox on Terry Croker's B8 jammed solid on the last lap, Lepp came through to win the 2-litre class in the first part, but Craft was beaten by the Lolas of Denny Hulme and Frank Gardner. Craft fought back in the second part, but his engine gave up, leaving Lepp with 17 agonising laps to complete to make sure of the title. He was happy to follow Willie Green's B8 round, staying close enough to preserve his lead in the class on aggregate and coming home to win his second sports car championship for Chevron.

One other Chevron driver who began to attract attention in 1969 was David Purley. The 24-year-old Army paratrooper had bought Barrie Smith's twin-cam engined B8 at the start of the season to replace his AC Cobra, which he had wrecked at Brands Hatch. Although somewhat impetuous, he was obviously very fast and soon took a couple of class wins in *Motoring News* championship races, and an outright win at Castle Combe.

By the end of the year, though, Chevron admirers had something new to enthuse about as Derek Bennett had produced what many people still believe was his finest creation — the B16 sports car.

CHAPTER 7

B16 – the ultimate Chevron?

WITH the B8 having established Chevron's international reputation, Derek Bennett realised that he had to try and keep a step ahead of the opposition by getting to work on its successor. The B8 had evolved to suit the requirements of Derek's customers over a three-year period. Now Derek wanted to put all that accumulated experience into designing a completely new car. The concept of the new car had been running through Derek's mind for much of 1968, but with so many other demands on his time he was unable to make a real start on the prototype until the 1969 season was under way.

The front end of the B16 was designed with a detachable nose sub-section to make repair work easier. The same principle was used at the rear. (*Photo Arthur Taylor.*)

Once again Derek set to work with his square tubes to build the basic spaceframe chassis, which was then reinforced with steel and duraluminium sheeting in the same way as the B8. The car was not bristling with technical innovations but reflected Derek's instinct of keeping the car as simple as possible and then refining it to work at its maximum potential. So the suspension followed the principles of the B8 with wishbones at the front and an upper link and triangular lower wishbone at the back. Bringing the centre of gravity down even lower was important and the overall height of the car was only three feet. The car incorporated a removable front subframe for ease of repairs. The basic design of the body to cover the new package was again Derek's but he took the decision to call in a stylist, Jim Clark from Specialised Mouldings, to make sure that everything was done properly. There were no aluminium bodies this time. Instead a plaster plug was made from which Specialised Mouldings produced a fibreglass body for the prototype.

The other problem for the new car was power. Derek saw little future for the BMW engine as it stood and as BMW themselves were not keen to develop something more suitable at that point, he went to Weslake to see if they could produce a batch of engines which would see the new car through homologation. The idea was to put a 16-valve Weslake head on the BMW block, but Chevron would have had to fund the entire project and they could not raise the capital to do so. So the next stop was Cosworth, who they thought might be interested in working with the BMW engine in the absence of a suitable 2-litre Ford block. Keith Duckworth was interested at first, but it was eventually decided that the potential conflict with their paymasters at Ford was too great, and so everyone sat down together to come up with an alternative scheme.

The four valves per cylinder 1598cc Cosworth FVA Formula 2 engine had already been run successfully in a number of Chevron B8s and Derek Bennett asked Keith Duckworth how much closer to 2-litres he could get the FVA. Duckworth liked the B16 and saw the potential in the growing 2-litre sports car scene. He felt that making a competitive engine available in quantity, and at a reasonable price, would help sustain the formula, to the benefit of both Chevron and Cosworth. Using a different crank and a longer stroke, the engine was brought up to 1790cc and designated the FVC. People at Chevron liked to joke that this stood for 'Four-Valve Chevron', but in fact it was merely the next acronym in Cosworth's naming system. Duckworth deliberately de-rated the engine, exchanging top-end revs for reliability, but the new engine was still expected to give 20 bhp more than the FVA and 40 bhp more than the BMW, so it looked like being a potent package when combined with the lighter, sleeker new car.

With the Chevron factory still very much an open house, Derek's new car was an open secret and by the time he finally took it along to Aintree one afternoon late in July 1969 it was eagerly awaited. No-one who saw the B16 that first time was disappointed. It looked perfect and people began to fall in love with the B16 in the way they have done ever since. Derek whisked the new car round Aintree inside the outright lap record and pronounced it 'very promising'. The prototype was running with a 2-litre BMW engine as well, so expectations were high as to what it would achieve when the new FVC engine was ready.

Derek tested the car again at Croft, equalling Chris Craft's lap record despite running with the Aintree gear ratios, and an ambitious decision was taken to give the B16 its début at the Nürburgring 500km on 7 September. Brian Redman agreed to drive the car, taking a break from his commitments with the World Championship-winning Porsche team, and Brian Hart was commissioned to rebuild an FVA engine which David Bridges' team had run in Formula 2 the previous year.

By the time they got to the Nürburgring, a second car had been completed for John Bridges, and the two new Chevrons turned heads from the moment they arrived. Carlo Abarth's cars had taken a convincing 1-2-3 victory in the previous year's race and he was confident that the race was theirs for the taking again in 1969. Toine Hezemans and Gijs van Lennep each had a Group 4 2000S, while the Group 6 2000SP was entered for Jo Ortner. After the Friday practice session the Fiat-Abarths held the first three places on the grid and Abarth told his drivers to sit out Saturday's session.

Setting a new car up round the 14-mile Nürburgring was a daunting task, but Derek Bennett had been working away on Friday to try and make the car more stable, cutting up bits of aluminium to make little fins at the front and a makeshift spoiler at the back. Negotiations with Bilstein also provided some new shock absorbers which Redman felt made the B16 much more stable over the bumps, and allowed him to dispense with the spoilers which were costing him about 400 rpm down the straights. In its new set-up the car went round almost 24 seconds quicker than it had the day before, and no less than 5.6 seconds inside Hezemans' previous pole position time. The whole Chevron team watched gleefully as the Abarth drivers looked on from the pits in disbelief.

Race day was very hot and Redman intended to run the car in easily, probably following the Abarths in the early stages — especially in the light of the rumours flying around which suggested that one of the Abarths had been fitted with a super-quick engine overnight to entice Redman into running the

CHEVRON

Chevron too hard. But Brian surprised everyone by diving into the South Turn first as the cars swooped out from behind the pace car, and at the end of the first lap he came round still at the head of the pack, with Hezemans leading the Abarths in formation behind him. Redman steadily extended his lead and at half-distance he was 30 seconds ahead, despite a slow refuelling stop.

It took nearly three-and-a-quarter hours to complete the 500km and the tension in the Chevron pit grew almost unbearable as the race drew towards its close. Redman was too busy concentrating to feel nervous. He remembers feeling tired after about two hours and his main concern was to survive the heat. In the pits Derek Bennett was as quiet as ever, his apparent calm belying the nervousness he was really feeling as he endlessly twisted a piece of wire between his fingers. In the closing minutes a wayward Sprite cut across the front of the Chevron as Redman was lapping it. He had no option but to run into the back of it, but the only damage was to a headlight and he continued to the finish and the greatest triumph in Chevron's short history. Once again a Chevron had won 'straight out of the box', not this time over 10 laps of Oulton Park but over 20 laps of the Nürburgring. Derek Bennett had no need to worry about keeping his workforce busy over the coming winter.

With unanimous agreement that it looked fabulous, and a fairy-tail début victory behind it, the B16 already looked like a hugely successful car. But Brian Redman's tremendous skill and adaptability had disguised the fact that the car actually had serious handling problems. A week after the Nürburgring, the works car went to Imola where John Hine and John

Brian Redman's Nürburgring-winning B16 in the factory. Note the small lip on the back of the rear body section with which the car was originally designed. (*Photo Arthur Taylor.*)

B16 – THE ULTIMATE CHEVRON?

Brian Redman's pit time sheet for the Nürburgring 500km. His race number was 19 - 53 and 54 were the Abarths of Toine Hezemans and Gijs van Lennep. Note the consistency of Redman's lap times on laps seven to nine.

Lepp shared the driving. Hine crashed the car in practice and went off again during the race in the torrential rain that eventually stopped the proceedings. Lepp was one of Derek Bennett's most devoted fans, but he was not impressed by his first experience of the B16.

'It frightened me to death — absolutely petrified me. It had got far too much downforce at the front and it was lifting the rear wheels off the ground. John Hine said the car was perfect. I said I was petrified of it and that there was something definitely wrong with it. As far as I was concerned it was dangerous, it frightened me. I couldn't tell you what was wrong with it, I just didn't like it. And then he had an accident in practice — coming down the hill at about 140 mph it turned left into the barrier. He admitted after that there was something wrong with it!'

Lepp drove a B16 again a month later when he shared John

CHEVRON

Tim Schenken, Digby Martland and Derek Bennett on the pit wall at Kyalami.

Bridges' car in the Paris 1,000km at Montlhéry. The race was shortened to 586km after fog delayed the start, but it was still two laps too long for the Red Rose B16, which went out with a defunct gearbox. A nose spoiler had appeared on the car to try and make it more stable, but Lepp remained unimpressed and decided against having a B16 of his own for the following season. Instead he had his own Group 6 open sports car, the Spectre, built by Les Redmond. Even John Bridges now admits that he thought the B16 was terrible at the Nürburgring. 'That really made me think Brian Redman was God!' he recalls, echoing a sentiment felt by many after Redman's giant-killing feat.

Tim Schenken was due to drive the works car with John Hine in the South African Springbok Series and went along with Brian Redman to a test session at Oulton Park. Paul Owens recalls that Schenken had 'a horrendous spin' at Knicker Brook, got out of the car, and promptly told Redman that he didn't know how the hell he could drive the car — it was terrible. Redman, meanwhile, knocked three seconds off the 2-litre Group 6 lap record as he put the newly-arrived Cosworth FVC engine through its paces. Derek Bennett had driven the B16 at Imola, sharing John Bridges' car until it went out with spluttering electrics. He accepted that the car was not as stable and forgiving as a B8 but, like Redman, he did not feel there was anything fundamentally wrong with it. So the works car and a new one for Digby Martland were shipped out for the Kyalami 9-Hours at the beginning of November.

The traditional tea-time thunderstorm at Kyalami was particularly bad that year and torrential rain flooded much of the track. Hine ran straight into a pool of water and slid off into a bank, damaging the back end. Digby Martland and Charles Lucas kept going, despite having to be pushed back to the pits with electrical problems, and were sixth at the finish. Tim Schenken returned to Britain after the race, but he had persisted in his view that the car was difficult to drive at high speed, and so with two weeks before the next Springbok race, Derek Bennett and John Hine went testing with the works car to try and isolate the problem.

The difficulty seems to have been that the initial reaction of the drivers was that the car understeered, which was why nose fins and spoilers were tried at the Nürburgring and at Imola. But the real problem was that the car was short on downforce at the back. This meant that drivers were instinctively wary of turning too hard into fast bends because the tail felt as if it was going to break away, and — because they were not turning in sharply enough — by the time they had the car stable it was starting to understeer. 'I know it sounds contradictory,' comments Paul Owens, 'but it only understeered because it oversteered.'

Eventually the nature of the problem became apparent and they realised that more downforce was needed on the back, not the front, to stop it lifting. Various spoilers were tried at the back and eventually the B16 gained the pair of 'orange box' rear spoilers with which it went into full production.

That experience with the B16 taught Derek Bennett some salutary lessons. 'I think he was discouraged a little bit,' recalls Owens. 'Although everybody kept on telling us how fantastic the car looked, I think deep down in our own hearts and minds, we knew that the car was not as good as it should have been.' Because Derek had been so keen to get the B16 absolutely right he had taken the unusual step of bringing in outside help, particularly with the styling of the body, where he had taken advice from Jim Clark. 'We thought that there were people outside our sphere who knew more than we did and we were influenced.' The aerodynamics were indeed very good when the car was travelling at high speed in a straight line, but Derek Bennett was also renowned for making his cars go round corners. 'Derek took advice,' says Owens, 'and it was the first and the last car that he took advice in from the outside'.

Digby Martland stayed on for the remainder of the Springbok Series and his best result was third place overall in the final race at Pietermaritzburg. But back at Bolton the orders were flooding in and Chevron had their eye on the new European 2-litre Sports Car Series, which was due to start in April. The B16 did not make its first racing appearance in Britain until 15 March 1970, six months after its win at the Nür-

Overleaf: Brian Redman poses in the 1970 works B16. Note the large rear spoilers which had been developed to overcome the early handling problems. (*Photo Arthur Taylor.*)

CHEVRON

B16 – THE ULTIMATE CHEVRON?

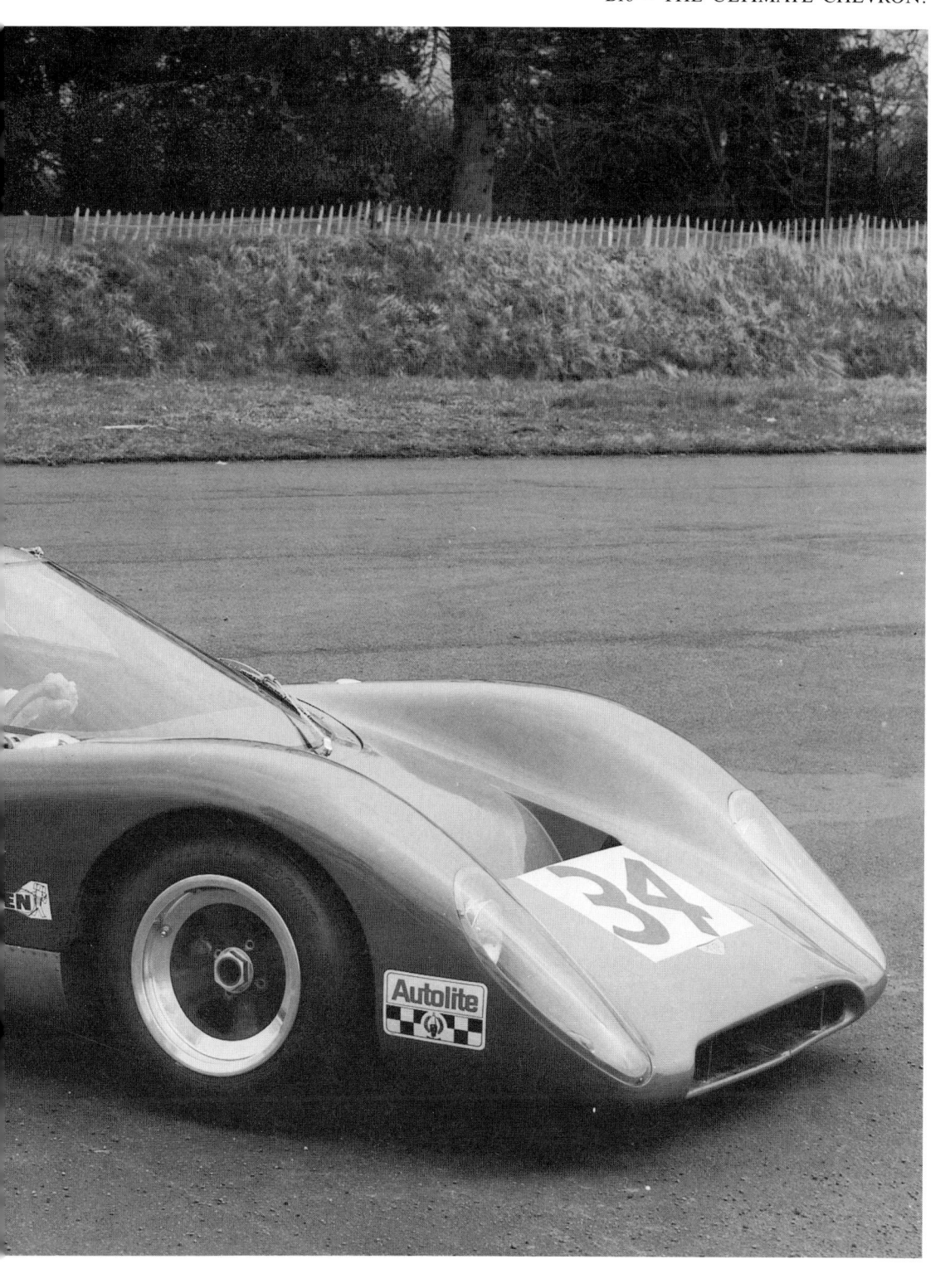

burgring. Ian Skailes and John Bridges failed to attract a lot of attention in the rain at Snetterton as electrical problems put them both out but, back at the Norfolk circuit a fortnight later on Good Friday, John Burton gave his new B16 a début win in the opening round of the RAC British Sports Car Championship.

The problems with the B16 had been resolved behind the scenes and had gone largely unnoticed, and the car was already being hailed as Derek Bennett's most successful yet. On Easter Monday the new works car appeared for the first time, running slightly lighter bodywork than the customer cars, and with Brian Redman at the wheel. The race, at Thruxton, only counted for RAC points, but as it supported a European Formula 2 Championship round, it drew a top international entry. Redman started from pole position, having got the best of the varying weather conditions in practice. It was no real surprise when Jo Siffert's 4.5-litre Porsche 917 went away to win the race comfortably, but Redman had qualified the 1.8-litre Chevron little more than a second slower than his own lap record in a Lola T70. He stunned everyone by holding off the challenge of Reine Wisell's 3-litre Porsche 908 to finish second overall, while Jo Bonnier and Barrie Smith trailed further behind in a pair of 5-litre Lola T70s!

After that performance, expectations were high for the opening round of the European 2-litre series, which was to be the inaugural race at the brand new Paul Ricard circuit at Le Castellet, near Marseilles, which had been completed in little more than six months by the French drinks magnate at a cost of over one million francs. Things did not start off well for the Chevron team as Redman's flight was delayed, causing him to miss the Friday practice session — not that this mattered because he would not have had a car as the transporter had broken down on its way across France.

Once everyone finally arrived at Ricard they were in for another shock when they saw Jo Bonnier's new Lola T210 for the first time. Bonnier had spent some time at Bolton discussing the possibility of becoming a Chevron agent and the potential market for the B16 in Europe, which left Derek Bennett's men feeling a little embarrassed at their own openness when he eventually went to Lola. Taking full advantage of the latest change in the regulations, the T210 was an open car and weighed in 70kg lighter than the B16. Redman practised only 0.3 seconds slower than Bonnier, but he knew he was going to have his work cut out in the race — and for the rest of the season. The duo soon pulled clear of the rest of the field as first Redman and then Bonnier held the lead. Halfway through the 100-lap race, Redman had slipped 12 seconds behind, hindered by the traffic. But in little more than 10 laps he clawed back the deficit and retook Bonnier for the lead.

Shortly afterwards the Lola lost a lap in an unexpected stop for fuel and suddenly the pressure was off Redman. The Chevron went on to win and the Lola was classified second, even though it dropped out two laps from the end with a broken throttle cable. With John Burton third and Ian Skailes fifth it was a good day for the B16, but the new Lola had sounded alarm bells. 'It was at that point that I said to Derek, "Please give me an open car" ', recalls Brian Redman. His memories of 1970 are of 'driving like a madman in the B16' and as the season went on his task became ever more difficult.

The transporter broke down again on the way back from Ricard, causing Brian to miss practice for the sports car race that supported the International Trophy at Silverstone. Starting from the back of the grid, he fought his way through to finish fourth as Chevrons took eight of the first 10 places. Unfortunately the all-important first place went to a Lola as Jo Bonnier's T210 held off a determined challenge from John Burton's B16 to win.

Burton and Bonnier renewed their battle when a small group of cars travelled to Finland for the second round of the European 2-litre series at Hameenlinna. With Redman away driving John Wyer's Porsche 908/3 Special to victory on the Targa Florio, it was left to Burton to uphold Chevron's honour in the two-part race. He swapped the lead with Bonnier in the first part until fuel pump problems sent the Lola into the pits. Bonnier was disqualified for pushing the car backwards into the pit lane, but he still raced in the second part. Burton diced with the Lola in the early stages of part two, but knowing his aggregate win was safe he let Bonnier get away by the end.

At Salzburgring, Redman was back with the works B16 and had to fight off Dieter Quester's Abarth as well as Bonnier's Lola. He battled for the lead with Quester in the first part and with Bonnier in the second, but the B16 didn't finish either race, dropping out of the first with a misfire and running out of petrol two laps from the end of the second.

In the next two rounds, at Anderstorp and Hockenheim, Redman continued with the unequal task of trying to keep the Chevron on terms with Bonnier's Lola, and at both races he was beaten into second place. Brian pleaded with Derek again for an open car, and this time, with the early season production rush at the factory out of the way, Derek got to work on the project. He must have been reluctant to admit that his new car was obsolete so soon after its début, but ultimately he was prepared to do whatever was necessary to keep his cars winning races. When I asked him a few years later whether he felt he had ever made any mistakes, Derek said

CHEVRON

The aluminium-bodied B16-Spyder prototype was tested at Oulton Park at the end of August 1970 before Brian Redman gave it its début at the Nürburgring. Here Brian talks to Derek Bennett before taking the car out as journalist Murray Taylor waits for a quote. (*Photo Jeff Hutchinson.*)

'The biggest mistake was that we didn't have the B16 out in time. That could have helped no end because then we would have had the Spyder out sooner.'

The first thing to do was to take off the heavy, coupé body. The rounded sills were replaced with square section sills but, apart from that, the chassis and suspension were left exactly the same. Brian Redman remembers discussing with Derek what the new, open bodywork should look like. Derek was concerned that they would be unable to do any wind-tunnel testing. Brian had been impressed with the flat wedge shape of the Porsche 908/3, so he said to Derek, 'Don't bother about the wind tunnel, copy the 908/3, that's got it all done'.

So Derek put together his ideas for a Porsche-like body and went back to Agnew and Clarke's, where the original bodies for the Clubmans cars had been made, to have one put together in aluminium. Away from the races themselves Porsche did not make many calls on Brian's time, so he was able to be involved with Derek throughout the building and testing of the B16-Spyder. 'I used to go round and see Derek, and he'd be there at 10 o'clock at night with his brown overalls on, and

B16 – THE ULTIMATE CHEVRON?

his goggles on his head, hammering.' While the car was being made, Brian was content to watch. 'My input was only as a driver. I've always purposely tried to stay away from the engineering side because I've seen a lot of drivers mix themselves up with trying to do both driving and engineering. So my input has always been to say what the car is doing, and to say what I would like it to do.'

Testing for Chevron was never like testing for anyone else because of Derek's own ability as a driver. Redman recalls: 'With Derek Bennett I did some of the fastest testing and development that I've ever done — either at that time or subsequently — because Derek himself was an extremely good driver as well as an engineer. So we would go and test any car at Oulton Park and I would say "the car's doing this at these particular corners" and Derek would then get in and drive it. He'd come back in two or three laps and say "Yes, it is, and I think it's this", and he'd leave right away with Paul Owens and the transporter and go back to Bolton and make changes — sometimes quite major — to the suspension, involving cutting and welding and all the rest of it, and come back the next day and we'd do it again. Incredibly fast development.'

Reine Wisell had similar memories of rapid progress in testing and development which he came to look back on wistfully during his time at BRM. 'If there was something I didn't like, I just told Derek how I felt about it and he'd say, "Oh, we'll see," and then just next day, or two days later, it would be ready.'

While the B16-Spyder was being built, Chevron tried to hold their place in the 2-litre championship with the coupé. Vic Elford drove the works car at Mugello, an unusual race run on the amazing 67km circuit of closed public roads in the mountains between Bologna and Florence. The cars started at 10-second intervals, racing against the clock. Unfortunately Elford began the race with his bag tank leaking onto him and as it took half an hour to get back round to the pits to change his petrol-soaked overalls, he suffered quite nasty burns. He continued the race but, distracted by the pain, he lost concentration and slid off into a ditch. With Bonnier's Lola giving the race a miss, Abarth took a clean sweep of the first three places as Arturo Merzario won the race for the second year running. Failing to score any points, Chevron slipped six points behind Lola in the championship, while Abarth closed to only three points behind Chevron.

Redman was back for the next round at Enna in August and had the distinction of giving the B16 its first Group 5 class win, as the necessary 25 cars had been produced for it to be homologated earlier in the month. But as far as the race overall was concerned, he was once again soundly beaten by

109

CHEVRON

Bonnier's Lola. Brake problems in the first heat and a pit stop to clean an oily screen in the second did not help Redman's chances and he was lapped by Bonnier in each of the 45 lap heats. He still finished second by the calculations of everyone but the organisers, who put him third, behind Merzario's Abarth.

Fortunately Redman knew he would have a Spyder for the next round, which just happened to be the Nürburgring 500km and the anniversary of his triumphant début in the original B16. He and Derek tested the new car at Oulton Park at the end of August and a week later it was flying round the Nürburgring. All of Chevron's problems seemed to be over as Redman took pole position with a lap in 8 minutes 12.4 seconds — more than 21 seconds faster than his pole-winning time the year before and a staggering 10.6 seconds quicker than second man, Arturo Merzario, in the Abarth.

Everything seemed to be going according to plan as Redman led away from the rolling start and pulled out a lead of more than two minutes. Then on the 13th of the 22 laps, a fuel line attached to the metering unit began to leak petrol onto the exhaust pipe. Redman takes up the story: 'There's a jump at the 14km point in top gear, very fast. And of course as the car comes off the ground you've got to lift off the throttle for a moment, which I did. And then as I came back on the throttle the engine started misfiring, and I quickly looked at the gauges and saw the fuel pressure was fluctuating badly.

Vic Elford took over the works B16 at Mugello on 19 July 1970. He didn't finish that race, but drove the car to victory in the Nürburgring 500 km seven weeks later. (*Photo Jeff Hutchinson.*)

Without even thinking about it I switched on the electric pump, and as I did that it just went "Boom" and caught fire. And so there I was, still in top gear, going at a pretty high speed, and quite well on fire at the back. I headed for the nearest marshals' post and stopped, and by the time I'd reached that it was really on fire — the marshal ran away. I got the fire extinguisher and ran back and we put the fire out, but it was well burnt, it was a pretty big fire.'

Chris Craft's Lola T210 took over the lead, only to go out when its FVC seized, which handed the race back to Chevron as Vic Elford brought the works B16 coupé in for an ironic victory, beating the Abarths of Merzario and Leo Kinnunen and Karl von Wendt's Lola.

Chevron's biggest problem now was getting the car, which had been almost completely burnt out, rebuilt in time for the final championship round at Spa two weeks later. Derek, Paul and the crew dashed back to Bolton and put it back together themselves with a heroic effort, and the team arrived in Belgium, three points behind Lola in the championship, needing to win the race to take the title. They could hardly have had anyone better qualified to win at Spa than Brian Redman. Earlier in the year he had won the 1,000km race there for the third successive year, sharing a Porsche 917 with Jo Siffert, and it would have been hard to find a driver who knew the demanding road circuit better.

Having given the previous couple of races a miss, Jo Bonnier was back to do battle for Lola in the closing race and he vied with Redman for pole position over the two days of practice. In the end Redman took the place, and the psychological advantage. He was incredulous at the speed of the little Chevron, which was lapping the $8\frac{3}{4}$-mile circuit little more than two seconds slower than the record he had set in his 3-litre factory Porsche 908 the year before. Of all the races Brian Redman has competed in, and won, in his illustrious career, he still remembers that day at Spa as one of his best. 'I've had other races which were much better known, and perhaps more important, but for sheer nail-biting, down–to–the–last–minute anxiety, that one took some beating.'

The story of the race is best told in Redman's own words:

'In the race Bonnier and I were really never separated by more than about a second, and although we pitted on different laps for fuel, we came out in exactly the same position. We kept breaking the record — lap after lap it kept coming down as we went faster, and I really couldn't see a good way to get an advantage, as Bonnier obviously couldn't either. Then on the next to last lap I couldn't get first gear at the hairpin and I lost perhaps

CHEVRON

Brian Redman on the way to his breathtaking victory at Spa on 20 September 1970 with the B16-Spyder. The win gave Chevron the European 2-litre Sports Car Championship title. (*Photo Jeff Hutchinson.*)

over a hundred yards. In that lap I really went faster than I thought was possible and that was when I set the lap record of 3 minutes 34.3 seconds, which beat my own lap record in a factory, 908, long-tailed Porsche — the best prototype in the world — and I went three seconds faster in this little 1.8 Chevron, which was crazy. But I caught Bonnier and passed him and still continued at what felt to be the same pace.

'We're now on the last lap, and coming out of Stavelot, which is the long, long right-hander at the far end of the circuit, glancing in the mirror he was well behind me — he wasn't closer, he was 70 or 80 yards behind. So we're now accelerating through the flat-out corners, up the back straight, and glancing in my mirror I was absolutely horrified to see he was catching me. And he just came past me, and cut me off in the way that he always did when he came past anyone. When he got halfway past he would just move over, and you'd to either lift off or hit him. So he did that, which I was expecting!

'But we then came into La Source hairpin, the final turn of the last lap, and I'm absolutely right behind him, but he's on the right hand side of the road, so he's guarding the inside line into the corner, which is the correct thing to do. We reached what had been my last braking point side by side and I thought that I probably wasn't going to make the corner. So I concentrated on braking in a straight line and was then hoping to make a last minute turn and come back inside Jo. So there I am braking, with the wheels locking and unlocking and I'm going straight up the escape road. And I made the late turn and as I turned, there was Jo sliding to a halt sideways — he'd spun. And there was just room between him and the wall on the outside, and I went through the gap, and of course managed to win the race, and the championship for Chevron by one point.'

In the Chevron pit, Derek Bennett was still sitting with his head in his hands, as he had been for the past half-hour. While Brian and the team were out getting drunk and pouring beer over each other's heads that night, Derek's celebrations would be as restrained as ever. Derek was usually more relieved than elated when things went well and his introspective reaction to important successes often made people think he was unconcerned. The glory embarrassed him, but underneath he still loved winning and his sisters remember 'Derek's grin — a sort of soft, little boy's grin on his face, which would say "That's good — I'm pleased with myself".' That day he must have looked like the Cheshire Cat.

Although BMW had not become involved with the production B16s, a development BMW engine did appear in a B16 during 1970. Koepchen Engineering, the tuning company run by Austrian Peter Koepchen, bought a car which BMW development engineer Dieter Basche drove initially. This was a version of the 1600cc Formula 2 engine, stretched to 2-litres with the help of the Apfelbeck crank. Basche finished fourth at Anderstorp in June on the car's début, then Dieter Quester defected from Abarth and took the car over at Hockenheim in July. The package was obviously very quick and Quester battled for the lead with Redman and Bonnier in the second heat before slipping back to third. Unfortunately it was destined not to finish a race after that as Basche and Quester both had big practice accidents, and then the engine blew up at Spa.

Another development on the engine front was the fitting of a 2-litre Mazda rotary engine into a B16. Mazda entered the car for Le Mans and Belgium Racing prepared it for their

At the beginning of 1970, graphic designer Andy Mylius got together with Nomad sports car designer Bob Curl to produce an open 'spyder' conversion for the Chevron B8, known as the Gropa CMC (Chevron-Mylius-Curl). Here Gerry Birrell is pictured at the wheel of the first Gropa, which he co-drove with Mylius to a Group 6, 2-litre class win in the BOAC 1,000km on 12 April. (*Photo LAT.*)

drivers, Julien Vernaeve and Yves Deprez. The dramatically noisy car made a promising début in the Spa 1,000km when it finished 15th overall. The Belgian pair followed this up with 10th overall and second in class in the Nürburgring 1,000km. Everything looked well set for Le Mans. But the team's hopes were quickly dashed when the car retired only an hour into the race when its carburettor system fell apart.

Two other B16s went to Le Mans that year, but neither finished. Ian Skailes and John Hine retired with a couple of hours to go when their FVC engine gave up, while Digby Martland and Clive Baker had gone out a couple of hours earlier when their BMW engine dropped a valve. That car was one of three which had been bought, through Swiss agent Jo Siffert, by Steve McQueen's Solar Productions film company to use in the film 'Le Mans'. One of the cars was entered for the race itself to give some continuity to the racing footage. Reliability was a vital concern as they wanted to film it for as long as possible, so a BMW engine — as used in the B8s — was fitted, complete with 'unbustable' double valve springs. In the event it was outlasted by the 'fragile' FVC. The film company ran into further unforeseen problems because much of the race was wet. Their own private filming sessions at the track after the race were all in good weather and they had to spray the track with water to match the sequences up with the actual race footage. All three of Solar's B16s were used in this additional filming and some of the close-up shots in the film give the impression that the race was full of Chevrons! Meanwhile, Digby Martland decided that Le Mans had been his last race. International sports car racing was becoming ever more competitive and new engine and tyre technology was escalating the cost enormously. The day of the gifted amateur seemed to be over and Digby decided to leave the professionals to it.

The European 2-litre Sports Car Series inevitably took away entries from the RAC's British Championship, but the title was once again won by a Chevron as Trevor Twaites took his two-year-old B8 to victory. With separate classes for Group 5 and

Group 6 cars, the B8s were not in direct competition with the B16s for points. While waiting for his new Spectre, reigning champion John Lepp borrowed his first B8 back from its latest owner and won the class in the first two rounds over the Easter weekend. But when his new car arrived he went off to upset the B16s in the Group 6 class, leaving Twaites with a clear run to the championship.

Lepp picked up a drive in his later B8 when he partnered its new driver, George Silverwood, in the BOAC 1,000km at Brands Hatch in April. As the new B16s fell by the wayside, the B8 was the highest Chevron finisher as Lepp came storming through in the closing stages to finish 10th overall, failing to snatch victory in the 2-litre Group 5 class from the Porsche 910 of John L'Amie and Tommy Reid by less than a second.

With Chevron concentrating their works effort on the B16, the customers were left to themselves in Formula 3. Reine Wisell's success in the B15 had brought in plenty of orders for the updated B17 version, but the Chevrons had to fight hard to beat the Lotus 59s as the cars screamed and slipstreamed their way through the 1-litre formula's final year. Jürg Dubler and Peter Hanson were the most successful B17 drivers, taking five international wins between them.

Dubler beat Gerry Birrell's Brabham BT28 to win at Montjuich Park in April, then a month later he beat the McNamara of a young Austrian by the name of Niki Lauda to win at Brno, in Czechoslovakia. The Swiss driver's third win came at Zandvoort, when he fought for the lead with James Hunt's Lotus 59A until Hunt's engine gave up with three laps to go. Hanson's wins came in Finland and Sweden. At Hameenlinna he led from start to finish to beat Conny Andersson's Brabham and Hunt's Lotus, while at Karlskoga he fought off Birrell's Brabham to win.

In Britain, the *Motor Sport* Shell Championship was intensely fought, while many of the leading drivers also took in the Lombank series. Again, Peter Hanson was frequently the strongest of the Chevron runners. At Cadwell Park in July he took on the Lotus 59s of Dave Walker, James Hunt and Carlos Pace, eventually coming in second to Walker. With Pace retiring, Hunt was third ahead of the Chevrons of Barrie Maskell and American Steve Matchett with Wilson Fittipaldi sixth in another Lotus. Hanson was second again at the Oulton Park Gold Cup meeting in August, losing the lead to Carlos Pace on the last lap. Jürg Dubler was also beaten by Pace in an equally close race at Croft.

Another driver who went very quickly in a B17 was the New Zealander Bert Hawthorne, who won a Lombank round at Brands Hatch in May. Steve Matchett's B15 was second as the Chevron duo beat the Lotus 59s of Pace and Wilson Fittipaldi

B16 – THE ULTIMATE CHEVRON?

Unfortunately, Hawthorne's efforts came to a premature halt when he wrote the car off at Oulton Park later that month. Lying third in his heat, he collided with the somewhat crossed-up Gold Leaf Lotus of Dave Walker coming into Knicker Brook. His B17 was thrown 20 feet into the air, flying clean over a safety bank and fence and coming to rest in the middle of a grandstand. Mercifully the stand was rather sparsely populated and no-one was injured. Gerry Birrell's Brabham had cartwheeled out of the race in a similar incident only minutes before and official fingers were sternly wagged at the survivors before the Formula 3 final.

Barrie Maskell's efforts were rewarded with a win at Oulton Park in September, which was handed to him when the leading trio got tangled up with each other at the last corner, letting his B17 through to win. The year ended with a popular win by Chris Skeaping, whose first season in Formula 3 had been a disaster. On a cold, wet, November day at Thruxton, driving without rain tyres, he spun his B17 on the second lap and then fought his way back through the field to beat Dave Morgan's March and the Lotuses of Dave Walker and Carlos Pace.

But as the British season petered out in the Hampshire winter, Chevrons were on the winning trail out in the sunshine of South Africa where the Springbok Series was under way again.

With no works car in 1970, privateers were left to wave the Chevron flag in Formula 3. Here Barrie Maskell's B17 leads Wilson Fittipaldi's Lotus 59 and Roger Keele's Palliser WD3 at the Oulton Park Gold Cup meeting in August. (*Photo Frank Hall.*)

117

CHAPTER 8

Classic sports cars and the path to Formula 2

THE Springbok Series was officially Brian Redman's swan-song. Increasingly concerned by the number of his friends who had lost their lives in motor racing accidents, he had decided to retire and had shipped his family and all their belongings out to South Africa, where he was going to work as a salesman for Franz Richter's Richter Motors BMW dealership in Johannesburg. Before he emigrated, Brian had a couple of Interserie wins in a BRM Can-Am car, and when he got to South Africa with the B16-Spyder, his winning streak continued. 'Somehow I couldn't manage to lose a race. I was in one of those incredible runs of success which occasionally come for no apparent reason.'

In the 9-Hours at Kyalami, Redman shared the car with John Hine and they won the 2-litre class comfortably by finishing fifth overall. The remaining five Springbok races were just for the 2-litre cars, and Redman won them all, despite strong opposition from the Lola T210s of Helmut Marko and Mike Hailwood. Richard Attwood shared the laurels with Redman

On 17 October 1970, Brian Redman made a farewell appearance in a B16 at Oulton Park before 'emigrating' to South Africa. John (left) and Charles Bridges were among the many people there to wish him well. (*Photo Frank Hall.*)

at Cape Town and Welkom, the Rhodesian John Love co-drove at Bulawayo, and Redman won the Lourenco Marques and Pietermaritzburg 3-Hour races single-handed.

As reigning European 2-litre and Springbok champions, Chevron proved a popular choice for drivers in 1971 and the production version of the B16-Spyder, the B19, was Derek Bennett's fastest selling model yet, with 35 being produced during the season. After the success of the opening year of European 2-litre sports car racing, the championship drew much bigger entries for its second season and packed grids of Chevrons, Lolas and Abarths frequently flew round in great slipstreaming bunches that were more reminiscent of Formula 3 than the gentlemanly pursuit of sports car racing. Although Lola did not run a works car, their Swiss agent, Jo Bonnier, entered two of the latest Lola T212s under the Scuderia Filipinetti banner, and with Helmut Marko heading the driver line-up in another two-car Lola team run by Karl von Wendt, a repeat of the previous year's Chevron v Lola battle was assured.

On the Chevron side, Chris Craft took over Brian Redman's seat in the works car, while Chevron director John Bridges ran two cars for himself and John Hine in Red Rose Racing colours. Great things were also expected of the Dobbie Auto Racing Team, known as DART. Scottish businessman Denys Dobbie had bought two B19s for John Miles and Graham Birrell, and Dave Wilson had left Chevron to run the team's attack on the European series.

The World Championship BOAC 1,000km at Brands Hatch provided a useful shakedown for many of the new cars two weeks before the 2-litre series started and Chevron continued on their high note as Miles and Birrell dominated the 2-litre Group 6 class in their DART B19, beating the new Lola T212 of Jo Bonnier and Peter Westbury comfortably on their way to seventh overall. For good measure Chevrons also took the first three places in the Group 5 2-litre class, headed by the B16 of Andrew Fletcher and Bill Tuckett in 12th place overall. Things got tougher for DART when the European Championship opened at Paul Ricard and Miles, sharing his car with Toine Hezemans, had to settle for third place as the Lola of Helmut Marko and Jean-Pierre Jabouille beat Vic Elford's Filipinetti Lola to win.

The championship moved on to Austria in May and with financial expediency to think about John Bridges stepped down from his own Red Rose B19 in favour of the 22-year-old Formula 3 driver, Niki Lauda, who had some sponsorship to buy a drive at his home circuit of Salzburgring and was keen to take on his fellow countryman, Helmut Marko. After starting the first heat from the second row, Lauda was soon battling for the lead with Marko's pole-winning Lola and found him-

CHEVRON

Niki Lauda won the only race he ever drove in a Chevron, taking victory at Salzburgring in this Red Rose B19 on 23 May 1971. (*Photo Jeff Hutchinson.*)

self ahead when Marko dropped out with falling fuel pressure. A lap later, Vic Elford's Lola dived past Lauda's Chevron, only to lose the lead with a pit stop after running over some accident debris. But still Lauda was not home and dry as John Burton's B19 and Arturo Merzario's Abarth came up to take over the battle. For a while Lauda was demoted to third place, but four laps from the end he retook Merzario and then shadowed Burton until the last lap when he outbraked him to snatch the lead. Burton began the last lap first and ended it third as Merzario dived through after Lauda and the trio crossed the finish line covered by 1.1 seconds. Hine trailed in fourth, held back by a misfire.

Elford's Lola broke clear in the second heat as Hine, his car running smoothly again, worked his way through to second place. But with aggregate victory in mind and Merzario right on his tail, Lauda could not afford to be beaten by his teammate. With eight laps to go he inched his way past Hine, going on to add second place to his earlier win as Hine held Merzario back by enough to ensure Lauda the overall victory by 1.4 seconds after almost two hours of racing. Hine was rewarded with a third place on aggregate.

John Hine's own day did come at the Dunes Trophy European championship round at Zandvoort in September, when he won both heats despite having to fight his way through from the back after being nudged off at the start of the second part. It was a performance which John Bridges still rates as the best by any of his drivers.

One casualty of the Salzburgring race was Graham Birrell, who broke his wrist when his DART B19 was nudged into the barriers by Elford's Lola. So when Silverstone got its first ever sight of the European Championship a fortnight later, Dutchman Toine Hezemans was at the wheel of the second DART Chevron. The race was probably the high point of the season with 32 cars lining up in 4-3-4 formation for two 40-lap heats. Only Vic Elford's Lola T212 on pole spoiled the Chevron monopoly of the first two rows of the grid and 19 of the starters had been made in Bolton. It also seemed that you had to be called John to drive a B19 with six of the 10 B19s present boasting a John at the wheel. (For the record they were, in grid order, Miles, Hine, Burton, Lepp, Bamford and Bridges.)

Undeterred by the dual handicap of not having a Chevron and not being called John, Vic Elford stormed round at the head of a screaming 10-car pack until his Lola ran over a discarded starter motor and damaged a water pipe. John Burton then went to the front until he hit a hare and damaged the B19's radiator, and so Chris Craft's works Chevron took up the running. The hectic chase continued unabated as Craft set a new lap record at more than 123 mph, only to spin off a lap later. This handed the lead to Hezemans, who hung on to win from Helmut Marko's Lola and John Lepp, now back in the Chevron fold following the demise of the B16. Ronnie Peterson was a tremendous fourth in one of the Filipinetti Lolas, which he had started 10 seconds after everybody else

Silverstone's Martini International in June 1971 was one of the most exciting races in the European 2-litre series. Here Toine Hezemans, whose DART B19 won the race on aggregate, holds off Ronnie Peterson's Lola T212. (*Photo Jeff Hutchinson.*)

after missing practice.

Peterson was late getting to the grid for the second heat and had to start from the back a second time, but he stormed through to take the lead off Hezemans, going into Woodcote on only the fourth lap. Hezemans was content to let him go and concentrated on consolidating his lead on aggregate. Second place at the end of the heat was good enough to give Hezemans that overall win, with Peterson claiming second and Lepp third.

With two wins from three races and a handy lead in the championship, things were looking good for Chevron once again but, as it turned out, John Hine's win at Zandvoort in September was the only other race they were to win as Lola picked up another four on their way to victory in the series. Two of those wins were scored by Helmut Marko, who deservedly won the Drivers' Championship as the only person to win more than one round. When Hine's Red Rose B19 led the Canon Cameras–sponsored cars of Ed Swart and John Burton to a Chevron 1-2-3 at Zandvoort, Lola's lead was cut to only six points, but the company's priority swung to the lucrative South African Springbok Series and Hine's car joined two works B19s to be shipped out to Kyalami. With sponsorship deals from Lucky Strike and Gunston cigarettes, Chevron could not afford to miss the Springbok Series, which had now become a traditional end-of-season jaunt for the men from Bolton, and the closest thing to a holiday Derek Bennett ever took.

Chris Craft was probably not sorry to leave the European series behind after his disappointing year. He had suffered a couple of accidents that were not his fault and a couple of engine failures, and he frequently struggled with his tyres as Derek Bennett stuck to his contract with Dunlop while the other front-runners had switched to Firestones. The new grooveless, slick racing tyres had been introduced to the formula by Firestone at the beginning of the season and Dunlop had struggled to keep up with their progress through the year.

Craft may have thought he had taken over from Brian Redman, but when he got to the opening 2-litre round at Paul Ricard, there was Brian Redman sharing the works car with him for the three-hour race. Redman's emigration must have been one of the shortest on record as it had taken him little more than three months to decide that he was not cut out to be a car salesman. If his emigration was brief, his retirement from racing had been non-existent. After winning the Springbok Series, Brian had gone on to do the South African Formula 1 Championship in a Formula 2 Chevron and then driven a Surtees TS9 to seventh place in a one-off drive at the South African Grand Prix. Redman knew he could not stop being a racing driver, so April found him back in Europe, sharing a Red Rose B19 with Richard Attwood at Ricard, as well as partnering Chris Craft. Redman did not race the works car as Craft crashed early on when the bonnet flew up and blocked his vision, but he and Attwood finished eighth.

Sid Taylor came up with a Formula 5000 drive for Redman, but Brian's season was abruptly halted in May when he crashed a John Wyer/Gulf Porsche 908/3 on the Targa Florio. The car exploded and Brian was badly burned, as the scars from the extensive skin grafts to his face still show. Barely a month after the accident, Brian was back behind the wheel of a racing car again as he tried the works B19 during some Dunlop tyre tests at Aintree. The Chevron recuperation therapy was working again! With preparation for the Springbok Series in mind, Derek Bennett came up with a second works B19 for Redman for the Nürburgring 500km in September and, for the third year running, Redman started the race in a Chevron from pole position. This time he got inside the eight minute mark, taking 17.5 seconds off his time in the B16-Spyder with a lap in 7 minutes 54.9 seconds. Unfortunately he went out of the race with a blown engine.

The Springbok Series provided a useful test bed for new ideas and in 1971 the important development work was with engines. For the two years since it first appeared in the proto-type B16, Cosworth's FVC had been virtually universal in 2-litre sports car racing. But in the search for more power, and with a new 2-litre Formula 2 on the horizon for 1972, engine builders had been looking round for an alternative during 1971. Cosworth's belt-driven 1600cc BDA engine was the favoured choice. Using the block of Ford's 'Kent' engine, it was designed primarily for the new breed of sporty, road-going Ford Escorts, but racing engine builders were becoming familiar with it as the power unit for the new Formula Atlantic. Brian Hart took the major step of dispensing with the cast iron Ford block and designing his own light-alloy version to bolt the BDA head onto. Doing away with the liners helped get the engine up to 1994cc and the new unit caused quite a stir when it appeared in John Miles' DART B19 at the Hockenheim 2-litre race on 4 July.

Later in the season, Derek Bennett installed a 2-litre Abarth engine in a B19 for Toine Hezemans, who put the car on pole position on its début at Zandvoort in September. The engine seemed extremely quick, but unrelated mechanical failures stopped Hezemans finishing any races using it. Meanwhile, Chevron themselves had been working with Race Engine Services, who produced their 2-litre BDA using the standard iron block for Chris Craft's works B19 at the end of August. The engine took Craft to his best result of the year when he finished second to Vic Elford's Lola in the Nürburgring 500km, but at Zandvoort the belt drive broke and Derek turned his attention to another new engine for the Springbok Series.

Inevitably Cosworth was again the source, but the engine this time was based on Chevrolet's Vega EA unit, which Cosworth had been working on for some months at the request of General Motors. Brought down from its original 2.3 litres to 1994cc, its light-alloy block gave it a weight advantage over the BDAs and figures from Cosworth's test bench showed it to be producing around 270 bhp — at least 25 bhp more than an FVC. Mike Hailwood shared the Vega-engined B19 with Chris Craft at Kyalami and, despite running with a low rev limit because the spare engine hadn't arrived yet, Hailwood put it onto the front row, alongside the two works Ferrari 312Ps and ahead of a couple of Porsche 917s. In the race the speed trap clocked the car at 164 mph — 15 mph faster than the best FVC-engined car — and Hailwood was leading the race overall when he came in for his first refuelling stop and the engine was found to have lost compression.

From then on, Paul Owens and Derek Bennett fought their way through a catalogue of disasters with the engine and the works car only finished one race, the Cape 3-Hours at Killarney where Brian Redman shared the car with Hailwood and came in second, despite losing time in the pits having a fuel leak repaired. Although Redman had put the car on pole position for that race, it was found to have a cracked block after practice and it ran the race on Vega engine number three. Overheating and loss of water were constant problems and by the end of the series they had got through four engines.

In the meantime, another young driver who was also destined to become a Formula 1 World Champion was making his mark in a Chevron B19. The South African Jody Scheckter had been brought in by Ed Swart to share his car, and after Scheckter had survived an enormous accident at Killarney when a rear tyre blew, they went on to win the Lourenço Marques 3-Hours a week later. Mike Hailwood joined Paddy Driver in the FVC-engined works B19 to win in the next round at Bulawayo, in Rhodesia as it then was; and then John Hine and Dave Charlton took their turn to win at Welkom in the Red Rose B19, with Swart and Scheckter taking second place.

Hine looked all set to win another one when the latest version of Brian Hart's alloy BDA arrived in time for the last round at Pietermaritzburg. In the early stages Hine pulled out a big lead over Scheckter, but he lost the place having a brake problem cured in the pits and then went out when the engine developed a misfire. John Love was the eventual winner in a Lola T212, his consistency having already won him the Springbok title.

Chevron did not leave 1971 without a championship title though as the DART team pulled in their horns during the summer for John Miles to concentrate on the RAC British Sports Car Championship, which his B19 duly won, giving Chevron the title for the third year in a row. The series was dominated by Chevrons and B16s joined in the fray in a closely fought Group 5 class, which was eventually won by Brian Robinson.

Various Chevrons continued to venture into long distance events and John Hine shared his Red Rose B19 with Spain's José Juncadella to finish third overall in the Barcelona 1,000km at Montjuich Park in October. They were not the first 2-litre car home though as the gruelling race, which ran for well over seven hours, was won by the Lola T212-FVC of Jo Bonnier and Ronnie Peterson. Even the ageing B8 managed to come up with a couple of World Championship class wins during the year. At a poorly supported Spa 1,000km, Tony Birchenhough and Brian Joscelyne came in 12th overall to win their class, while a week later at the Targa Florio, brothers Mike and Richard Knight came out on top of the three Group 5 2-litre class runners, despite failing to complete their last lap. An even more curious class win was that of Tony Goodwin and Ray Nash from a lowly 22nd place overall in the Nürburgring 1,000km in Goodwin's four-year-old B6, which had been converted to open form and renamed the Redex-RPA.

In British club racing, many older Chevrons continued to prove competitive, and more than six years after its début, Derek Bennett's own original B1 Clubmans car, then owned by Geoff Temple, won at Croft, beating the B2 of Dave Rees to the flag. Earlier in the year Croft had also been the scene

Graham Hill tries a B19 for size as Dave Wilson looks on. Plans for the former World Champion to race the DART car at Brands Hatch on August Bank Holiday 1971 had to be dropped because of clashing fuel contracts. The drive went instead to Wilson Fittipaldi, who finished well down after a controversial collision with John Hine's B19. (*Photo Bolton Evening News.*)

of Derek Bennett's last race. The pressure of being a racing car designer and manufacturer meant that Derek had not raced regularly since 1968, although he still tested all his prototypes and development cars. But he was never one for hanging around watching other people. If he was not racing himself he would much rather be back at the factory getting on with work that needed doing. Circumstances had squeezed out his own ambitions of becoming a professional racing driver, but once or twice a year he still managed to get himself back onto the starting grid.

John Bridges had entered two Red Rose B19s, for himself and John Hine, in a two-part British Championship round at Croft. But John had to go to London with his daughter, who needed an eye operation, so he persuaded Derek to race his car. In practice Derek fell out with the notorious Croft chicane and kinked the monocoque. But, with Chris Craft away winning an Interserie race at the Norisring in Ecurie Evergreen's Can-Am McLaren M8E, the works car was not being used, so Derek shot back to the factory and got that one instead. He was lying sixth in the second part of the race until a bonnet pin came loose and the front bodywork folded up. As far as anybody is aware, he never made a conscious decision to give up racing, but 10 July 1971 turned out to have been Derek Bennett's last race.

One strand of Chevron's development which has not yet been mentioned is Formula 2, but Derek Bennett had been progressing steadily in the Formula and 1971 saw Chevron add a Formula 2 victory to its increasingly impressive list of achievements. Chevron's Formula 2 début had been at Hockenheim on 7 April 1968 — a date which is sadly etched in the motor racing history books for more sombre reasons as that same race claimed the life of Jim Clark.

Impressed with Chevron's first Formula 3 car, Peter Gethin had encouraged Cheshire team owner, Frank Lythgoe, to commission Derek Bennett to build a Formula 2 version for 1968. Based on the B9 Formula 3 chassis, the B10 had a wider engine bay to accommodate the Cosworth FVA engine, and incorporated bigger brakes and driveshafts. Lythgoe originally intended to run two cars and the first one was ready for Gethin to race at Hockenheim. It was also Gethin's own Formula 2 début and he was a little overawed at the thought of being in the same race as his hero, Jim Clark. Peter had been 11th fastest in practice, qualifying the Chevron two rows behind Clark's Lotus 48. On race day he had been having breakfast in his hotel when Clark came and joined him. 'All I remember about that day,' says Peter, 'is that he was my hero and I had breakfast with my hero that day.' Wondering what it was that heroes talked about over breakfast, Peter had plumped for tyres, and they had discussed what compounds they would be using if the threatened wet weather materialised.

In the first heat, Gethin was only running a couple of places behind Clark when the Lotus crashed, but like everyone else he saw nothing. The accident moved him up to seventh place, but he lost two laps repairing a broken throttle out on the circuit, and retired from the second heat. Like everyone else, he was stunned as the news of Clark's death began to sink in. 'I've never seen tough, hard drivers, as there were there that day, so upset,' Gethin recalled.

Two weeks later Gethin scored Chevron's first Formula 2 championship points when he finished fourth at Pau, in a race won convincingly by Jackie Stewart's Matra MS7. But when he only managed seventh place at Zolder the team began to get frustrated at their lack of progress. After the extraordinary début of the Formula 3 Chevron, there had been an expectation that the Bennett touch would produce a Formula 2 car which was just as competitive straight away. But it was an unrealistic hope — the car had not been designed for Formula 2 and it needed a testing and development programme to make it fully competitive as the suspension geometry did not work as well with the extra weight and power, and the bigger tyres.

Derek had been reluctant to build the Formula 2 cars as he already felt overstretched producing GT and Formula 3 cars, and he was unable to turn his attention to a development project. So Frank Lythgoe put the Chevron on one side and bought Gethin a Brabham for the rest of the season. The second chassis was nearly completed at this point, and when

Derek Bennett in the Formula 2 B10 at Mallory Park on 14 July 1968.

CHEVRON

the early season rush quietened down, Derek finished the car off and took it to Mallory Park to do a *Libre* race himself. He finished a close second to Steve Thompson's Lola, after leading for more than half the race. Derek shared the fastest lap and convinced himself that there was nothing fundamentally wrong with the B10. Somewhat disappointed that the car had been unable to make a stronger showing in Formula 2, he resolved not to get involved in the formula again until the opportunity arose for him to take a more active role.

It was the beginning of 1970 before Derek considered Formula 2 again. After winning at Sebring for Fred Opert at the end of 1969, Reine Wisell was impressed with the Formula B version of the B15 and thought it would adapt well to Formula 2, which he was keen to move into. He got himself a fairly modest budget from Publicator, a Swedish advertising company which had Mantorp Park and Anderstorp circuits amongst its clients, and Chevron agreed to run him in a works B17C — a Formula 2 version of the 1970 Formula 3 car. Reine made his Formula 2 début at Thruxton on 30 March, finishing eighth in his heat, but spinning out of the final while avoiding John Watson's rotating Brabham. He liked the car, but its reliability suffered because of the team's small budget and it almost always failed to finish.

Reine Wisell did a handful of Formula 2 races during 1970 with a B17C. Here his car poses on the startline at Oulton Park. (*Photo Arthur Taylor.*)

There was another B17C built, but it was not raced in Formula 2. Instead Steve Thompson drove it, first with an FVA engine and then the bigger FVC unit, in British *Formule Libre* events. Thompson was only beaten once all year, ending the season as BOC Champion with 14 wins and numerous lap records to his credit. Thompson's success seemed to draw attention to the failure of Wisell's car and Derek became increasingly unhappy that Chevron were being dismissed as incapable of building a competitive Formula 2 car.

So, with the B16 sports car project out of the way, he turned his mind to designing a brand new single-seater, which would be primarily a Formula 2 car. For three years Chevron's single-seaters had been basically developments of Derek Bennett's original design and, just as he had done with the sports car, Derek decided to put his accumulated experience into a completely new design.

Chevron's Formula 3 cars had already come to be known as semi-monocoque because of the practice of 'plating' the chassis — riveting steel and aluminium alloy sheeting between the steel tubing of the spaceframe to add strength and rigidity. But with the B18 Derek took another step towards true monocoque design, using aluminium panels in a semi-monocoque centre section, and attaching them to a steel frame which joined the front and rear tubular steel bulkheads rather than directly to the bulkheads themselves. This system meant that the rear sub-frame could be easily detached and the car converted to Formula 3 or Formula B specification. The steel frame also satisfied Derek's constant concern that his cars should offer drivers as much protection as possible in an accident. He was also reluctant to embrace the concept of the monocoque totally because it did not suit his way of working. New Chevrons were still built first and drawn later. As long as the blow torch and the pile of tubes was the basis of racing car chassis construction Derek could build his own prototypes the way he had always done, testing them himself and altering them where necessary until he was happy with the car. Only at that point would the race-ready prototype be handed over to the draughtsmen so they could make the drawings which suppliers and Chevron's own machine shop would need to produce parts and jigs for manufacturing the car. Modifying a spaceframe was just a matter of taking one tube out and putting another one in, whereas monocoque construction left you much more heavily committed to the design you had first come up with.

Aerodynamics was a persistent source of fascination to Derek and one of his prime concerns was to keep the airflow over the new car as clean and as effective as possible. To keep the flow cleaner along the side of the B18 he moved the front suspension inside the bodywork, a step which attracted comment as going against the current trend, although inboard suspension is now an accepted part of single-seater design. It was also the first car Derek had designed with wings and it was his thinking here which was the most controversial aspect of the car. The B18 had a conventional aerofoil at the back, but the front wing was mounted above the bodywork, its v-shaped leading edge giving it the appearance of an oversize Chevron badge. Derek was concerned that conventional front spoilers did not act directly onto the chassis and that much of their effect was diverted into flexing the nose rather than providing downforce on the chassis. He believed that a wing mounted above the front sub-frame rather than in front of it would create greater downforce, and would function better for being in a less turbulent airstream. This set-up also allowed enough space under the wing to place the radiator right at the front of the car, which he felt was another important consideration.

The end result was a stubby, angular car that seemed to possess none of the smooth good looks which people had come to associate with Chevrons. Where the attractiveness of the B16 had caused its early shortcomings to be almost completely overlooked, the ungainly appearance of the B18 convinced people that it would not work. 'It was a good car, but a very ugly one,' admits Paul Owens, 'and we couldn't sell them because people just didn't like them because of their looks.' Paul believes the car did look good to Derek because he could see the practical ideas which its design boasted, but convincing customers was an uphill battle and a frustrating experience for Derek, who found such unexpectedly fickle behaviour difficult to understand.

Ironically, the B18 was a big step forward for Chevron and the successes it did achieve are remarkable when you consider

Without its bodywork, the B18 displays its monocoque construction and inboard front suspension. The high front wing sat on top of the near-vertical radiator. (*Photo Jeff Hutchinson.*)

how few of the cars were raced. The prototype, which was built completely at Bolton, was finished towards the end of August 1970 and plans went ahead for Reine Wisell to give the B18 its début in the European Formula 2 round at Mantorp Park on 30 August. Derek tested it himself at Aintree, and then went out to Sweden with Reine for some additional testing at Mantorp Park a few days before the race. Testing was cut short when Reine crashed the car, but fortunately his home town of Motala was only 20 miles away and he was able to get the car repaired there the next day, in time for official practice. Wisell was fifth in the first heat and ran a promising fourth in the second part behind the Brabhams of Rolf Stommelen and Tim Schenken, and François Cevert's Tecno until his gear linkage broke.

Wisell flew back to England to race Sid Taylor's Formula 5000 McLaren M10B at Snetterton the next day. He beat Mike Hailwood to begin a sequence of three wins which shot him to such prominence that Lotus signed him up for the United States Grand Prix at Watkins Glen in October. Suddenly the Formula 2 Chevron was not a priority for Reine and plans to race it again in Europe that year were shelved.

Instead Brian Redman took the prototype with him to South Africa as a memento of Bolton to keep him company in his new homeland. A week after racing the B16-Spyder in the Kyalami 9-Hours, Redman went back there to test the B18, and promptly wrote it off when he swerved to avoid a 'turkey-sized bird' which came wandering across the track. Paul Owens and Derek Bennett had been hoping to use Brian to get some development work done on the B18 while they were in South Africa with the sports car for the Springbok Series, so they had a second car built up at Bolton and sent out. When Derek went home at the end of Brian's runaway victory in the series, Paul stayed on to help prepare the B18 for the forthcoming South African Formula 1 series. Driving to Kyalami one day, Paul was involved in an accident when another car shot a stop sign and hit him broadside on. Paul was thrown out of the car and critically injured. He spent a month in hospital with a fractured skull and damaged vertebrae. He also lost his hearing and sense of balance on his left side, which still affects him now.

When the news reached England, Derek was the most emotional his sister, June, could ever remember seeing him. His loyalty to Paul was something many of those who had known Derek a long time found hard to understand. Those who knew Derek well had a respect and admiration for him, rooted in the days of the model aircraft 'fan club', which bordered on hero worship. In contrast, Paul often seemed to them truculent and disrespectful, undeserving of the special relationship he appeared to have with Derek. There was perhaps more than a hint of mutual jealousy in the way Paul and June did not get on with each other. June worked at the factory for five years, running the office, and the only time she remembers ever seeing Derek lose his temper was during a row she was having with him over Paul.

But Paul's independent manner merely disguised his devotion to Derek. His own elder brother had died when Paul was 20 and Derek had taken over that role in his life. With only sisters of his own, the idea of having a younger brother must have appealed to Derek, and Paul was the one he taught to do things his way, as he had done with his sister, Wendy, in the aeromodelling days. Paul Owens has gone on to become tremendously successful in his own right, and now runs Reynard's composites facility. But he is happy to give Derek Bennett the credit for his success. 'I think I owe all my success to him,' says Paul, 'because he instilled in me the will to do it better than anybody else. His preparation was always immaculate. Whatever he did, he had to do it better than somebody else could do it, and that was his motivation. He taught me a lot which still stands now.' Derek knew he could depend on Paul to do exactly what he wanted in the way he would have done it himself, and the thought of being without Paul obviously shook him.

Paul had been due to go out to South America for a two-race Formula 2 series in Colombia at the beginning of February. Jo Siffert was still a Chevron agent and he had ordered two B18s for himself and Xavier Perrot to race there. The cars had been built up at Bolton, incorporating some of the developments which had come out of Brian Redman's test sessions in South Africa, and shipped out to Colombia where Paul Owens was due to join them. With Paul still in hospital in South Africa, Steve Sheldon was dropped in at the deep end to make the trip on his own. Derek Bennett drove him

Jo Siffert scored Chevron's first Formula 2 victory at Bogota on 7 February 1971. His winning B18 is shown here at Mallory Park a month later.

down to Portsmouth to pick up the bag tanks for Perrot's car, and with those in one arm and a holdall of used pound notes in the other, Steve was left to find his way to Paris to pick up a charter flight to Bogota.

No-one took too much notice as Siffert lined up for the first heat halfway down the 18-car grid. But after only six laps he was second and gaining on the leading March 712M of Henri Pescarolo. Just before half-distance Siffert outbraked the March to take the lead and the Chevron hung on to win, despite a misfire caused when a plug lead came loose. Back on all cylinders, Siffert led the second heat from start to finish as Graham Hill's Lotus 69 gave chase in vain. The European season had not even started and already the B18 had given Chevron its first Formula 2 win.

The second part of the Temporada one week later was again at the new Autodroma in Bogota and while Steve Sheldon checked over the cars, Siffert and Pescarolo disappeared into the jungle to shoot crocodiles. On his return, Siffert planted the B18 on pole position and broke his own lap record as he led the first heat from start to finish, leaving Rolf Stommelen's Brabham BT30 more than 10 seconds behind at the finish. Then, just as he looked all set for a clean sweep in the second heat, Siffert slipped back from the lead when a cog on the distributor drive broke. The distributor shaft finally gave way on the last lap and the Chevron was not classified.

But the disappointment of losing the series at the last minute did little to detract from the euphoria of the earlier win and Derek Bennett felt confident that he had silenced the critics who said Chevron could not build a Formula 2 car. Unfortunately they were unable to sustain that momentum in Europe. On his return, Siffert was confirmed as the number two driver to Pedro Rodriguez in the new BRM P160 and the Chevron effort was pushed into a corner. Siffert made only occasional appearances in his B18, hiring it out, along with Perrot's car, for the races he could not get to. François Mazet gave the car its best result in Europe when he finished fourth at Pau in a race which, ironically, saw Reine Wisell score his first Formula 2 win in a Team LIRA Lotus 69.

Seeing their grip on Formula 2 slipping away again, Chevron tried to keep up a development programme on the B18 with their own works chassis, but much of the effort at Bolton was going into meeting the demand for the successful B19 sports car and there was neither the time nor the financial resources to devote to the B18. Chris Craft was given a couple of races in it, by way of compensation for the frustrating time he was having trying to keep the works B19 competitive on inferior rubber, but nothing was achieved.

The B18 did find some buyers in Formula B trim in America.

Mike Eyerly dominated the 1970 American Formula B Championship in his Fred Opert B17B. Opert believes Eyerly could have been a better driver than Keke Rosberg.

Fred Opert, who was still selling Brabhams as well as Chevrons in the States, had run a five-car team in Formula B the year before, which included B17Bs for himself and the defending champion, Mike Eyerly. Opert still rates Eyerly as one of the best drivers that ever sat in a Chevron, with a natural talent that outshone anyone who drove for him subsequently — and he includes Keke Rosberg in that assessment. In 1970, Eyerly dominated Formula B, winning nine races and taking the championship title again. That performance helped Opert sell four B18s the following year. The B18 also had potential for the British version of Formula B, Formula Atlantic, which was launched in 1971.

Formula B cars used 1600cc twin-cam engines, but the 1600cc BDA was permitted in Britain, although the new engines were still in very short supply when the first Formula Atlantic race was held at Brands Hatch on 7 March. The B18 which Graham Eden had ordered for Cyd Williams was not ready for that race, but Chevron was represented as Bob Ellice finished second to Vern Schuppan's Palliser, driving the B10 which Derek Bennett had raced himself in 1968.

When Williams appeared in the B18 he was immediately quick, but getting the engine reliable took some time. Meanwhile, Schuppan, who had stuck to twin-cam power, was piling up the points in the *Yellow Pages* Championship. But at Brands Hatch on 20 June it was Schuppan's engine that failed and Williams who went through to give Chevron their first Atlantic win, although his BDA sounded far from healthy as Williams spluttered across the finish line. Two weeks later he beat Schuppan in a straight fight at Brands Hatch and from then on the Chevron was the pace-setter as Williams took the lap record at five circuits. A gritty driver who always seemed to thrive on adversity, Cyd put in one of his most impressive performances later in the year at Brands Hatch. His mechanics were unable to free a jammed throttle in time for the race, so Cyd started with the throttle stuck open and only the ignition switch with which to control the car's performance! After spending a few laps getting used to a completely new driving technique, Cyd began to climb through the field and he broke the lap record four times on his way to the finish, crossing the line one second behind Schuppan's Palliser and Norman Cuthbert's Brabham, as they took the flag side by side.

With four rounds to go Cyd needed four wins to snatch the championship. A hectic weekend with races at Castle Combe and Snetterton saw him clock up the first two victories, but he went out of the penultimate round at Mallory Park when the head gasket blew. Williams won the last round, but the title had already gone to Schuppan.

The new 1600cc Formula 3 also began in 1971 and Rodney Bloor decided to run a B18 for Barrie Maskell, who had been very impressive on a negligible budget over the last two years of the 1-litre formula in a succession of Chevrons. He did not win a race and Bloor looks back on the season as something of a failure. But, nevertheless, Maskell was always among the front runners in a year that turned out to have provided some particularly talented opposition. When he came a close third in his heat at Crystal Palace, for instance, it was to two future World Champions — James Hunt and Jody Scheckter. And when he qualified for his heat at Brands Hatch at the end of the year on pole position, he had James Hunt and Colin Vandervell alongside him, with Alan Jones and David Purley behind. Barrie lost a few races because of mechanical failures, and he had one or two collisions when his enthusiasm got the better of him, but he did show that the Chevron could run with the best of them and finished in the first three on a number of occasions. He led several races, but his best result was at Snetterton in October where he was lying second to Dave Walker's Lotus 69 when a crash stopped the race.

Despite some good results and that all important first Formula 2 win, the B18 was regarded as a disappointment, so Derek Bennett put his head down to try again for 1972.

CHAPTER 9

The fairy story continues

THE new B20 was a logical development of the under-rated B18. The aerodynamic thinking which had been responsible for the B18's ungainly appearance was jettisoned and the front wing was replaced with an equally unusual — but far more attractive — deep, full-width nose, which was modelled on the front body section of the B19 sports car. With the airflow now directed up over the front wheels the front suspension could be brought outboard again, which removed the problems they had had getting the inboard top links stiff enough. Derek also made the B20 a true monocoque, dispensing with the central frame and joining the aluminium central 'tub' straight to the bulkheads.

Derek realised that they would have to run a works car in Formula 2 themselves to make sure the car achieved the success he knew it was capable of, and Paul Owens arranged backing from Castrol and Champion to support the effort. It was still hardly a big budget operation, with Castrol providing £6,000 and Champion around £1,200 for the season, but they reckoned they could make a good showing on it. The press took their intentions seriously when Peter Gethin was announced as the works driver. Peter was now in demand as a Formula 1 driver, especially after his stunning win for **BRM** in the Italian Grand Prix the previous September, and although it was nearly four years since he had given the first Chevron Formula 2 car its début, he had maintained his links with the company, acting as their South of England agent for a couple of years.

Despite the disappointments with the B10, Gethin was keen to race the new car. He got on well with Paul and Derek and, as a committed Chevron fan, he was confident that Derek had the ability to get it right. But early problems, largely to do with the engine, made the opening two British rounds of the European Formula 2 Championship a disappointment. Gethin was unable to do the next race, at the Nürburgring, as he was at Jarama driving for BRM. Chevron's other tame ace and Nürburgring specialist, Brian Redman, was racing Sid Taylor's Formula 5000 McLaren in Ireland, but Vic Elford had won the Nürburgring 500km for the previous two years — one of them in a B16 — so he was called in as a good bet.

A new Alan Smith-prepared BDA engine seemed to possess none of the quirks of its predecessor and Elford soon had the B20 handling to his liking as he qualified fourth fastest at the 'Ring. In the race he was running with the leading group until his rear wing came loose. Paul Owens had put a new wing on the car, moving it further back than the original one on a metal frame, and it was this frame that had come apart. After two pit stops to put it right, Elford was eventually classified 10th as the March 722 of Jochen Mass beat Derek Bell's Brabham BT38 to win the race.

The team went straight from Germany to the south of France, where Gethin rejoined them for the round-the-houses race at Pau. After the first couple of races Peter had been growing impatient with the new Chevron, but the car that greeted him at Pau was transformed, thanks to its new engine and the suspension modifications Paul Owens had worked out with Elford. Pau was one of his favourite circuits and Peter went into the race confident. 'I could drive better there than most people — I love Pau,' said Gethin. 'The car was beautiful and it suited my style round there. The whole thing was easy!'

Gethin started his heat alongside François Cevert's March 722 and was shadowing the Frenchman when the March broke down only three laps into the race, leaving the Chevron to a comfortable win in a time that gave Gethin pole position for the final. But the French were not about to hand victory on their circuit to an Englishman and Patrick Depailler challenged Gethin hard in the opening laps of the final in his John Coombs March 722. But as the race wore on, the Chevron's Firestone tyres held up better than the Goodyears on the March and Depailler began to fall back. Soon Gethin was half-a-minute ahead and enjoying himself. 'I remember going through the park and waving to a photographer called Jutta Fausel because I had so much lead, and looking at the trees, and the crumpet at the side of the road, and all sorts of things.'

Then suddenly the ball-joint broke on the fuel-metering unit, jamming the mixture on full rich with 18 laps still to go. 'It meant you either got full power or nothing.' Whenever he applied the throttle the car would snap viciously out of line and as Gethin struggled to keep the Chevron under control, Depailler was eating up his lead. With four laps to go, the March was on the Chevron's tail, but Gethin was not going to be deprived of his win now. 'I was determined to win it, and I did win it. But people didn't realise how hard I'd worked — I drove my balls off! That was one of my best ever races, in my book. I probably got as much satisfaction out of win-

Peter Gethin struggles to keep his B20 under control as the March of Patrick Depailler closes on him in the final laps of the 1972 Pau Formula 2 race. (*Photo LAT.*)

ning that race at Pau as I did winning the Grand Prix at Monza.'

Derek Bennett, of course, was not at Pau, but Paul Owens remembers him being delighted when he heard the news that they had won. By winning a prestigious European Championship round he had finally proved that Siffert's win at Bogota had not been a fluke and that Chevron really could build a winning Formula 2 car. The B20's full-width nose was still an oddity among the narrow, chisel noses of the other cars, but within a year Derek Bennett's approach had been copied by everyone. Chevron's reputation received a tremendous boost on 7 May 1972 because, while Peter Gethin was winning at Pau, John Hine and John Bridges were taking their Red Rose/Tergal B21 to the marque's best ever sports car World Championship result, collecting 12 points in the World Championship for Makes as they finished third overall in the Spa 1,000km. Well clear in the 2-litre class, the Chevron was beaten only by the 3-litre Ferrari 312Ps of Brian Redman/Arturo Merzario and Jacky Ickx/Clay Regazzoni, as Redman won the race for the fourth time to secure the championship for Ferrari.

Chevron maintained their high profile through May. Two weeks later Dieter Quester won the Salzburgring round of the

THE FAIRY STORY CONTINUES

John Hine makes a pit stop during the Nürburgring 1000 km on 28 May 1972. He and John Bridges finished fifth overall in their Tergal B21, winning the 2-litre class comfortably. (*Photo Jeff Hutchinson.*)

European 2-litre Championship in a new B21 fitted with a development BMW engine. The 16-valve crossflow engine was said to be the basis for the following year's Formula 2 power unit, but BMW denied that the entry had official works backing — indeed BMW Competitions Manager, Jochen Neerpasch was at Salzburgring to deny it himself! Then, a week after that, John Hine and John Bridges took another impressive long-distance result, beating the Lola T290 of Gerard Larrousse and Jo Bonnier to win the 2-litre class of the Nürburgring 1,000km by two laps as their B21 came home fifth overall. The next day was a Bank Holiday Monday in Britain and Vic Elford finished a strong fourth with the works B20 in the European Formula 2 round at Crystal Palace, only 4.6 seconds behind Jody Scheckter's winning McLaren.

But even these performances were overshadowed by what was happening at Oulton Park that Bank Holiday, 29 May. After taking his Ferrari 312P to second place at the Nürburgring, Brian Redman had flown back for the Rothmans European Formula 5000 Championship round at Oulton, and appeared not in Sid Taylor's McLaren, with which he was leading the championship, but in a brand new Chevron — the B24. After a disappointing season with the McLaren M18, Sid Taylor had gone back to the older McLaren M10B at the start of 1972 while he looked around for a suitable new chassis. There did not seem to be an obvious choice, so Brian asked Derek Bennett if he could build one. He said yes, so Brian asked him if he would like to. When he answered yes again, Brian wanted to know how much and how long. Coming up with a price was beyond Derek, but he was quick to answer '10 weeks' to the second part of the question. 'So Sid came and

CHEVRON

Brian Redman gave the B24 Formula 5000 car a début victory at Oulton Park on 29 May 1972. Here he springs away from the front row of the grid with Alan Rollinson's Lola T300 on his left and Trevor Taylor's Leda on his right. (*Photo Charles Briscoe-Knight.*)

provided the engine and the gearbox,' Redman recalls, 'and I paid Derek the princely sum of £3,250 for a rolling chassis 10 weeks later.'

Before going out to Spa, Redman had tested the new car at Oulton Park with Derek Bennett and it was immediately on the pace when Brian took it out for the final practice session on Monday morning. On a damp track he was more than three seconds slower than he had been in testing, but his time was still good enough for the middle of the front row. Alan Rollinson's Lola T300 led for just half a lap before Redman put the Chevron in front. A bout of 'flu made the race hard work for him, but choosing intermediate tyres gave him an advantage over those on wets on the drying track. Once in

THE FAIRY STORY CONTINUES

front Redman left the rest behind and beat Rollinson by a minute. Derek Bennett had done it again and Brian Redman had helped write another chapter in the fairy story of Chevron, winning first time out in a brand new car, just as he had done three years earlier with the B16 at the Nürburgring. With Paul Owens at Crystal Palace, Derek Bennett had been overseeing the new Formula 5000 car at Oulton. With characteristic understatement he described the win as 'satisfying'. Redman himself is a man in much the same dry, Lancastrian mould and he was happy for Derek to take the credit for the results. 'I never really thought "what a fantastic race I drove" because I know how much it's tied in with the car and the team. The best driver in the world can't make a bad car win a race.'

Barely two hours after its début win the B24 was racing again as a Chevron lined up alongside Formula 1 cars for the first time in the Oulton Park Gold Cup. Redman amazed everyone by planting the Chevron on the back of a tight leading quartet, happily hanging onto Denny Hulme's McLaren M19, Peter Gethin's BRM P160 and Emerson Fittipaldi's Lotus 72. When Gethin dropped out, Redman moved up to third, but he eventually dropped back to fourth, behind Tim Schenken's Surtees TS9B, after a quick pit stop when he thought something might have broken on the chassis. He still won the Formula 5000 category by more than a lap and broke his own lap record in the process.

Like so many major steps in the development of Chevron Cars, the move into Formula 5000 was a response to a customer's request, rather than a planned piece of company policy. So nothing was done to capitalise on the initial success of the B24 and no more were built that year. British drivers did not have to worry about beating the B24 as the prototype went immediately to America, where Sid Taylor was keen for Redman to race. 'We'd seen some of the prize money that was being paid in America,' said Brian, 'and we'd decided to go to Watkins Glen to try and gather a little bit of our money back. And so we went! Sid bought an estate car for $400 in New York, the car was shipped over on an open trailer, and we had no spares. It was a two-heat race with $20,000 for first place — which at the time was about £8,000 — so we would have paid for the entire car if we'd won!'

The B24 very nearly won them all their money back at Watkins Glen. After winning the first heat, Redman was ahead in the second when the battery went flat a few laps from the finish. He still took fourth place on aggregate, picking up enough prize money to convince Sid Taylor that it was worth continuing with the rest of the American series. Redman led again in the next race, at Elkhart Lake, but went out when the right front suspension collapsed as a locating bolt on the top link broke.

Redman was unable to drive at the Donnybrooke Speedway in Minnesota two weeks later as he had been called up to drive for McLaren in the German Grand Prix. But, ironically, Peter Gethin had been stood down from his BRM drive by the idiosyncratic Louis Stanley, so he stepped into Redman's seat in the Chevron. Again the car showed well as Gethin fought off a strong challenge from David Hobbs' Lola T300 to lead the first heat. But this time something in the rear suspension gave way and Gethin went out. With the car repaired he won the second heat comfortably and was still classified fourth on aggregate.

Concerned by these failures, Derek Bennett flew out to

THE FAIRY STORY CONTINUES

America, making some modifications to the suspension in time for the next race at Road Atlanta. Redman was back at the wheel and cruised to victory in the first part, beating Brett Lunger's Lola T300 by more than 17 seconds. But he lost the lead in the second part when the B24 began to handle badly. Brian was initially worried that it might be another suspension failure, but it turned out to be a broken front spoiler.

As Redman pondered his problem, forked lightning announced the start of a torrential downpour and he dived straight for the pits to get some wet tyres. While the Chevron was up on the jacks, half-a-dozen cars crashed on the starting straight in the impossible conditions, and as the officials reached for their red flags to stop the race, Sid Taylor slammed the Chevron down off the jacks and sent Brian off to do another lap, still on slicks. After two spins, he made it to the finish line and was initially declared the winner. But when Lunger's team protested, the results were wound back to the lap before the accidents, relegating Redman to second place.

At Lime Rock, Redman again had to settle for second place to Lunger's Carl Hogan Lola, but Chevron's long-threatened first American Formula 5000 win finally came on 24 September when Redman won both heats of the last round of the L & M Series at Riverside.

With the American series over, Redman brought the B24 back to Britain for a confrontation at Oulton Park with the New Zealander Graham McRae, also back from the States after winning the L & M title in his McRae GM1. Redman still had a chance of winning the Rothmans European Championship and he stunned the opposition by taking pole position with a lap 0.4 seconds inside Denny Hulme's outright lap record in the Formula 1 McLaren. Although Redman led away, McRae kept him under pressure and as the leaders came over Hill Top for the 13th time Redman resisted his natural instinct to slow down when he was confronted with a cloud of dust across the track. It turned out to contain a slow-moving backmarker and another car bouncing off the bank, and Redman was unable to avoid clipping one of the cars and damaging the Chevron's nose. Somehow McRae steered his way through the confusion, going on to win as Redman retired.

A week later Redman took his revenge, beating McRae and Frank Gardner's new Lola T330 at Brands Hatch. The race was a supporting event for the following day's JPS Victory Race, which Redman was due to contest in a Formula 1 McLaren M19A. When the McLaren needed an engine change during practice, Redman qualified the Chevron as well, just in case he might need it. But with the McLaren pronounced ready for action, Sid Taylor promptly sold the Chevron to Keith Holland, who started the race from the back of the grid and came through to win the Formula 5000 category. The weekend ensured that Derek Bennett would have plenty of customers for a production version of the B24 the following season.

As Brian Redman developed the new Formula 5000 car in America, Peter Gethin continued with the B20 in Formula 2, where he remained one of the front runners. But the team's limited budget handicapped the effort and relatively minor mechanical or engine problems conspired to stop Peter winning another race after Pau. Nevertheless, he came tantalisingly close on a couple of occasions. At Imola in July he snatched victory from Mike Hailwood's Surtees on the last lap of the first heat, only to retire from the second part with a broken fuel line. Two weeks later at Mantorp Park he looked all set to make up for that disappointment when he lined up on pole position with the Marches of Ronnie Peterson and Patrick Depailler alongside him, and Mike Hailwood's Surtees and Carlos Reutemann's Brabham behind. Depailler led for the first lap, but Gethin was soon past him and went on to win the first part by 38 seconds. He had the measure of his illustrious opposition once again in the second part and was leading by more than 10 seconds when he went off the track with a flat tyre.

Gethin was to have driven the B20 at Brands Hatch at the end of August in the Rothmans 50,000 — a curious, 'anything goes' *Formule Libre* race with a £10,000 first prize to lure some Grand Prix teams to take on the best Formula 2 and Formula 5000 cars. BRM entered a couple of cars and although Gethin was not asked to drive either of them, he remained under contract to BRM and Louis Stanley objected to him driving the Chevron. One suggestion was that Stanley objected to one of his contracted drivers racing a car that would have to make a refuelling stop, in the light of the Formula 1 Association's opposition to pit stops. Gethin's contract was also said to preclude him from racing another make of car in direct competition with BRM. More cynical observers felt that Stanley was just worried about the nimble Chevron showing up his flagging Grand Prix cars. But whatever the real reason, Gethin found himself threatened with legal action if he drove the Chevron. 'I must have been crazy to be intimidated like that,' says Gethin now, 'but in those days drivers didn't have the say they've got today.'

With practice already under way, Paul Owens had a car and no driver. Wondering what to do, he bumped into journalist Mike Doodson, who immediately suggested he call John Watson. When Bert Hawthorne had been killed at Hockenheim that April, Watson had been called in by Alan McCall to replace him in the Tui Formula 2 car. But the team's budget had run out and Watson was once again sitting at home

THE FAIRY STORY CONTINUES

without a drive. He had followed Chevron's progress with great interest since meeting Derek Bennett and Paul Owens in Ireland back in 1965, and he jumped at the chance of racing one for the first time.

Having raced the Tui against the Chevron in Formula 2, Watson arrived at Brands Hatch with some preconceived ideas about the car, particularly its full-width nose and long wheelbase, which would make it different to what he was used to. But his apprehensions vanished as soon as he took the Chevron out for practice. 'As I drove it I discovered it was a very sympathetic car to my driving style and technique. It was a very comfortable car to drive and a very confidence-inspiring car, and the more I drove it the more I enjoyed it.'

Although Chevron could only afford to risk running a 1.8-litre FVC sports car engine in the car, Watson still qualified on the fifth row and when the race started he moved quickly up amongst the Formula 1 cars, running fifth as he challenged Henri Pescarolo's March 711. When the Chevron came in for refuelling a fuel valve stuck and with petrol blowing back through the quick-fill cap breather, Watson had to come back into the pits. He returned to the race in eighth place, but fought his way back up to fifth again. In the end he had to settle for sixth place after spinning at South Bank in the closing stages while lapping a Formula 5000 car. The race was won by Emerson Fittipaldi's JPS Lotus, but the sight of the little Chevron harassing the Formula 1 cars was one of the highlights of the race, and Watson's spirited performance had put him back in the limelight.

Following the buzz that the Rothmans race had created, Chevron were keen to run John Watson again, both as a thank-you to him and as a sales pitch for the following year's cars.

John Watson revived his career when he put the works Formula 2 B20 in among the Formula 1 cars in the Rothmans 50,000 race at Brands Hatch on 28 August 1972. The tape over Peter Gethin's name bears witness to the last-minute driver change. (*Photo LAT.*)

So a second works car was built up for him to race at Oulton Park in the final round of the John Player British Formula 2 Championship. In the event, the day proved a big disappointment as Peter Gethin failed to start after damaging two engines in practice, and Watson retired with fluctuating oil pressure. But Watson had again demonstrated the potential of the Chevron, setting a new lap record, which he shared with the works March 722s of Ronnie Peterson and Niki Lauda, and James Hunt's March 712, while closing on the leading bunch on his way up from a poor grid position. Watson's enthusiasm for the B20 remained undampened. 'Round Oulton Park the car was brilliant. Had the engine had more power I think that was a race that could have been won very easily.'

John Watson was called up again at the beginning of November to help Chevron try to win the European 2-litre Sports Car Championship for a second time. With the final round at Jarama thought to have been cancelled, Chevron believed they had already won the title in October when John Burton's Canon-sponsored B21 won at Montjuich Park. When the Jarama race was reinstated the works Chevrons were already on their way to South Africa for the Kyalami 9–Hours, which was to be run on the same weekend. So John Bridges put together a three-car Red Rose team, consisting of the one B21 which had not gone to Kyalami and two B19s. Watson was brought in to bolster the regular Tergal-sponsored drivers, Niki Bosch and José Juncadella, and he claimed pole position in Bridges' own B19 from the previous season. Osella-Abarth had won four of the previous eight rounds. But with their star driver, Arturo Merzario, committed to Kyalami with Ferrari, they wheeled in Derek Bell for the showdown.

Pursued by three Abarths, Watson had pulled out a big lead in the first part of the race when he was knocked off as he tried to lap the Porsche 911 of Erwin Kremer. With Watson losing time in the pits having the B19 checked over, Nanni Galli's Osella won the heat and the title slipped away from Chevron. Watson fought tooth and nail with Bell to try and win the second heat, spinning off and catching him up again at one point. But Bell kept him in second place to win the race on aggregate, and the championship, for Osella-Abarth. It was a disappointing end to a frustrating year for Chevron's 2-litre sports car runners. Derek Bennett had had his hands full developing the Formula 2 car and then building the Formula 5000 prototype. But the week after Redman had won first time out in the B24, Derek was at Dijon helping John Hine to set up a new Red Rose B21, which he had fitted with a Chevrolet Cosworth EA engine. Although the engine had been at Bolton since the beginning of the season, the problems the Vega units had posed in the Springbok Series had made him reluctant to use it straight away. Cosworth had meanwhile continued their development with Jo Bonnier's Lola, and then with Guy Edwards' Lola, although they still seemed some way from solving the engine's inherent problems.

The engine ran well at Dijon and Hine led the race until being passed by Dieter Quester's B21, which had won on its début two weeks earlier with the potent new BMW engine. Hine then made contact with Walter Frey's Chevron as it slowed with gearbox problems, damaging his own car quite badly. Hine was having probably his best season in racing, but the successes had been punctuated by accidents. After the Springbok Series he had gone on to the opening round of the new 3-litre World Championship for Makes at Buenos Aires, where he and José Juncadella had finished fifth overall and first 2-litre car in their Red Rose/Tergal B19. A week later he had won the inaugural race at Balcarce, the birthplace of Juan Manuel Fangio, 250 miles to the south of the Argentine capital. Fangio himself had graciously declined John Bridges' invitation to be photographed in the winning Chevron, but just meeting his childhood hero qualified the occasion as one of the highlights of his life as far as the Red Rose boss was concerned.

When the new B21s arrived, Hine had finished third in the opening round of the European 2-litre Series at Paul Ricard and looked certain to win the second round at Vallelunga when the first of his disasters struck. Having won the first heat, he was again holding off Toine Hezemans' Abarth in the second race when he came round a bend at 120 mph to find the burning wreckage of Jean-Louis Lafosse's Lola upside down in the middle of the track. A piece of debris broke a rear wheel as Hine's Chevron ran over it and Hezemans was handed the race. Hine continued to show his form with the World Championship class wins at Spa and the Nürburgring before another accident put him out of the Dijon 2-litre race.

Two weeks later the Cosworth Vega engine was back in a new chassis for the Martini International at Silverstone, but as Hine completed his first flying lap the nearside front tyre deflated as the Chevron came into Woodcote Corner — still without its chicane in those days — at 130 mph. 'I just turned the wheel and nothing happened,' Hine remembers. The B21 spun into the armco and exploded. Hine dragged himself out with his overalls on fire. 'I couldn't see anything because the visor had gone black. All I heard was a marshal say, "For Christ's sake, put him out". Then I felt a fire extinguisher being sprayed all over me and I thought "Sod this, I think I'll sit down" and I sat down in the middle of the road apparently.' Only at that point did he realise that he could not get up again. His burns were only minor, but he had broken his back and was immediately taken to Stoke Mandeville hospital. John was moved by the number of visits he received from his fellow drivers and their generosity in bringing him flowers and chocolates. Only later did he discover that they were all going back to John Bridges, shaking their heads and saying, 'Well, he'll never drive again'.

In fact, Hine raced again in October when he co-drove a Red Rose B21 to fourth position in the Paris 1,000km at Montlhéry with José Juncadella. But he did miss the rest of the 2-litre season and the Chevron effort suffered, with John Burton's win at Barcelona being the only real high spot. The Vega engine was salvaged from the wreckage of Hine's car and put into yet another new chassis, which went to Enna for Jody Scheckter to drive. He led the first heat until a pit stop to repair a jammed fuel metering unit, and then finished off a disappointing weekend by retiring from the second heat with a broken oil pump. In the same race, Dieter Quester destroyed his B21 in a high speed crash, which brought the development programme on the 2-litre BMW engine to an abrupt end. Howden Ganley took over the Vega-engined car for the Nürburgring 500km, but went out when the engine blew. Chevron went to the Springbok Series that winter without the Vega engine and Cosworth soon dropped the time-consuming project.

Chevron's presence in the Springbok Series was its strongest so far. Two works cars went out to run in Team Gunston colours, and Peter Hanson's B21 joined one of the Red Rose B21s in a two-car team in Lucky Strike colours. The B21 was an updated version of the B19, the internal dimensions of its monocoque altered slightly to take account of changes in the regulations. Derek Bennett was always extremely reluctant to produce a new car when he could modify one which already worked, so when the B21s started to lose their edge in the European series he had gone out to Enna to cast around for development ideas. The result was a revised front suspension which lowered the front of the car by four inches and allowed it to take full advantage of the latest low-profile Firestone slicks. The works Team Gunston cars appeared in South Africa with these modifications and were soon being referred to as B21/23s.

Jody Scheckter was not available to drive a Chevron in the Springbok Series for a second year as he had been signed up by March to give their much-publicised BMW-engined 2-litre sports car, the 73S, its debut at the Kyalami 9-Hours, partnered by Niki Lauda. Chevron retaliated with the potent partnership of Jochen Mass and Gerry Birrell in a B21 with Brian Hart's latest alloy block BDA engine. Hart's engine was being developed in close co-operation with Ford, whose name

THE FAIRY STORY CONTINUES

appeared, along with Hart's own, on the cover. Birrell was contracted to Ford and Hart had close links with Chevron, so the package came together naturally. Its success was immediate as Birrell and Mass finished second overall at Kyalami, beaten only by the 3-litre Ferrari 312P of Clay Regazzoni and Arturo Merzario. The Red Rose/Lucky Strike B21 of John Hine and Dave Charlton, now running with an Alan Smith 1.9-litre FVC, swapped the class lead with the Gunston car until two lengthy pit stops to solve problems with the clutch and the battery. But it still finished third overall, pushing the new March down to third place in the 2-litre class.

The Springbok Series continued for the 2-litre cars and Birrell won the next three races to tie up the championship with one round still to run. The works March provided some potentially strong competition, but Birrell and Mass rose to the challenge and the March only finished in the first three once after a string of problems. The Chevron too had to overcome its fair share of incidents. At the Cape 3-Hours Birrell and Scheckter were both penalised a minute for jumping the start and it took them until half distance to take the official lead off Dave Charlton in the Red Rose B21. But when the March lost time in the pits with a broken throttle cable, Birrell and Mass went on to win comfortably as Chevrons took the first four places.

Jochen Mass at Lourenco Marques in November 1972 at the wheel of the Team Gunston B21 which he and Gerry Birrell took to victory. Both drivers won four times in the Springbok Series, but Birrell just took the title. (*Photo Jeff Hutchinson.*)

Over the border in Mozambique for the Lourenço Marques 3-Hours the works Chevron had another one-lap penalty to overcome, imposed this time for having a push start when the engine refused to fire up after the refuelling stop. Birrell had built up a big enough lead before handing over to Mass for them to stay ahead despite the penalty, but when an errant saloon car sideswiped the Chevron, Mass found himself limping towards the finish at much reduced speed. With 25 minutes to go, Dave Charlton — now sharing Scheckter's March — took over the lead, only to hand the race back to Mass when he spun trying to get past a back marker.

Mass was not able to do the Welkom 3-Hours so Birrell's fourth win came in partnership with Peter Gethin, who solved the nagging mystery of why he could not keep up with Birrell in his regular car as soon as he got his first taste of Hart power. Birrell handed over to Gethin with a comfortable lead, but the car spent five minutes in the pits when it was discovered that the gearbox plug had pulled out, dumping all the oil. Now two laps behind Scheckter and Charlton in the March, Gethin seemed to have an impossible task, but he came through to win when the March developed an oil leak. Back in his usual car for the final round at Pietermaritzburg, Gethin had a 2-litre Smith BDA to give him a little more power, but it was the great equaliser of wet weather which helped him win his second consecutive race and complete Chevron's clean sweep.

In the opening laps Gethin ran ahead of Mass and Scheckter until Scheckter fought his way to the front with the March. But Gethin was soon back in the lead when Scheckter went off as his rear brakes failed. With the rain worsening Gethin handed over to Mass, who was taking a stint in both Team Gunston cars to try and equal Birrell's points score in the championship. Half-an-hour later, the torrential rain forced the race to be halted with the Gethin/Mass B21 four laps clear of the rest. A series of pit stops to change tyres dropped the Mass/Birrell car down to sixth place, but Chevron still took the first four positions as John Hine and Dave Charlton came in second, ahead of the B21s of Roger Heavens/Guy Tunmer and Brian Robinson, who added fourth place to the two second places he had already collected in a fine single-handed effort.

With barely a pause for Christmas week, Chevron were flung straight into the 1973 season. Team Gunston had taken delivery of three brand new B25 Formula 2 cars and Peter Gethin stayed on to drive one in the opening round of the South African Formula 1 series, accompanied by Paul Owens. The coming year would prove a watershed for Chevron with its fairy tale story reaching new heights — and harsh reality bringing it back down to earth.

CHAPTER 10

Squaring up to real life

AS Chevron moved into 1973, Formula 2 was still at the top of their agenda. Although they still wanted to compete in the formula because it was a showcase for the company — the highest level at which they could conceivably afford to race — the feeling was growing that it could also be a lucrative market. Selling three of the latest B25s to Team Gunston in South Africa before the year had even begun set them off on a good footing and a strengthened works effort for the European Championship was soon being planned.

Lack of finance and fully competitive engines had hampered Chevron's efforts with Peter Gethin's B20 the year before, but after the successful Springbok Series with the sports cars they were able to extend the link with Gerry Birrell and Brian Hart into Formula 2. Birrell came to the team with Hart engines, paid for by Ford and, with the continuing support of Castrol and Champion, Chevron decided they could run a second car for Gethin. They got more starting money for two cars and a new transporter that could carry both cars kept their overheads not much higher than they had been for just one.

The new set-up would enable them to take a much stronger crack at March, who had been stealing the limelight with their ambitious 'straight in at the top' approach. Jackie Stewart had given March their first Formula 1 win at the Brands Hatch Race of Champions early in 1970 little more than six months after Ronnie Peterson had first raced the prototype March Formula 3 car at Cadwell Park. During 1970 March had taken over from Brabham as the biggest supplier of Formula 2 cars, and in 1971 Peterson had won the European Formula 2 Championship for them. Derek Bennett's attitude to March was mixed. Such a strong competitor obviously posed a threat to his company and it was important to keep a careful eye on what they were up to. But at the same time he welcomed the challenge of pitting his wits against Robin Herd in the contest to design the best racing car.

Sometimes, though, the odds seemed dauntingly stacked in March's favour. Instilled with the northern ethic of 'knowing your place' and aware of his lack of formal qualifications,

Derek could feel intimidated if he let himself think too much about Herd's double-first from Oxford University. With his background Derek expected to be inferior to such people and he often surprised himself when his best proved more than a match for theirs. It was not that he did not believe in himself, he just thought they should be so much better. His sister June remembers how he often felt uncomfortable about people who were better educated than he was, or had far more money than he did, as many of his customers did. 'He had this thing of thinking they were better than he was,' she says. 'He didn't know how to talk to some of these people. I can remember having to drum into him that he was better than them all.'

With March conveniently close to London at their Bicester base, the 'North-South divide' was beginning to rear its head with customers becoming reluctant to travel to the distant north. This syndrome affected the media more than anybody and Derek would get extremely agitated when he opened his weekly *Motoring News* or *Autosport* to find it full of what March had done, were doing, and were about to do, while life in Bolton was overlooked. Derek Bennett was not about to change the habits of a lifetime and become a gregarious, publicity-seeking, company figurehead. So he agreed to get someone in who could play the rôle of Chevron's front man. Grahame White, who was working out his notice as General Manager of the British Automobile Racing Club, was available and willing and in February of 1973 he was appointed Chevron's Sales and Publicity Director.

Such an appointment had also been recommended in a report by a team of business consultants that Derek had been persuaded to have in to look at the company, and White was given a roving brief covering media publicity, customer relations and general promotion, which aimed to exploit his considerable contacts, built up over eight years organising race meetings for the BARC. A southerner, who had been commissioned in the Army before becoming involved in motor sport professionally, Grahame White was not an obvious 'Chevron person' and the workforce was once again suspicious. White had a smart office, a good car, wore a suit, and lived in the 'Big Smoke'. Many of those who built the cars did not see why they needed him to come up to Bolton a couple of days a week to help sell their cars. But Derek was quite happy with the arrangement because it got him off the hook. Now somebody else could talk to sponsors, customers, and the press while he got on with building racing cars.

Among the rest of the people at Bolton though, a feeling began to grow that things would never be quite the same, that the spirit of those early years of Chevron was beginning to slip away. A couple of months after Grahame White was appointed, Doug Linton left the company. As Chevron became a bigger organisation he felt less comfortable and more isolated from Derek, and his job became increasingly administrative. In the absence of anyone else to do it, he had taken over most of the financial transactions of Derek Bennett Engineering, and kept the books for the accountants. Juggling the company's debts to see it through the lean winter months was an increasingly difficult task which Doug did not relish. The more successful the company became the more its cash-flow problems grew as money had to be found to keep suppliers sweet until the new season's customers began paying for the completed cars. In December of 1972 he had had to go cap in hand to the bank manager to get the money to pay the staff over the Christmas holiday. The business consultants were in at the time and Doug got back from his meeting with the bank manager to be chastised for not telling them what he had been up to. It all added to his feeling that the time had come to move on.

Meanwhile work on the B25 Formula 2 cars was in full swing, with the two works cars to build as well as a customer car for Dave Morgan in time for the early start to the European Championship at Mallory Park on 11 March. Morgan had won the Premier Grovewood Award in 1972 on the strength of his showings in Ed Reeves' Formula 2 Brabhams, which included winning the Mallory Park race. At the end of the year he had taken the works Chevron out to Brazil for a series of races at Interlagos and surprised everyone by his speed. He had liked the car and so property developer Reeves had decided to run him in a new Chevron for the 1973 European season.

Derek stuck to his principle that the customer always came first and Morgan's was the only car that was ready in good time for Mallory Park. Gethin's car was completed in time for practice, but there were too many problems with it for Gethin to get in a decent time and it was decided not to start the race. Morgan struggled through the first heat with his engine cutting out intermittently, but finished a strong third in the second part to secure an encouraging fourth place on aggregate. Even more impressive was the performance of John Lepp, who finished fifth overall in his first Formula 2 race, driving the underpowered Formula Atlantic version of the B25 with a 1600cc BDA engine.

After competing successfully in sports cars for so long, Lepp had wanted to dispel some doubts about sports car drivers not being good enough to race single-seaters. So the previous year he had done a deal with the Manchester racing car dealer, Bob Howlings, to run a B20 in the *Yellow Pages* Formula Atlantic Championship. Lepp was soon on the pace and he broke the lap record at Brands Hatch in April as he chased

CHEVRON

A dream comes true as the winning B24 sets off on a lap of honour after winning the Race of Champions. As Peter Gethin waves to the crowd Paul Owens sits clutching the trophy in apparent disbelief. In front of Gethin, Grahame White marvels at how much easier his new job as Chevron's Sales and Publicity Director has just become. (*Photo LAT.*)

Vern Schuppan's March 722 on his way to second place. He finally beat Schuppan to take his first Atlantic race win at Croft in August, proving to himself that sports car drivers could win races in single-seaters. For 1973 Lepp was concentrating on the European 2-litre Sports Car series, driving a Red Rose B23, but Derek Buller-Sinfield had bought a B25 to give his driver, George Silverwood, a crack at Atlantic, and the car was offered to Lepp when his sports car races did not clash.

Fifth in a Formula 2 race did not seem such a bad start to Lepp's season. But for Chevron, that opening race was rather more ominous as the March 732 of Jean-Pierre Jarier won both parts. A week later, the slow start to Chevron's works Formula 2 effort was forgotten as Peter Gethin's Formula 5000 B24 won the Race of Champions at Brands Hatch. Everybody who worked for Chevron shared the elation that their car had beaten some of the world's best professional Formula 1 teams. Much of the fun and excitement of working for Chevron had been the David and Goliath nature of the company's success, and the thrill of getting the better of ever-bigger giants. John Lepp describes it as the story of the nut cracking the sledgehammer, and the fairy tale way in which Chevron had a habit of beating all the odds was often hard to believe, even for those involved. But this time Chevron's success was on the television and the front page of a national newspaper and everyone felt that Chevron had really arrived.

Of course, if you beat enough giants, you eventually become one yourself and if Chevron now had the credibility they had always wanted, they also had an awful lot to live up to. The two works Formula 2 cars made a hesitant showing at Hockenheim, but then the Easter Monday meeting at Thruxton gave both drivers the chance to show what the B25 was capable of. The race was run as two heats and a final and Gethin qualified well by finishing third in his heat. Birrell would have to fight through from a more lowly position after finishing 11th in the other heat following a pit stop to change a flat tyre.

A multiple pile-up on the startline put Jarier's works March out of the final almost before it had begun, but both Chevrons got safely through the chaos and were soon part of a tightly-knit bunch in pursuit of the leading March of Jacques Coulon. The race ended in disappointment for Gethin when his experimental Cosworth FVD engine exploded, but Birrell continued to work his way through to the head of the group. Just before half distance, Coulon dropped out and Birrell inherited the lead. For lap after lap he fought off a trio of the new Motul-Rondel cars, driven by Jody Scheckter, Henri Pescarolo and Bob Wollek, and looked all set to win. But Mike Beuttler caught the Motuls in his March, and picked them off to mount his own challenge on Birrell.

With a little over two laps to go the Chevron was still in front but Beuttler made a poorly-judged attempt to get alongside as they came into the chicane. His nearside front wheel hit Birrell's offside rear, flipping the Chevron up into the air. As the Chevron lurched back onto its wheels in front of the March both cars came to a halt and the surviving Motuls of Pescarolo and Wollek sped past before Beuttler and Birrell could get going again. Birrell was moved up to third place when the race stewards disqualified Beuttler for dangerous driving, but it was scant consolation for the frustration of losing a race which all agreed he should have won.

Gethin missed a round of the series racing Doug Shierson's B24 in America and Birrell missed one to drive a works Group 2 Capri at Le Mans, but both cars were out together again when the Formula 2 championship moved to the Rouen road circuit at the end of June. Hopes were high that Birrell would

Gerry Birrell was on course for victory at the Thruxton Formula 2 race on 23 April 1973 until Mike Beuttler's March collided with his works B25. Here he leads the Motul of Henri Pescarolo, which inherited victory. (*Photo LAT.*)

claim the win he had been deprived of at Thruxton, but tragedy struck in practice. As Gerry came through the fast downhill swerves after the pits, flat-out at 160 mph, a punctured front tyre began to deflate and he lost control just before the fifth-gear right-hander at Six Frères. The car went straight on, ploughing almost head-on into a protruding section of armco barrier around a new access road. The barrier had been inadequately secured and the two layers peeled apart, letting the front of the car force its way between them. This left the driver to take the full impact and the tremendous force killed poor Gerry instantly.

Paul Owens jumped on his monkey bike and rode round the back of the circuit to the scene of the crash. He arrived just in time to see them carrying Birrell's body into the ambulance. The shock was numbing and everyone there was distraught. Reading of Gerry's death in the papers back in Bolton the following morning, Chevron's employees were as sickened by the shock. He had been extremely popular and they all felt they had lost a good friend. But more than that, the tragedy had burst the Chevron bubble. Just three months after the fairy tale of winning the Race of Champions, real life had taken its revenge. In eight years Derek Bennett had built more than 250 Chevrons, but nobody had been killed in one before.

Derek's cars had earned a deserved reputation for being strong and safe and the accident reinforced his concern with safety. The car itself had stood up to the impact very well and the failure of the armco barrier was not something that could have been predicted. Nevertheless Derek immediately had forward-facing stays added to the roll bar to deflect a barrier over the driver if any such freak accident were to happen again — a safety feature which was incorporated into every single-seater Chevron made from that day.

For Peter Gethin, Gerry Birrell's crash was a chilling reminder of a near identical accident which had happened to him exactly a year earlier. Coming into the same, flat-out, downhill, right-hand bend Gethin had felt a wheel nut come loose and seen the nearside front wheel fly off his B20. As the car veered left, out of his control, he had time to think. 'I remember thinking — this is it, they won't find me for ages because I'll be so far in those trees,' he recalls. He hit the guard rail very hard, but the curve of the armco retained the car and it performed a wall-of-death act before coming to a halt. Peter got out having done no more than scrape some skin off a knuckle, but it was the first time an accident had ever affected him psychologically. That night he went into Paris with Mike Hailwood — 'we had a date with a couple of birds' — and Peter spent the whole evening being sick as the shock hit him.

SQUARING UP TO REAL LIFE

Twelve months later he was back at Rouen and he and Gerry were practising in separate sessions. By the end of his session they had worked out which compound of tyres was working best, and because there was not time to fit that same compound to Birrell's wheels before his session, they just fitted the wheels from Gethin's car. So it was one of Peter's tyres that failed, pitching Gerry into the armco barely five yards from the spot where he had hit it the year before. Only in the meantime, the gradual curve of the armco had been opened up to make room for an ambulance access road. There was now an overlapping break in the armco and Gerry's car hit the end of one section of it almost head on. The twists of fate occurred to Peter immediately and he did not have the slightest second thought about the team's immediate decision to withdraw from the race.

Once Chevron had begun to get over the personal loss of Gerry Birrell, they realised that they had also lost their Formula 2 team. Their Brian Hart engines and much of their commercial support was linked to Gerry, not to Chevron Cars, and so the works effort was virtually stopped in its tracks. Instead the emphasis switched more towards Formula 5000, which until then had been purely a customer-led enterprise, in the tradition of so many of Derek Bennett's projects. Gethin was contesting the L & M Series in America for Doug Shierson. But after its spectacular win in the Race of Champions, his B24 had failed to live up to expectations, and a close second place to Jody Scheckter's Trojan at Laguna Seca had been the most encouraging result. After that, the team seemed to be going backwards with the car, and its problems echoed those which Brian Redman had had with the prototype the year before.

The difficulties centred on differences in the prevailing tyre technology in Britain and America. In Britain, Chevrons ran on Firestone tyres and the suspension geometry of the B24 suited the tyres on which it was raced in its home country. Shierson, however, had a contract with Goodyear, whose Formula 5000 tyres had a much lower profile than the British Firestones on which the car had won at Brands Hatch. The apparent mismatch between the car and its tyres brought handling problems and suspension failures, reminiscent of those which Redman had suffered. In desperation, Shierson persuaded Goodyear to let him run British Firestones on the car for one race, at Watkins Glen the weekend before Rouen. Things looked promising when Gethin ran second in the final, holding off Brian Redman's Carl Haas Lola T330. But then a rear suspension upright broke and Gethin was out again. Shierson reckoned the Firestones were too sticky for the conditions and the way they set the car up, and the strain on the suspension had proved too much.

Derek Bennett agreed to redesign the rear suspension to suit the American Goodyear tyres, but although this brought an end to the suspension failures, Gethin was never really happy with the car's handling and the season continued to be a disappointment. The year at least looked like ending on a high note at Seattle in September when Gethin won his heat, but engine failure put him out of the final and he had to watch Brian Redman take his fifth win of the series in his Lola. The championship, though, went to Jody Scheckter in Sid Taylor's Trojan, who had taken advantage of Redman's absence from the first two rounds of the series to pile up a points advantage which he never lost. Despite being overshadowed by Redman and Scheckter, Gethin still finished fourth in the series. But there was no denying that he and Doug Shierson were bitterly disappointed. Shierson, now an Indianapolis-winning team manager, feels that Chevron never really understood the severity of the problems they were up against in the States, which was understandable given the tremendous success the B24 was having in Britain. Even so, looking back on that year, Shierson still cannot feel badly done by. 'I paid $8,500 for a complete car and spares,' he remembers. 'That doesn't pay our tyre bill for an Indy Car weekend now.'

In Britain, the B24 was generally a match for the Lola T330 and the Trojan T101 and Chevrons ended the year in the first three places in the Rothmans European Formula 5000 Championship. When he won the opening round on the day before the Race of Champions, Peter Gethin commented that the B24 suited Brands Hatch perfectly. Chevron's 'home' circuit, Oulton Park, is a similar track, undulating and with a demanding mixture of fast and slow corners, and where much of Chevron's testing and setting up was carried out. So it is interesting that five of the six races Chevrons won that year were at Brands Hatch or Oulton Park.

Once Gethin had left for the American series, the Chevron driver on form soon proved to be Steve Thompson, driving the prototype B24 which he had taken out to Australia and New Zealand for the Tasman Series over the winter. Thompson had taken an impressive start-to-finish win in torrential rain at Warwick Farm in round six of the Tasman Series, and when it rained at Brands Hatch in April he dominated the race in similar fashion to win his first European Championship round, and take the lead in the series. The next round, at Oulton Park on 13 May, saw the first of Chevron's two 1-2-3 victories, although Thompson finished on the tail end of the trio. The race was the first Formula 5000 win for Belgian Teddy Pilette in the VDS Chevron owned by Count Rudi van der Straten, the Belgian brewing magnate. The team had taken a while to get their car fully sorted, but everything came together at Oulton as Pilette scored a runaway win to become the sixth different winner in six rounds of the Championship. Peter Gethin made a surprise appearance at the wheel of Bob Brown's Anglo-American Racing B24 and finished second, struggling with handling problems as he fought off a determined challenge from Steve Thompson.

Thompson's third place kept him ahead in the championship, but disaster struck when he wrote the car off during a tyre testing session at Silverstone, hitting the Woodcote barriers at 140 mph after a punctured tyre came off the rim. He immediately ordered a new car, but it could not be built in time for the next race at Mallory Park, at which Keith Holland became winner number seven in his Trojan. Thompson's new B24 was ready for Mallory Park in July, but he only managed sixth place and lost his championship lead to Brett Lunger, whose victory in Sid Taylor's Trojan made him the first driver to win twice. The Chevron drivers failed to get back into the ascendancy until the series returned to Brands Hatch on August Bank Holiday Monday. In response to the problems Gethin was having with the B24 in America, Derek Bennett had built a works development chassis, and Gethin had managed to squeeze in a race at Mondello Park between his other commitments. After that, Derek had tested the car himself and Gethin put in on pole position for the Brands Hatch race. Everything went perfectly as Gethin led the race comfortably until eight laps from the end of the 65-lap race when the car's Morand Chevrolet engine blew up. But Pilette came through to win and took over the lead in the championship.

Gethin made up for his disappointment a fortnight later when he won the Oulton Park Gold Cup, the prestigious event now no longer a Formula 1 race but a Formula 5000 championship round. In one of the most exciting races of the year, Gethin had to fight through from third place after making a poor start from pole position. Pilette came in second after getting the best of a scrap with Tony Dean, whose B24 finished third to complete an emotional clean sweep for Chevron in the most important race at their home circuit. Having won the Race of Champions, Peter Gethin confirmed his hero status by putting his name on the Gold Cup under those of Stirling Moss, Jack Brabham, Jim Clark, John Surtees and Jackie Stewart.

The championship justified its European status with trips to Denmark and Holland next. At the Jyllandsring, Pilette won the second part of the two-part event, but Ian Ashley's Lola T330 had beaten him by a bigger margin in the first part and he had to settle for second place. At Zandvoort Tony Dean got his best result of the year when he finished second, only half a length behind Guy Edwards' Lola in a wet race which had seen first John Watson, in a Hexagon Trojan, and then Teddy Pilette, slide off while leading. Dean continued in good form when the series returned to Britain and led from pole position at Snetterton until a spin when his brakes started to fade dropped him back. Pilette took over the lead, but was eventually beaten narrowly by Bob Evans' Trojan.

Although Dean had not won a race, his consistent results meant that, with double points at stake in the final round at Brands Hatch in October, it was still possible for him to take the championship from Pilette. The Belgian made a bad start from pole position and eventually went out with a blown engine. If Dean could finish in the first three, he could win the title. In the end he could only manage fourth as Guy Edwards' Lola beat the Trojans of Keith Holland and John Watson to win. It was only the second time all year that a Chevron had failed to finish in the first three, but when the championship points were tallied up, Chevrons were first, second and third with Pilette the winner from Dean and Thompson.

Not wanting to lose their momentum in Formula 2 altogether, Chevron ran a single works car in a handful of races later in the season. Derek Bennett continued to develop the B25 and raised some eyebrows when he took it round Oulton Park in testing under the Formula 2 lap record that John Watson had set the previous September. With Gethin at Road America, Watson was invited to race the car at Mantorp Park at the end of July as the works team raced for the first time since Gerry Birrell's death. They had managed to hang on to a Hart engine and Watson started from the front row of the grid, alongside Jarier's March and Depailler's Elf. As Jarier won both heats to take first place on aggregate, Watson wound up an encouraging third overall.

Two weeks later, Gethin was back in the car at Karlskoga, where he produced another one of his sensational drives in what the press were happy to call the 'Formula 2 race of the

Teddy Pilette's VDS B24 won the 1973 European Formula 5000 Championship. The Belgian is pictured here at Brands Hatch in the final round on 21 October 1973. (*Photo LAT.*)

year'. After beating Mike Hailwood's Surtees to win his qualifying heat comfortably, Gethin took on the impressive Jarier in the final. Torsten Palm's Surtees split them for 31 of the 48 laps until he missed a gear, allowing Gethin to dive through into second place. For the rest of the race Gethin harried the March, his Hart-BDA losing out to Jarier's powerful BMW engine on the straights, but getting it all back on superior handling through the corners, Jarier became increasingly ragged as he fought to block Gethin, but although Gethin got the Chevron alongside the March on a number of occasions, Jarier hung on to win by half a length.

Spurred on by Gethin's performance, Chevron borrowed John Lepp's Formula Atlantic B25 from its new owner, Irishman Patsy McGarrity, and put a Hart-BDA in so Watson could drive alongside Gethin at Albi. But fuel leaks afflicted both cars. Gethin ran out of petrol in the closing stages and Watson finished tenth, having run with the leading group until making a pit stop to have a leak in his fuel pressure gauge sealed off. It was a disappointing end to the season, but Derek Bennett was happy that his car had shown itself to be competitive enough to drum up some custom for the 1974 version.

Throughout the company's history it was axiomatic that Chevron *was* Derek Bennett. This close identification between the designer and his cars was responsible for the tremendous loyalty felt to the marque by so many of its customers, but it could also have its drawbacks. Doug Shierson had come to believe during his Formula 5000 season in America that your success was directly related to the distance you were from Derek Bennett and, for much of 1973, Chevron's sports car drivers suffered from the same problem. The B19 had gone through another update to become the B23 for that season, and with plenty of orders for the car, Chevron did not feel any need to run a works team. But a large number of the B23s built went outside the high profile arena of the European 2-litre Series — a number went to Italy, via agent Eris Tondelli, where they were popular in a national series, and others went to Japan and even Venezuela. Meanwhile, John Bridges' Red Rose team drew in its horns, daunted by the cost of running its four-car team the previous year. The sponsorship deal with Tergal came to an end and the team reverted to two cars, back in the traditional Red Rose dark blue.

John Lepp and John Burton were signed to drive and they started the season in fine style with a 1-2 victory in the opening round at Paul Ricard. It was Lepp's first international victory and a fine performance from the Chevron stalwart who still ran his jewellers shops during the week and took on the professional racing drivers at weekends. He had been fourth in the first heat, despite a pit stop to have a loose plug lead

CHEVRON

John Lepp's Red Rose B23 leads Chris Craft's Lola T292 on its way to victory in the opening round of the 1973 European 2-litre Sports Car Championship at Paul Ricard. (*Photo Jeff Hutchinson.*)

replaced. Then he had won the second heat, climbing back into the lead after dropping to fourth place with a stop to change tyres. But with wet weather and many new cars not fully sorted, it was a race of attrition and only five cars were classified in the aggregate results. The Chevron was still basically a three-year-old car racing against up-to-date machinery from Lola, Osella, March and GRD, and Ricard was its first and last championship race win of the year.

The main opposition for the Chevrons were two of Lola's latest T292s, driven by Guy Edwards and Chris Craft, who won two rounds each. Gerard Larrousse gave Lola the win that secured them the championship title in the final round at Montjuich Park, and Vittorio Brambilla and Arturo Merzario each won a race for Osella-Abarth. Aerodynamic developments, coupled with suspension changes to make the most of the rapidly developing slick-tyre technology, had given the other manufacturers an edge, and Lepp and Burton would generally qualify well down the grid. It was only the tenacity of their driving and the high standard of the team's preparation that enabled them to get to the finish in more flattering positions. Indeed Chevron led the series with two rounds to go and Burton only lost the drivers' championship to Chris Craft at the last race. Privateer Martin Raymond proved a revelation in his updated B21 and helped Chevron's points tally by taking second place twice, at the Nürburgring and the Osterreichring, and coming third at Barcelona, He was rewarded with fourth place in the drivers' championship. Tim Schenken even made a contribution as he finished third in the Nürburgring 500km in a one-off outing in one of Roger Hire's cars.

With neither Derek Bennett nor Paul Owens directly involved with the sports car series in any way it proved extremely difficult to get a response to the SOS messages which were constantly heading back to Bolton. 'At the end, the B23 was an absolute lemon,' recalls John Lepp. 'To keep up with *anything* you had to drive it semi-suicidal.' Over the years, Lepp had become used to the problems involved in getting Derek's attention. The first step was generally to walk into the factory, scour the shop floor for Derek, and then walk up to him and switch his gas off — that way at least you were not drowned out by his welding torch as you tried to make your point. John did his fair share of switching off the gas that year, but with Derek's mind on the Formula 2 and Formula 5000 cars, getting him to turn his attention to the sports car was all but impossible. 'If you could get Derek's attention onto whatever it was you wanted, it was sorted out in a matter of minutes,' says Lepp. 'But until you got to the stage where somebody was hitting his product with a hammer and making it look like a load of junk, he wouldn't actually do anything about it.'

The first sign of progress came at the beginning of July. Lepp was not going to be available for the non-championship 2-litre race at Vila Real so John Bridges had got Gerry Birrell to agree to drive his B23, hoping that the input of his own works driver might encourage Derek to take an interest in the sports car. But Birrell was killed a week before the race and Derek suggested that John call up Peter Gethin to race the car. Although all the other cars were now running with a full-width rear wing, Derek had long been adamant that the car's bodywork should create better airflow and downforce by itself and he was reluctant to consider following the trend. But he finally succumbed in time for the Vila Real race and Red Rose mechanic Tony Galland flew out to Portugal clutching the first Chevron rear wing.

Although Gethin qualified on the front row, he was a little shocked to find himself more than four seconds a lap slower than Dave Walker's GRD. Although the wing made the car more stable, Gethin was still unable to get anywhere near Walker in the race. When the GRD began to slow, local ace Carlos Gaspar started to challenge Gethin in his Lola T292. Gethin was also struggling with tyre problems and Gaspar got past him, going on to pass the ailing GRD and win the race as Gethin followed him through into second place.

Lepp tried the car himself the following weekend at a second Portuguese non-championship race, at Estoril. The car's handling had settled down noticeably in the corners, but the wing was reducing the car's straight-line speed. Again Walker set the pace, but the GRD crashed while leading and Lepp went on to win the race. With Peter Gethin's none too complimentary verdict on the car to work from, Derek Bennett began to show an interest in improving the B23. Lepp was pushing for a new car and wanted Derek to build a full monocoque like the Lola and graft the rear end of the successful B25 Formula 2 car onto the back of it. But Derek never liked to start on a prototype until he was convinced that no more development work could be done on an existing model, and so he took a B23 out a few times himself to try and restore its competitiveness. The result was revisions to the front and rear suspension geometry to enable the car to run lower profile tyres. Mechanical and engine failures on the Red Rose cars at the next couple of races made the outcome of the modifications inconclusive, but the drivers still felt the car had a long way to go.

Back at the factory Derek's workforce also wanted to know what he was going to do with the B23. If there was going to be a new car for 1974 they knew he would have to get working on it pretty quickly. The staff did not like to see the cars they built being rubbished by drivers and in the press, and the idea of a new monocoque sports car was being widely canvassed. But with the modifications to the B23 complete, Derek seemed to favour leaving things as they were, especially as the new bodywork he had designed for the car, featuring an integral rear wing, had brought its times down considerably in testing. Then one morning he walked in and announced, 'I've been thinking. We'll go to a monocoque on the B23.'

By the first week in October Derek was out testing the prototype B26 at Oulton Park and Croft. It featured a full monocoque mated to the rear suspension of the B25, and had an integral full-width wing on the rear bodywork. In back-to-back tests with one of the Red Rose B23s, Derek was more than three seconds a lap quicker round Croft in the new car. With the Springbok Series coming round again, Chevron seemed once again to have a car that would win races.

Motor racing usually manages to exist in a cosy vacuum, able to carry on unaffected by political and economic upheaval in the world around it. But as Derek Bennett was driving his new Chevron round Croft, the Middle East had been thrown into a turmoil which would have far reaching consequences even in the world of motor sport. The Egyptian invasion of Israel at Yom Kippur had started the Arab-Israeli War and although the conflict was soon over, the Arab world was quick to extract retribution from the West for its supposed support of Israel. At first this meant the virtual cutting off of oil supplies from the Middle East. Then came a rapid increase in prices as the Organisation of Petroleum Exporting Countries turned the taps back on slowly enough to keep demand way ahead of supply. Before the end of the year oil quadrupled in price. The West was forced to cut back its consumption and in Britain petrol rationing seemed imminent as the Government printed ration books. Against this background, such a conspicuously wasteful occupation as motor racing was not going to meet with much approval.

As this situation was unfolding, a new works B26 was loaded up to be flown to Kyalami where John Watson and Ian Scheckter were to drive it in Team Gunston colours in the 9-Hours on 3 November. With the Middle East still at war, the plane had to fly a diverted route to South Africa round the bulge of Africa and some cars had to be left behind to make way for the extra fuel that was needed for the longer flight. Running with a 2-litre Hart-BDA, the new car did everything that was wished of it. After qualifying on the second row, it was leading the race when Scheckter ran out of fuel. He dashed to meet his pit crew, who were already sprinting out to the car with a can of petrol, and the car was soon on its way again, now second to the 3-litre Porsche 908/3 or Reinhold Joest and Herbert Mueller. When the Porsche came into the pits to have a misfire cured, Watson took the Chevron through into the lead and when the Joest Porsche came out again it was right on his tail, albeit two laps down. The battle that ensued between the two cars was the highlight of the race as the Porsche powered past on the straight only to be eaten

The B26 was Derek Bennett's first monocoque construction sports car and transformed Chevron's fortunes in the category. (*Photo Arthur Taylor.*)

up through the corners every time by the nimble Chevron. Watson still remembers the race as one of his most enjoyable. Unfortunately, the B26 eventually succumbed to overheating problems, and the Porsche went on to win. The 2-litre category still went to Chevron, though, as 21-year-old Ian Grob partnered John Hine to an impressive third overall in the KVG B23. The B26 was classified fifth, although it was not running at the end.

Shortly after Kyalami, South Africa banned motor racing as the oil embargo began to bite. The Government gave a special dispensation for the first of the 2-litre races to go ahead, at Cape Town's Killarney circuit, but the remainder of the Springbok Series was cancelled. In Watson's words: 'Killarney makes Phoenix Park seem quite safe,' and during testing he discovered it had something even the Dublin circuit did not have, namely sand dunes. Coming out of a corner the B26 snapped into sudden oversteer and spun across the dune. 'It literally skipped across the sand dunes like a stone over water,' says Watson. 'The car got filled with sand and that prevented us from qualifying. To this day I still don't know what happened. I was absolutely sure that something had broken on the car, but there didn't appear to be anything.'

After missing official practice while the sand was removed from the car, Watson had to start the three-hour race from the back. In just three laps he had made it through to fifth place and, despite losing time with a brief spin, he was comfortably in the lead when he handed the Chevron over to Ian Scheckter just after half distance. Scheckter hung on to beat the Lola T292 of Eddie Keizan and John Nicholson by three laps. Watson was delighted to have scored his first international victory and Derek Bennett had again shown how quickly he could produce a race-winning new car when he turned his mind to it.

With the rest of the series cancelled, everyone flew back to Britain where the oil crisis was being compounded by a coal miners' strike. Oil was now far too expensive to be used to make up the shortfall of coal at the power stations and shortly before Christmas the Prime Minister, Edward Heath, put industry onto a three-day week to conserve coal supplies. A State of Emergency was declared and the television stations were ordered to do their bit for energy conservation by closing down at 10.30 each night. Rallying had already been banned and a question mark hung over the prospects for the new racing season. It was not a good time to be trying to make a living building racing cars.

CHAPTER 11

Surviving the oil crisis

AS Britain struggled through to a General Election in February 1974 Derek Bennett was faced with the unpleasant prospect of having to lay off staff at Bolton. Orders for cars had all but evaporated and there was not enough work to keep everybody employed. One of those to go was Paul Rice, who had spent seven years working a lathe in the machine shop. He had been an apprentice in Derek Hughes' machine shop behind the mill when Chevron bought the business out in 1967. Motor racing was completely new to him, but he had soon settled into the family atmosphere and enjoyed working for Derek Bennett. He remembers the tremendous pride in the finished product, the care you gave to your work when you knew someone's life could depend on it, and the enthusiasm that kept him working there until the early hours of the morning, riding home on his pedal bike afterwards. He still says they were the best people he ever worked for.

With its usual winter cashflow problem exacerbated in this way, Chevron's survival could have been seriously threatened if it had not been for two of its staunchest supporters, Fred Opert and Count van der Straten. Chevron had fallen out with Opert the previous year and he had not sold any cars for them in 1973. As well as importing Chevrons, Opert was also an agent for Brabham and a feeling had grown up that he could not be doing a 100 per cent job for Chevron if he was also selling cars built by one of their competitors. Brian Redman suggested to Derek that Geoff Freeman, who he had met in Ohio while racing the prototype Formula 5000 car in the States during 1972, would be able to do a good job for them. So it was decided to shake Opert up and give Freeman the agency. Opert had always got on well with Dave Wilson, but with Wilson then working for GRD he had lost his main ally in Bolton.

Ironically, Opert knew that Brabham — which Bernie Ecclestone had recently bought from Ron Tauranac — was planning to stop building customer cars the following year, so he had planned to put all his efforts into the Chevron side of his operation during 1973 as these would be the only cars he could sell in 1974. He also had plans to run Swedish driver Bertil Roos in some Formula 2 races in Europe. Roos had taken over as the instructor at Opert's Bridgehampton Racing School, replacing Bert Hawthorne when he was killed at Hockenheim. With no Chevrons available Roos stayed in Formula Super Vee, winning the championship for Opert in a Tui. Through Dave Wilson Roos made his Formula 2 début in a GRD 273 at Mantorp Park in July, but as John Watson's B25 sat on the front row of the grid for the race, Opert could not help wishing he had a Chevron for his man.

Dave Wilson went back to his old job at Chevron at the end of that season and he was quick to point out that he thought they had made a mistake in dropping Opert. Freeman had only sold a handful of cars for them and Wilson was convinced that Opert would do a better job, especially now he was no longer selling Brabhams. They came up with a deal, which would let Opert and Freeman sell Chevrons in different parts of the States. Freeman put in an order for one B27 chassis for 1974 — and Opert promptly ordered six, convinced that the oil crisis was not going to hit motor racing in America the way it had done in the rest of the world.

The other vital order which got Chevron through the early months of 1974 was from Count van der Straten, who had decided to run a team of two B28s in Formula 5000 for Teddy Pilette and Peter Gethin. Van der Straten had taken a liking to Derek, with his straightforward, no-nonsense ways, and he became something of a patron of Chevron. Everyone at the factory was in awe of the Count and when word got round that he was coming for a visit there would be 'a right clean-up' to make the place presentable for him. But for all his tendency to feel awkward with people who were rich, successful, or both, Derek got on very well with the Count. He liked his lack of pretension and van der Straten liked Derek's honesty. So they would go up the road to 'the caff' together and discuss racing over egg on toast, which Derek would dissect the way he always did, clinically removing the egg white, which he never ate, and somehow always managing to have enough yolk left for the final piece of toast.

Aware of Chevron's cashflow problems, van der Straten used to pay for his cars in advance and keep his account with Chevron topped up by paying his prize money straight to them. So payment up front for two Formula 5000 cars was a lifesaver. When Derek once asked him why he paid his prize money into their account, the Count replied that it was because they needed it more than he did. Derek did not argue with that and would not have felt that his pride had been wounded in any way. Derek had always operated on the same principles himself, always happy to help out someone whose need was greater than his, so he accepted van der Straten's help in the spirit it was given.

Before the new season started in Europe, VDS took their two B24s out to Australia and New Zealand for the strenuous Tasman Series — eight races in as many weekends. Gethin led the championship after winning the second round at Pukekohe, but by the time they reached Australia at the beginning of February the Lola drivers seemed to have the edge and Paul Owens was sent out with the latest modifications to convert the cars to the new B28 specification. New rear suspension uprights, a longer wheelbase, and a wider track seemed to overcome the handling problems and Pilette and Gethin bounced back to take first and second places at Surfers Paradise. A week later, Gethin won at Sandown Park, Melbourne, to put himself firmly at the head of the points table as they went into the last race at Adelaide. Max Stewart had to win the race with Gethin unplaced to snatch the title, but Stewart's Lola blew its gearbox while leading, and Gethin cruised round to win the championship by finishing second to Warwick Brown's Lola T332.

He was the first Englishman to win the Tasman Series and he still remembers it as a high point in his career. All of his heroes had won the Tasman in its days as a Formula 1 series and it meant a lot to him to add his own name to a list that included Jim Clark, Jackie Stewart, Chris Amon — and Bruce McLaren, who had died testing one of his own cars four years earlier and whom Derek Bennett reminded him of in so many ways. 'Bruce and Derek Bennett were the same,' says Peter. 'Both could drive things, both could design, both could build things. And they were able to get people to do things. You felt that they wouldn't ask you to do something that they wouldn't — or couldn't — do themselves.'

Peter Gethin leads the Lola T332s of Brian Redman and Guy Edwards round Druids Bend at Brands Hatch on his way to a début win for the B28 on 16 March 1974. (*Photo Tim Tyler.*)

Back in Britain the Rothmans Formula 5000 series was more closely contested than ever and the pressure was on the works-supported VDS B28s. In keeping with tradition, the new cars were finished at two o'clock on the morning of practice for the opening round at Brands Hatch. Gethin then followed the traditional plot by winning the race, beating Mike Wilds' March 74A and Brian Redman in Sid Taylor's Lola T332.

Gethin looked on course to win his third Formula 5000 championship as he won again at Zolder, Zandvoort and Monza. But when the series returned to the UK in the summer, Bob Evans put together three wins in a row in his Lola T332 and Gethin's championship lead suddenly vanished. Over the season Lola had refined the latest development of their successful T330 into a good all-round car that was a match for the Chevron on the twisty circuits as well as the fast ones, and Gethin began to be unhappy with his B28's handling as he struggled to stay with Evans's Lola.

Derek Bennett responded in the same way he always responded when a driver was critical of one of his cars — he jumped in and tried it himself. After trying a few alterations to the suspension, Derek became the first person, albeit unofficially, to lap Croft in under a minute as he took Gethin's car round in 59.7 seconds — $1\frac{1}{2}$ seconds inside the outright circuit record held by Tony Dean's B24. Derek was happy that the car was OK, but Gethin's faltering enthusiasm was not helped by three non-finishes, two of them in chaotic wet races, and one when vibrations from an experimental Morand engine caused his gearbox to seize.

By the time the double-points final at Brands Hatch came round, Gethin needed to win the race with Evans finishing lower than fifth if he was to take the title. Gethin was right behind Evans in third place when the Lola's engine failed. Boxed in behind the slowing car, Gethin lost a couple of places, but with Evans out a win would give him the championship. Gethin had taken a gamble with his tyres, fitting some hand-grooved slicks on the rear in the belief that they would warm up quicker in the cool October weather and give him an advantage. Unfortunately, they warmed up too well, slowing him down again as they overheated. Gethin eventually finished a distant third, with one of his rear tyres flat and pouring smoke. Ironically, it was a VDS Chevron that won the race as Vern Schuppan scored his first Formula 5000 victory having a one-off drive in an updated B24.

That race at Brands Hatch also saw Alan Jones make his Formula 5000 début in a Chevron. Jones had been going extremely well in Formula Atlantic driving a March 74B for Harry Stiller, and Stiller entered him at Brands in John MacDonald's B24. The Australian made a promising start and

SURVIVING THE OIL CRISIS

Alan Jones made his Formula 5000 début in a B24 at Brands Hatch on 20 October 1974. (*Photo LAT.*)

was running fifth until an electrical fault caused his engine to cut out.

If Gethin's season had been a disappointment, Pilette's had been a disaster as the reigning champion failed to win a single race in 1974. He actually led every one of the first eight races, only to fall back or retire with a succession of mechanical failures or punctures. At Thruxton he even lost the lead on the last lap when he ran out of petrol. Practice crashes prevented him even starting two of the later races and two second places — to Gethin at Monza and to Ian Ashley's Lola at Oulton Park — were his best results. There was one more Chevron win as Tony Dean mastered the rain at Brands Hatch in a race that had to be stopped and restarted because of the British summer weather.

In Britain Lolas had far outnumbered Chevrons in 1974 and in America Chevron had not been represented at all. In the tight economic conditions that still prevailed after the oil crisis, Derek Bennett decided that the market for Formula 5000 cars was not big enough to justify the expense of developing a new car, and at the end of the year Chevron announced that they would be dropping out of Formula 5000 to concentrate on Formula 2 and Atlantic with the new B29.

Sales of Formula Atlantic cars to America were a major contribution to Chevron's survival through a difficult year. As

British industry got back to full-time working and the world began to adjust to permanently higher oil prices, the racing car industry could breathe again. But during that year only 24 cars left the factory at Bolton — well under half the previous year's production and the smallest number of cars to be built since 1967.

Obviously there had been no question of continuing with a full works Formula 2 team, but Fred Opert kept up the Chevron presence in the opening rounds of the European Championship as Bertil Roos put in a couple of encouraging performances before he and his B27 returned to the States to contest the North American Formula Atlantic series. Derek Bennett meanwhile had kept up a full testing programme with the B27 to make sure that the car was fully competitive when Chris Marshall's Team Baty eventually pulled together its ambitious plans to run a works-supported Chevron for James Hunt.

Team Baty were not ready to race until Salzburgring on 2 June and shortly before the race it was announced that Japan's Hiroshi Kazato would be joining Hunt in a second B27. But within days of the announcement Kazato was one of two drivers killed in a pile-up, driving his B23 in a sports car race at Mount Fuji. A dispute over starting money also kept Hunt out of the race, and so Tom Pryce was brought in to drive the car. Pryce had won the top Grovewood Award in 1973 after several early season wins with a Royale in Formula Atlantic, and some promising showings in Formula 2 later in the year with a Motul. The week before Salzburgring Pryce had won the Monaco Formula 3 race in a March 743, and he was already being tipped to take over Brian Redman's drive in the Shadow Formula 1 team. His appearance in Formula 2 provided a welcome relief from the March domination as he put the Schnitzer BMW-engined B27 on pole position. Overnight Chevron emerged as a serious threat to March as Pryce was backed up by two more new B27s, driven by David Purley and Dieter Quester. Hong Kong businessman Bob Harper had been running a pair of March 742s but, unhappy with the apparent superiority of the works Marches over the customer cars, he had taken his BMW engines to Bolton and asked Derek Bennett to put them into a couple of Chevrons.

For three laps Pryce led the race, but problems with the fuel pump slowed him down, and finally brought him into the pits. Jacques Laffite went on to win the race in his BP March 742, but Purley came through from well down the grid to take a fighting second place for Chevron. Purley took a couple more second places in the car, but Quester never seemed to get to grips with his Chevron. Having pronounced the car undriveable after Karlskoga, he handed it over to Tom Pryce for Enna a fortnight later — and Pryce promptly qualified it on the

SURVIVING THE OIL CRISIS

Tom Pryce caused a sensation at Salzburgring on 2 June 1974 when he put the Team Baty B27 on pole position for its first Formula 2 race. Pryce led until fuel pump problems sent him into the pits. (*Photo LAT.*)

second row. Unfortunately, he went out of the race in a spectacular accident, which sent the car rolling end over end high over the armco barrier before it came to rest in the reeds at the edge of Enna's notorious lake. The monocoque was ruptured but Pryce escaped unhurt.

Baty finally got Hunt into their Chevron for a non-championship race at Rouen at the end of June. He qualified seventh fastest, despite his practice being curtailed when the car's Schnitzer-BMW engine dropped a valve. But the race brought chaos as a sudden downpour on the opening lap caught the field on the wrong tyres. Hunt joined a gaggle of cars heading into the pits for a tyre change, but he pulled up behind race control, jumped out of the car and attempted to get the race stopped because the conditions were too dangerous. The officials were not prepared to have their authority challenged and Hunt's team eventually persuaded him to go back into the race on wet tyres. A lap later he was black flagged and reprimanded by the organisers. Hunt apologised politely and took his ball home. Not all future World Champions had auspicious races in Chevrons!

Pryce took third place in the car at Mugello, but the team had to withdraw him at Karlskoga because of a clash of tyre contracts. With his new status as a Shadow Grand Prix driver he was contracted to Goodyear, but the team was contracted to Firestone and the car had been designed to run on Firestone's 23-inch rear tyres, which were two inches smaller than the Goodyears. With the team in disarray, the car was rented to Austrian journalist and racing driver, Harald Ertl, who then bought it.

In Britain, Formula Atlantic continued to grow in popularity, and Dave Morgan and Jim Crawford won half-a-dozen races between them to establish Chevron as a force in the formula.

Morgan put a 1600cc BDA into the B25 he had raced in Formula 2 the previous season, and showed well in the second half of the year, winning championship rounds at Thruxton, Mallory Park, and Dublin's Phoenix Park. Crawford, meanwhile, had been writing himself into the thick of the Chevron fairy tale, launching the kind of career that could only have been scripted in Bolton.

Since he moved to America, making a name for himself in Can-Am racing, and then by leading the Indianapolis 500, Crawford has been known as a Scotsman. Admittedly, he was born in Dunfermline and has a name that conjures up images of shortbread biscuits in tartan-clad boxes, but when he opens his mouth he is as Lancashire as they come, having lived most of his life in Bolton. There was only one thing that Chevron's staff could think of that would top their dreams of a Formula 1 car from Bolton winning the World Championship — and that was having a driver from Bolton in it when it won. Crawford became part of the dream and looked forward to the day when they would all be invited to tea with the Mayor of Bolton.

Crawford was introduced to Derek Bennett by his friend, Neil Edwards, who had been working for Chevron since 1970. Until then Jim's racing career had been confined to a handful of races in cars owned by another friend, Stephen Choularton. Choularton had bought a March 73B Formula Atlantic car for 1973 and Jim helped him out with the preparation. He was rewarded with a drive in the car at a *Libre* race at Croft in June and caused a sensation by not only winning the race but also breaking the outright circuit record and winning the Man of the Meeting award. Three weeks later the Atlantic championship contenders raced at Croft and Choularton shocked the regulars by winning. David Purley sat fastest time in another March, but failed to beat Crawford's lap time.

Neil Edwards decided that now might be a good time to mention his friend to Derek Bennett, and soon after they ambushed him in the Blundell Arms, a pub a couple of miles up Chorley Old Road from the Chevron factory, where he knew Derek used to call on a Friday night. Derek had heard of Crawford and as no slouch round Croft himself, he was impressed by his times in the Atlantic car. Before he dashed off he said he would be testing at Aintree the following week, and why didn't Jim come and take a look. As Jim downed a pint in the Aintree Clubhouse after the session, Derek asked him could he do the rest of the Atlantic series if he had a car. Jim said 'no problem', and Derek told him to be at the factory the next morning as he dashed off at his usual high speed.

As Crawford stood in the middle of the factory the next

SURVIVING THE OIL CRISIS

day watching Derek Bennett bustle past him three or four times, apparently oblivious to him, he began to feel he might have got it wrong. But then Derek stopped, asked him who he was and, his memory jogged, bounded off up the wooden stairs that led from the machine shop into the stores. After making a rapid mental note of what he had got in there, he came back, threw Jim a part and said 'Make yourself a car'. Over the next few weeks Neil Edwards built up a B25, using a spare Formula 2 chassis and the rear suspension and a lot of the bits off Gerry Birrell's car. They found some works body panels, but Jim was not allowed to keep the broad yellow 'works' stripe down the middle, so they painted over it in red. Jim's helmet was painted black with a red stripe to match, and has stayed that way ever since. Jim had got to know Race Engine Services very well from picking up Choularton's engines from them. They too had been impressed by his showing at Croft, so they agreed to lend him their works engine. After a shakedown win in a *Libre* race at Aintree, the car was ready for Jim to make his Formula Atlantic début at Oulton Park on 7 October.

In practice he was under the lap record and qualified on the middle of the front row. As the flag fell he shot off into the lead, to the general astonishment of the main championship contenders, David Purley, John Nicholson and Colin Vandervell, who found themselves scrapping over second place. As the lap record tumbled, Crawford held off his pursuers for 11 of the 15 laps, but his lack of experience finally told and Nicholson slipped by in the Lyncar to win the race. Nevertheless, Crawford shared the new lap record with Nicholson and successfully fought off the March of championship leader Purley to finish an impressive second.

Jim Crawford came close to winning at Oulton Park on his Formula Atlantic début. Here his B25 leads the Lyncar of John Nicholson through Old Hall Corner. (*Photo Frank Hall.*)

Setting the car up for unfamiliar circuits proved more difficult, but Jim still came fifth at Brands Hatch a week later, and started from the front row at Snetterton before going out of the race with a gearbox failure. He had certainly done enough to prove himself a serious championship contender for the following year. Bolton's own son had also demonstrated the capabilities of Chevron's Atlantic chassis, so it came as something of a surprise when he and his mentor, Steve Choularton, appeared at the start of 1974 with a pair of March 73Bs. Not having served the many years' apprenticeship it took to get to know Derek Bennett, Jim had made the mistake of expecting some sort of reaction when he returned the car, triumphantly, to the factory, polished and gleaming. Instead someone just said 'Thanks', with all the praise that would be heaped on someone successfully returning a library book on time. He thought they must have been disappointed with the results, and sloped off to build a second March out of Choularton's spares.

It was only well into the next season, when he was winning races in the March and leading the John Player Championship, that he felt confident enough to ask Derek, when they were both at the same test session, why had he not offered him a car? 'Why didn't you ask for one?' came the reply, and he had gone again before Jim could think of anything to say. He began to realise that Derek was not as cold as he appeared and that if he ignored you it was nothing personal and should not be taken as a snub. Realising that he had not fallen out with Chevron after all, Jim became a regular visitor to the Chevron factory again. Meanwhile Crawford's reputation had spread as far as Team Lotus and Peter Warr offered him a 12-month testing contract with the Formula 1 team, barely a year after he had won that *Libre* race at Croft.

He also did some testing for Team Harper when they were running one of their Formula 2 B27-BMWs at Silverstone at the same time as Jim was testing his Atlantic March. Pleased with the results they offered him a drive, and Crawford made his Formula 2 début in Dieter Quester's car at a non-championship race at Nogaro in September. He qualified on the fourth row, alongside David Purley in the team's other car, and went on to finish fifth despite tyre problems and having to drive most of the race with a shattered visor. Purley crashed out of the race, which was won by Patrick Tambay's Elf. Also making his Formula 2 début that day, in an Elf, was Frenchman René Arnoux, who had been given an identical contract with Lotus. There was a general feeling that the two drivers were being played off against each other for the chance of greater things and it niggled Crawford when Arnoux beat him by one place at Nogaro.

SURVIVING THE OIL CRISIS

Crawford went to the final round of the John Player Atlantic Championship at Oulton Park in October, one point ahead of John Nicholson and favourite to take the title exactly 12 months after his Atlantic début. As Alan Jones stormed away to win the race in his March 74B, Nicholson and Crawford tangled. Crawford's March was unable to continue, but Nicholson's Lyncar struggled on to finish fifth and win the championship.

Crawford's disappointment was palpable, but he was still well placed in the less important Southern Organs Championship, which had a few rounds left to run, and saw a chance to salvage something. Steve Choularton had overspent to get Jim through the John Player series, largely without sponsorship, and he could not offer a car any more. So Jim called up Fred Opert and asked if he could borrow the B27 which he had sitting at the back of the factory in Bolton. The car had been bought for young Mexican driver, Hector Rebaque, who had done a few British Atlantic races in it earlier in the year. Having met him around the factory on many occasions, Opert counted Crawford as 'a mate', so he said that as long as he replaced anything he broke on it, he could borrow the car. By the time the deal was done Jim had missed two races, but there were still two more to go, at Snetterton and Brands Hatch. The fairy tale writers seemed to be back on the job as Crawford snatched last lap victories from Alan Jones' March in both races and won the championship by two points. Shortly after winning at Brands, Crawford was made the BP Superman of the Year and given a special commendation in the Grovewood Awards.

In sports car racing, the B26 proved to be a tremendous car, but John Lepp's efforts in Roger Hire's works-supported car were overwhelmed by the appearance in the European 2-litre series of the works Alpine Renaults. John Bridges' Red Rose team had reluctantly pulled out of the championship because of the escalating cost, and the appearance of the no-expense-spared, three-car works Renault team proved a fatal turn of the screw for the series. As Renault took a clean sweep of all seven championship rounds, the highlight of Lepp's season came at Hockenheim in August when he finished second on aggregate, only 0.8 seconds behind Alain Serpaggi's Alpine-Renault.

On that occasion, Lepp was at the wheel of a full works B26 which had made a sensational début in May, using an all-new Brian Hart engine. Hart's strongest connection with Chevron had always been through Fred Opert. Ever since Opert first put Hart twin-cam engines into his Formula B cars in 1969, every Chevron he had sold had come as a package, complete with Brian Hart engine. That continuity maintained the link with Chevron even after Gerry Birrell's death and when Hart finished building his first completely original engine he asked Derek Bennett if he would like to try it out in a sports car. After the success of his own alloy block with the Cosworth BDA, Hart realised there was a growing market for a 2-litre alloy racing engine. Cosworth themselves had now developed the cast iron 'Kent' block of the BDA up to 1975cc for Formula 2, as the BDG. That engine was Hart's performance target and his own four-cylinder alloy block, 16-valve head, belt-driven, engine was 30 lbs lighter than the BDG, with an immediate 15 bhp advantage. Not being a production engine, the new 420 would be ineligible for Formula 2 until the rules changed in a couple of seasons, but it was an obvious choice for 2-litre sports car drivers.

Chevron put the engine into a brand new B26, which was just ready in time for Peter Gethin to drive at an Interserie race at Silverstone in May. The engine had never been run in a car before, but Hart was quietly confident about its performance. Nevertheless, the dream début that resulted was beyond even Brian Hart's hopes as Gethin enlivened a dull race by flying round in the midst of the Porsche 917s and Can-Am McLarens to finish fifth overall and win the 2-litre class comfortably from John Lepp in his regular B26 with its alloy block Hart BDA. After struggling with the B23 at Vila Real the previous summer, Gethin was delighted with the B26 and its new engine. The car itself was christened 'Chocolate Drop' because of its unusual brown bodywork, and it became one of those cars that everyone who had anything to do with developed a soft spot for.

A week after Silverstone, Chocolate Drop went to Nürburgring where the new Hart engine was to make its World Championship début in the 750km (the oil crisis had caused the races to be shortened from their usual 1,000 km). John Watson was paired with Gethin for the race and he too, was delighted with the car. 'The pleasure of that car on that circuit that weekend was pretty special,' Watson recalls. His main reason for doing the race was as preparation for the German Grand Prix, when he would be driving the Hexagon Brabham. But there did not seem to be much wrong with his knowledge of the circuit in practice when he lapped in 7 mins 35.5 seconds, well inside the 2-litre lap record and almost seven seconds faster than the next car in the class. Watson still remembers the race as one of his best, even though the car went out in the closing stages, with Gethin leading the class, when a wheel bearing broke.

When John Lepp drove the car in the last-ditch attempt to stop Renault walking away with the 2-litre championship at Hockenheim, both Brian Hart and Derek Bennett were there to will the B26 on. In his best showing of the year, Lepp was

SURVIVING THE OIL CRISIS

only narrowly beaten on aggregate by Serpaggi's Renault, but when he got back to the pits Brian and Derek had already gone, both obviously disappointed.

Away from the disappointments of the 2-litre series, the B26 continued to perform extremely well in long distance events, and Chevron ended the year fifth in the World Championship for Makes. At the Osterreichring in June, Rafael Barrios and Richard Scott took one of the Domecq-sponsored Forge Mill B26s to seventh overall and a class win, despite starting at the back of the grid after missing practice when their transporter broke down. John Lepp teamed up with the South African Guy Tunmer for the Kyalami 6-Hours, which was the final round of the World Championship in November and they, too, won their class, finishing fourth overall in a Team Lexington B26.

However, the best result of the year for the B26 was at the British Airways 1,000km at Brands Hatch in September when the two drivers who had become most synonymous with Chevron's success, Brian Redman and Peter Gethin, teamed up together for the first time in the Hart-engined works car. Despite an agonising eight-minute pit stop to change a shock absorber, they were still fourth at the end, only 38 seconds behind the 3-litre Gulf GR7-DFV of Derek Bell and David Hobbs. The next runner in the 2-litre class had been left 15 laps behind.

But the Brands Hatch race underlined the steady demise of sports car racing. The bulk of the entry was made up of 2-litre cars and only 6,517 adults paid to watch the race, compared with the 33,000 who had been there on the day Brian Redman drove a Chevron in the race for the first time in 1967. It seemed that Derek Bennett's decision to concentrate on the B29 for 1975 was the right one.

Chevron's most successful drivers, Brian Redman and Peter Gethin, only ever drove together once – in the British Airways 1,000km at Brands Hatch on 29 September 1974. They won their class convincingly. Here Redman takes over from Gethin during a routine pitstop as Derek Bennett lurks nervously behind the tyres on the pit counter. (*Photo LAT.*)

CHAPTER 12

Finding a successful formula

MOTOR racing emerged from the shadow of the oil crisis into a year of transition with manufacturers having to turn their attention to new markets as established formulae fell by the wayside.

With Chevron having decided to concentrate on the B29 for 1975 it was important for them to have a strong team in British Formula Atlantic. This time there were no misunderstandings as a 'two for the price of one' deal was put together with Stephen Choularton for SDC Racing to run a pair of B29s with Brian Hart BDA engines for Jim Crawford and Choularton himself. Crawford was also pulled in to help with the sales campaign, going out to West Palm Beach, Florida, with Derek Bennett in February to share the driving as the works B29 was put through some extensive testing in front of potential customers. With Crawford lapping more than two seconds inside the Formula 5000 track record, the spectators were impressed and a dozen B29s were sold for North American Formula Atlantic events.

Back in the depressingly familiar cold and wet surroundings of a March day at Mallory Park, the John Player British Atlantic Championship opened well for Chevron with B29s taking the first three places. The surprise winner was Formula Ford graduate and Grovewood Award winner, Richard Morgan, in a B29 bought for him by Donington circuit owner, Tom Wheatcroft. Morgan took the lead when Crawford spun the length of the main straight in the appalling conditions. Unlike Tony Brise, who had spun out of the lead earlier in his Modus, Crawford did not damage his car and he recovered to finish second, ahead of Choularton.

Morgan was unable to match that opening performance again, but Crawford's championship hopes were dashed by Brise, who completely demoralised the opposition by winning the next six races in his works Modus. Crawford was second in three of those races, but his attempts to solve a persistent handling problem seemed to be making his car slower. He became even more baffled after trying his team-mate's car during a test session at Oulton Park and immediately going

$1\frac{1}{2}$ seconds faster than he could in his own. As frustration set in, he persuaded Derek Bennett to try his car. After a couple of laps, Derek brought the car in and pronounced that something was wrong with the chassis. 'It was bending, and I wasn't experienced enough to pick that up,' said Crawford.

Putting a stiffening bar into Crawford's car transformed it and Jim went to Mallory Park in June and won. Ironically, Brise's winning run came to an end when the Modus broke a half-shaft on the grid, but Crawford was confident of being able to beat him at last.

When the Atlantic championship went to Silverstone to support the British Grand Prix, all eyes were on Brise and Crawford, both of whom were also racing in the Grand Prix itself. With a few weeks of his Lotus test contract still to run, Crawford was making his Formula 1 début in a Lotus 72. Brise had made his début for Frank Williams earlier in the year, but now he was fitting his Atlantic races around a regular place in Graham Hill's new Embassy-Hill team. The day should have been a high point in the careers of both drivers, but it turned out to be one of those perverse days when the motor racing fates decide to dash the hopes of the best drivers.

The Grand Prix was brought to a premature end when a rainstorm sent half the runners into the catch fencing. Crawford had already slithered off on the wet track some laps earlier, while Brise got caught up in the final chaos and found himself being taken to hospital for treatment to facial injuries when he should have been climbing into his Modus for the Atlantic race. Crawford started his B29 from the front row but, while disputing third place, he tangled with Nick May's Lola to put the finishing touches to a day to forget. American Ted Wentz kept everything under control to win his first John Player race in his Lola T360B, while Alo Lawler drove the race of his life to bring his B29 in second.

Crawford bounced back with another win at Mallory Park in August and, when the championship final came round at Brands Hatch in September, he found himself in the position of having to win with Brise failing to score if he was going to snatch the title. But by this point, another ace had come to the fore and Crawford's task was complicated by the presence of Sweden's Gunnar Nilsson on pole position. Nilsson, who was already on his way to winning the BP Formula 3 Championship in a works March, had been a surprise replacement for American Matt Spitzley in Ted Moore's Rapid Movements Chevron at Mallory, where he had acquitted himself well to finish fourth.

In practice at Brands, Nilsson had proved the master of the heavy rain which had characterised the season. Determined not to be beaten to the title two years running, Crawford led

CHEVRON

away, but Nilsson carved past him after four laps. In the dreadful conditions, Brise had no intention of making a race of it and was concentrating on keeping out of trouble. At half distance he was lapped by Crawford, whose dogged pursuit of Nilsson looked like being rewarded as the Swede's car developed a chronic misfire. But just as Crawford started to reel in Nilsson, his own engine cut out completely and he freewheeled out of the race. Nilsson lapped Brise three times on his way to victory, but with Crawford out, sixth place was more than enough to give Brise the title.

The inevitable lack of finance kept Crawford out of the late season Southern Organs championship rounds that remained. But Nilsson stamped his authority on the formula by winning all four races. Meanwhile, the B29 had also been claiming its share of success in North America, and Bill Brack won the Canadian Formula Atlantic Championship for the second year running in his.

It is a sad postscript to what turned out to be the best season of Formula Atlantic racing in Britain that both Tony Brise and Gunnar Nilsson died before they could truly fulfil their promise. Brise was killed only a few weeks after the end of the 1975 season when Graham Hill's Formula 1 Team was wiped out in a plane crash while flying back from a test session in France, with Hill himself at the controls. Nilsson progressed rapidly into Formula 1 and had already won a Grand Prix for Lotus when he was found to have cancer. After a valiant battle against the disease, Gunnar died in October 1978.

As Formula Atlantic grew in status, Chevron kept up a fairly low-key presence in Formula 2. Fred Opert felt his young Mexican charge, Hector Rebaque — who was still only

Gunnar Nilsson took a string of Formula Atlantic wins at the end of 1975. Here his B29 holds off the Lola of a hard-charging Ted Wentz on the way to the third of those wins, at Oulton Park on 4 October. (*Photo Eric Yuill.*)

19 years old — was ready for Formula 2 after his year in Atlantic and his was the only Chevron on the grid for the first round of the 1975 European Championship at Estoril. Rebaque went out of that race with a puncture, but he surprised everyone by finishing fourth in the next round at Thruxton. By the following round, at Hockenheim in April, another Chevron team had joined the championship as Christian Ethuin and Xavier Lapeyre appeared in a pair of B29s run by French Chevron agent Fred Stalder's Race Organisation Course. The team were introducing Chrysler to Formula 2 and had to wait until April before the alloy heads for their steel-block Simca engines were homologated. ROC struggled to get the new engines quick enough or reliable enough and even when Jean-Pierre Beltoise was brought in to boost the driver line-up, championship points eluded them.

Harald Ertl continued to race his ex-works/Baty B27 while he waited for a new B29, but he took his — and Chevron's — best result of the year in the older car when he finished third at the Nürburgring in April, behind Jacques Laffite's Martini and Patrick Tambay in the works March 752.

There was no direct works Chevron involvement until late in the year when a development chassis was built for Brian Redman to test with a works BMW engine. Dissatisfied with his Schnitzer BMW-engined March, Austrian Hans Binder approached Chevron about running him in the car, and he appeared in it for the first time at Silverstone at the end of August. Binder qualified promisingly on the third row, but he must have been a little surprised to see Jim Crawford a place ahead of him, running his Atlantic B29 with a Richardson BDG. Binder was running behind Crawford in the race when he holed his radiator and went out with the engine overheating. Crawford lost a fine fifth place a few laps later when his gearbox gave up. Binder did the three remaining races in the series and the works team was rewarded with fourth place at Zolder.

During the course of 1975, Chevron had clawed their production back up to 35 cars, but they were still less than halfway to regaining their earlier sales levels. They had only sold six of their latest B31 sports cars, and as the decline of sports car racing continued Derek Bennett realised that it was important for Chevron to find another formula where they could sell cars in volume. He looked back nostalgically on the old 1-litre Formula 3 of the late 1960s as the best formula they had been involved in. He could not bring that back, but he was still very keen on Formula 3 which seemed to be having a resurgence despite competition from the introduction of what he called 'daft formulas'. So he set to work to produce Chevron's first Formula 3 car for nearly five years, the B34. Tackling once again the eternal problem of the balance between downforce and speed led Derek this time to produce a smart, small car with a wide, flat-bottomed monocoque. He stuck with a full-width nose, although the scooped, concave nose had evolved considerably from the tradition of the sports car-like front, which went back to the days of the B20. Stylist Jim Clark, now working as a freelance, was brought into the factory to help with the bodywork design, and the combined result was an especially attractive, new-look Chevron with sharper, clean lines and a sense of purpose that marked it out as another of Derek Bennett's winners.

By the time Derek tested the prototype at Oulton Park early in December, orders for the car, and its Formula 2 B35 version, were already coming in. A boost to Chevron sales in Europe also came with the news that the Italian March agent, Pino Trivellato, was changing his allegiance to Chevron and had just signed a three-year deal to import the Bolton cars. Trivellato Racing also promised a high racing profile with plans to run a pair of B35s with factory BMW engines in Formula 2, and a B34 in the European Formula 3 series.

As Trivellato were casting round for a young Italian to race their Formula 3 car, Mario Patrese was looking for a drive for his son. Riccardo, who was 21 years old, had won the world karting championship two years before and had moved into circuit racing for 1975, where he finished runner-up to Bruno Giacomelli in the Formula Italia Championship. His father went to Vicenza hoping to see Pino Trivellato. Instead he found Trivellato's Formula 3 Team Manager, Ugo Kloden, who he discovered was already a fan of Riccardo's. Kloden sold the idea of running Patrese to Trivellato and Riccardo began testing the B34 in readiness for a Formula 3 baptism of fire at the Nürburgring on the first weekend of April.

Having never seen the Nürburgring before, Patrese decided to go and take a look a few days before the race. They could not get out onto the circuit in a car because of a racing school session on the pits loop. But it was a nice sunny day, and they had nothing else to do, so Patrese and Kloden decided to walk the first few kilometres to get the feel of the track. After the first three kilometres they decided to walk on another three, and before they realised it they were on the other side of the circuit. Now they had come this far they might as well finish their walk. 'It took us about seven hours to walk around the circuit,' Patrese recalls. 'I was writing down all the crucial points, because 23km of circuit is not very easy to remember. The following day I could study the circuit on paper and when I went out for first practice I already knew the circuit quite well!'

Paul Owens went out to the Nürburgring to oversee the

FINDING A SUCCESSFUL FORMULA

début of the B34. Like most people he had never heard of Patrese and when he arrived in Germany he was not too optimistic when he discovered that he had never raced a Formula 3 car or driven at the Nürburgring before. On top of this, Riccardo's English was as non-existent as Paul's Italian, and Paul made a mental note just to treat the meeting as a weekend out. But as the two struggled along in a language of their own invention, Paul became impressed at how much Riccardo knew about the 'Ring. Maybe putting this together with his own experience of working with 'Ring experts like Brian Redman and Vic Elford could produce something after all.

The day before the European Championship race there was a round of the German National Series, which Patrese did for the experience, and finished in an impressive second place. The following day he looked even better and was leading the European round until heavy rain set in. Conscious of his inexperience, Patrese eased off and eventually settled for third place, behind Conny Andersson's March 763 and Bertram Schafer's Ralt RT1. Two weeks later, at Zandvoort, he fulfilled that tremendous early promise and took his first win. It also meant that Chevron had a winning Formula 3 car once

Riccardo Patrese prepares for the start of his first European Championship Formula 3 race at the Nürburgring on 4 April 1976. His Trivellato B34 finished third. (*Photo Jeff Hutchinson.*)

again and guaranteed that the factory would be kept busy building B34s for the next few months.

Trivellato ran their two B35s in the European Formula 2 Championship, but their two Italian drivers, Roberto Marazzi and Giorgio Francia, rarely shone. Marazzi's fifth place in the opening round at Hockenheim in April looked promising, but he never improved on that performance and another fifth place, at Rouen in June, was the only other time he finished in the points. Two seventh places were the best Francia was able to manage.

With the Trivellato cars proving disappointing, Fred Opert's team drew some useful attention to the B35. For the first time Opert planned to contest the whole of the European Championship, and he started out with two cars for Frenchman José Dolhem and Venezuelan-born Yugoslav Juan Cochesa. But during the year, some lucrative deals began to come Opert's way and some extremely famous names started to appear in his B35s — most notably at Pau in June when his line-up boasted the reigning Formula 2 champion, Jacques Laffite, and the 1973 Champion, Jean-Pierre Jarier.

Opert's 'French Connection' stemmed back a couple of seasons to the Trois Rivières Formula Atlantic race in Quebec, where the organisers had offered him Gitanes sponsorship money if he could bring a French driver into the race. Opert took the money and brought them Jean-Pierre Jaussaud, who he ran in a B27 alongside Tom Pryce. Pryce went out with brake problems, but Jaussaud finished second. The Gitanes money was available again for the race the following September and Opert got them a couple of Jean-Pierres this time — Jarier and Jaussaud — and José Dolhem, putting them in three B29s. Opert paid meticulous attention to getting the Gitanes colour scheme exactly right, and the cars were prepared to his usual immaculate standards. When Gitanes' head marketing people came over to Canada for the race, they were immediately impressed. They were even more impressed in the race when Jarier looked to be heading for victory. But then he spun three laps from the end after tangling with a back marker and Vittorio Brambilla's works March slipped through to win. Nevertheless, Opert's Chevrons took the next four places as Jarier recovered to finish second, ahead of Jaussaud and Dolhem, and Hector Rebaque followed the Gitanes trio across the line.

Over the winter, Opert kept in contact with Gitanes, making the most of his ability to speak French to set up a series of meetings in Paris. Eventually he did a deal to run two Chevrons in Gitanes colours at the three French rounds of the European Formula 2 Championship — and with their Ligier Grand Prix star, Jacques Laffite, as the main driver.

As Formula 2 was now open to full racing engines, the latest version of Brian Hart's alloy 2-litre sports car engine, the 420R, had become eligible. Because of his strong ties with Opert, Hart had encouraged the American to expand his activities in Europe, using 420Rs in his Chevrons. But Laffite's deal required him to run a BMW engine, so Opert came to an arrangement with Harald Ertl to enter his car for the season if Laffite could use it for the three French races. Opert's cars were run from the same German garage as Ertl's, and the team kept a complete spare set of body panels in Gitanes' colours to transform Ertl's car for Laffite.

Laffite and Jarier caused quite a stir when they appeared for the first time at Pau. Despite getting through two engines in practice, Laffite qualified on the second row, behind the Martinis of Patrick Tambay and René Arnoux and alongside Jean-Pierre Jabouille's Elf. Behind him, Jarier, in one of Opert's Hart-engined B35s, shared the third row with Michel Leclere's Elf, making it six Frenchman at the front of the grid.

Laffite got left behind at the start, but he fought his way back to third place, with only the Martinis of Tambay and Arnoux ahead of him. Just when Tambay's lead was looking secure, he spun out of the race, which meant that Laffite was chasing Arnoux for the lead. Unfortunately, Laffite had developed cramp in his right leg as the seat in the Chevron was not quite right for him. In considerable discomfort, he was struggling to work the pedals, and brushed the armco at one point. Having closed to a couple of seconds behind Arnoux, he had to ease off and settle for second place, but he did take the lap record and he had shown that the B35 was definitely a winner. Jarier brought the second Opert car in fourth, trailing smoke from an oil leak.

One spectator who watched Laffite's performance enviously was Hans Binder, who had become totally disillusioned with his Osella after failing to qualify it for the race. Paul Owens was there working on Laffite's car and Binder asked him if Chevron could run a car for him for the rest of the season. Paul was keen to run Binder again if he could come up with enough money for a proper works effort, and in the meantime, Opert's cars were available at Rouen as Laffite and Jarier were both committed to driving for Alpine Renault in a World Sports Car Championship race at Enna. Binder found himself in the Hart-engined car as Opert secured the services of Tom Pryce, now established in Formula 1 with Shadow, for the BMW-powered B35. Tom was delighted with the car and left it virtually as it had been set-up for Laffite as he claimed third place on the grid, less than two-tenths of a second slower than Alex Ribeiro's works March. Binder was relieved not only to make the grid, but to qualify seventh fastest in the

Hart-powered car. In the race, Pryce found his BMW engine was reluctant to pick up coming out of slow corners and he slipped to the back of the leading group. Experimenting with using lower gears in the tight corners, he got into a slide and momentarily lost his grip on the steering wheel as he snatched another gear. The car lurched into a catch fence and Tom was out of the race after only five laps.

Engine problems put Binder out of the race too, but a new BMW-engined works car was ready for him by the time the championship reached Mugello in July. But it was another Chevron that created a sensation at Mugello when a B35 appeared on the front row of the grid, driven by the Australian Bob Muir, who just a few weeks before had been unable to qualify his own Minos at Pau. Unfortunately, problems with the clutch pushed Muir well down in the race, but Binder came in a promising seventh.

As the season continued, the new names kept popping up in Chevrons, and at Estoril in August the latest name on the side of one of Fred Opert's cars was Keke Rosberg. Opert had been urged to keep an eye on Rosberg in Super Vee the year before by Ian Williams of Tui, who also encouraged Keke to write to Fred introducing himself. Opert saw him race a couple of times during 1975 when the European Super Vee series supported Formula 2 races, and he was impressed enough to take up Williams' suggestion that he run him, in a Tui, at Watkins Glen in the Super Vee race that supported the United States Grand Prix. Keijo Rosberg was only just beginning to be known in racing circles as 'Keke' — and either way Opert's American signwriters were confused — so he arrived in America to find his car sign-written for K.K. Rosberg. American spectators were happy to assume they were watching Kevin Karl in action.

Opert is unsure why Keke did not finish better than fifth in that race, but he does remember that they all enjoyed themselves enormously the whole weekend, and that the seeds of his relationship with Rosberg were sown. For 1976, Rosberg was offered a Formula 2 drive in Jorg Obermoser's Toj, but the car was cumbersome and uncompetitive and Rosberg often struggled even to qualify. Then, for the Estoril race, he managed to persuade Obermoser, and his sponsor, Warsteiner, to hire one of Opert's Chevrons. On the Portuguese circuit, Rosberg was an immediate sensation, ending up third fastest in practice with only Arnoux's Martini and Ribeiro's March in front of him on the grid. Running with a Hart engine, he even outpaced the BMW-engined works Chevron of Hans Binder, which started the race alongside him on the second row. As Arnoux went away in front, Binder and Rosberg fought over second place with Ribeiro. But Rosberg's fine race came to an end two-thirds of the way through when a water pipe broke. Desperate to make a good showing after his unimpressive results in the Toj, Rosberg was tremendously disappointed, but his performance had not gone unnoticed. Meanwhile, with Derek Bennett on hand to oversee the latest suspension modifications on the works car, Binder took a good fourth place.

Binder continued to show well in the remaining couple of races, picking up two more fourth places, at Nogaro and Hockenheim. Jochen Mass also appeared in a Chevron at Hockenheim, taking a new ATS B35 to sixth place. Opert had his Gitanes twins back for Nogaro, and Jacques Laffite again finished second. Jarier was running well until a deflating front tyre brought him into the pits where, much to Opert's surprise, he climbed out of the car and retired. During testing at Nogaro Opert had given another promising young French driver his first taste of a Formula 2 car. José Dolhem had introduced Fred to his cousin, Didier Pironi, and Fred had been very impressed by Pironi's form in Formule Renault. The Frenchman was due to graduate into Formula 2 with Martini in 1977, but Opert let him try Laffite's car at Nogaro. 'The boy's just got to be good' was Opert's comment after Pironi got down to Laffite's times in two laps, using the wrong gear ratios and worn-out tyres.

For the Hockenheim final round Rolf Stommelen drove one of Opert's Hart-engined cars, but he was delayed by a broken exhaust. Making his Formula 2 début in the second Opert car that day was Rupert Keegan, who had been the revelation of the British Formula 3 Championship in his B34. Chevron had planned to run at least one works-supported car in Britain to help boost sales of the new car, and back in early February a group of hopefuls had been on hand at Silverstone to try Patrese's B34 before it was shipped out to Italy. After Derek Bennett had given the car a shakedown, the would-be customers and works drivers took their turns and triple British Formula Ford Champion, Geoff Lees, was particularly impressive. Geoff's dominance of Formula Ford the previous season had earned him a Grovewood Award and his Formula 3 début was eagerly awaited. If he could contribute some sponsorship, the works drive was his.

Unfortunately for Geoff, Patrese's success in Europe filled the order books before Chevron could get round to building their own works car and it was not until the end of June that his B34 — chassis number 24 — was finished, inevitably at three o'clock on raceday morning. It was the first time the car had raced in Britain and Lees looked good as he brought it in fourth in his first Formula 3 race. At that point the formula in Britain was very much a March benefit. Twenty-one-year-old Rupert Keegan had started the year with a string of wins in an old March 743, shaking off his wild image and establishing himself as a respected driver. But the works March 763 of Bruno Giacomelli was getting more competitive all the time as the Italian newcomer found his feet in the formula and Keegan prepared to replace the stop-gap 743 with a brand new car, designed and built specially for him.

Rupert's car always ran in the colours of British Air Ferries, part of the air cargo group owned by his father Mike, who was an enthusiastic supporter of his son's racing, and had recently bought the Hawke racing car company. A young designer by the name of Adrian Reynard had been brought in to design a Hawke Formula 3 car for Rupert, but when it was ready there were initially problems with the chassis and Rupert was reluctant to put his faith in it for an all-important BP Championship round. Giacomelli had beaten him for the first time in May and then gone on to win the Formula 3 race at the Monaco Grand Prix, so Keegan was feeling the pressure. With the Hawke still not properly sorted, he went back to the old March at Oulton Park in July, and was soundly beaten again by Giacomelli. But the Keegans had already seen another possible solution and six days later Rupert appeared at Brands Hatch to practise for the British Grand Prix supporting race at the wheel of a brand new Chevron.

Keegan went out of the race when he put a hole in the sump after running over a kerb while chasing Geoff Lees' third-placed B34. But he soon had the car sorted to his liking and beat Giacomelli's March to win three of the next four races. Keegan went into the final BP Championship round at Thruxton on the last day of October defending a three-point lead. But the last race showdown came to a controversial end as Keegan and Giacomelli headed determinedly for the same piece of road at the first corner and collided with

Rupert Keegan switched to a Chevron midway through the 1976 season and went on to win the BP Formula 3 Championship. Here his B34 leads the Ralt RT1 of Geoff Brabham at Brands Hatch in October. (Photo Tim Tyler.)

each other. The March and the Chevron were both out of the race and heated discussions with the stewards followed, but the title was Rupert Keegan's and Chevron could now add the British Formula 3 Championship to the European title, which Riccardo Patrese had made sure of a few weeks earlier. The Thruxton race also proved a welcome boost for Geoff Lees. He had beaten Giacomelli and Keegan in his works B34 for the first time in the final round of Silverstone's ShellSport Championship the previous month, and in their self-imposed absence from the Thruxton race he took his first BP win, claiming the lap record in the process.

A week later Chevron had the chance to collect yet another title as the Italian national F3 series ended at Magione. Although Patrese had been concentrating on the European Championship, some of those races had also brought in Italian championship points and he found himself sharing the lead with only one race to run. Convinced that Patrese, who had won four European rounds, had some sort of special car, one of his Italian rivals had bought the Chevron from Trivellato straight after the last race at Vallelunga. Pleased with the tidy sum they had got for the 'special' car, Trivellato put together another B34 for Magione and Patrese went out and won that race too, becoming the Italian champion.

The B34 had also been selling very well in Formula Atlantic trim, but ironically none of those sales was in Britain, where the formula was flagging and drivers on tight budgets were content to stick with the successful B29. The Chevrons were not competitive with the works Lola T460 of Ted Wentz or the Boxer of Tony Rouff but, when the two Americans tangled with each other at Thruxton, Chevrons poured through to take the first four places, headed by Phil Dowsett in Stephen Choularton's old B29.

The B29 had had another late moment of glory earlier in the year when Fred Opert got Brian Redman to drive the BMW-engined Formula 2 car that Binder had raced in Europe in the New Zealand Formula 5000 Tasman Championship in January. Despite his power disadvantage, Redman gave the big cars quite a fright, finishing fourth at Pukekohe and second at Manfeild, where he was only 11 seconds behind Max Stewart's Lola T332 at the finish — even after two spins on the wet track. Redman's hopes of snatching the championship faded away as engine problems and a broken wheel brought his giant-killing exploits to an end in the two remaining races.

On the day Redman was giving the B29 its last race in New Zealand, the B34 was making its début in the opening round of the South African Formula Atlantic Championship at Killarney, near Cape Town. Tony Martin, a long-time South African Chevron customer, finished second in his B34, with

CHEVRON

New York Chevrolet dealer Bobby Brown was a successful Chevron customer in North American Formula B and Atlantic for a number of years. Here his B34 leads the Lola T360 of Tom Klausler on the way to victory in an IMSA Atlantic race at Road Atlanta in April 1976.

Canadian Atlantic Champion, Bill Brack, following him home third in a second Chevron.

Fred Opert continued to run an Atlantic team in North America, as well as selling B34s to a number of other teams. Howdy Holmes, Bill Brack and Gordon Smiley all took Chevrons to top-three finishes in the Players Championship, and Chevron's North American presence reached a high at the increasingly prestigious Trois Rivières Atlantic Race, for which 10 B34s and a B29 practised. Opert again had Gitanes backing for the race, and his star line-up included Patrick Tambay and Alan Jones. The man the French-Canadians were all cheering for, though, was their own Gilles Villeneuve. He had dominated the Players Canadian Atlantic series all year and now they wanted to see him beat the Grand Prix stars, who included James Hunt, who was about to become World Champion.

Villeneuve did not disappoint his fans and dominated the race in his March 76B. But Alan Jones fought his way through from a poor grid position to take a good second place in his Chevron, holding off the Marches of Hunt, Vittorio Brambilla and Bobby Rahal. Tambay drove a steady race to finish sixth.

Although Chevron had officially been out of Formula 5000

192

FINDING A SUCCESSFUL FORMULA

for two years, a couple of one-off cars appeared in the struggling formula during 1975 and 1976. The most successful of these was David Purley's B30, which took advantage of a change in the rules that allowed the 3.4 litre Cosworth-Ford V6 engine to compete in the formula alongside the traditional 5-litre Chevrolets. He persuaded Derek Bennett to adapt a B29 Formula 2 chassis to take the engine and the new car surprised everyone when it took second place in the opening round of the 1975 ShellSport 5000 series at Brands Hatch.

Two weeks later, in the Easter Monday race at Brands Hatch, the B30 won for the first time as Purley headed Dave Walker's B28 and Tony Dean's B24 across the line in Chevron's last 1-2-3 in the formula. Lola had been struggling to get their new T400 working properly and, just as they did, Purley began to hit trouble, losing races as engine and gearbox problems combined with punctures and the odd spin to keep him out of the results until September when he won the Oulton Park Gold Cup. It was a good win for Purley as he beat Vern Schuppan in Sid Taylor's Lola T332 and the VDS Lola T400s of Teddy Pilette and Peter Gethin, but the race also demonstrated the terminal decline of Formula 5000 in Britain with a mere 12 cars taking the start.

On 19 October the formula bowed out at Brands Hatch, with Peter Gethin winning the last race just as he had the

Good Friday 1975 at Oulton Park sees David Purley pressing on in his unique B30 Formula 5000 car, here in its original specification with B29-style front bodywork. With melting snow running across the track, Purley chose to use hand-grooved slicks and finished third in the treacherous conditions. (*Photo Eric Yuill.*)

CHEVRON

The sleeker, revised version of the B30 took David Purley to the ShellSport 5000 Championship title in 1976. (*Photo Eric Yuill.*)

first some six-and-a-half years before when he took the Church Farm McLaren M10A to victory at Oulton Park.

In Britain the ShellSport 5000 series continued, run to Group 8 regulations to let in Formula 1 and 2 cars alongside the old Formula 5000 machines. David Purley continued with the B30, but while he was away driving in the Tasman Series over the winter, his Lec team, under the guidance of Team Manager Mike Earle, revised the car considerably, replacing the full-width front with a chisel nose and wings. Derek Bell tested the car extensively and the car was well sorted by the time the new championship got under way at Mallory Park in March. Purley beat Damien Magee's V6-engined March 751 to win the race. It was the first of six wins for Purley in what was to prove the most successful season of his career as he took the championship title comfortably, a convincing 65 points clear of Magee.

Count van der Straten's team decided to switch their efforts to America, where Formula 5000 was continuing, but they were in something of a quandary over which chassis to use. The Lola T332 seemed to have had the edge on Chevron's B28 during 1974, so when Chevron pulled out of the formula at the end of that season, Lola had been an obvious choice. But the new T400 had not lived up to expectations and had frequently struggled to keep up with the older T332s. Frustrated with the situation, Peter Gethin returned to his faith in Derek Bennett, and told van der Straten that he wanted Chevron to build him a car. Others in the team thought they should stay with Lola, so the Count agreed that Gethin could have his Chevron and they would take it to Paul Ricard before the season started and run it in back-to-back tests with the latest Lola T430.

FINDING A SUCCESSFUL FORMULA

'It was very expensive for poor old van der Straten,' comments Gethin. 'But I was a great believer in Derek Bennett and I thought that he had the ability to build a one-off.' In the end the tests proved inconclusive and the VDS team made the rather unsatisfactory decision to let Gethin race the Chevron B37, while Teddy Pilette would race the Lola. In the end, neither car met with much success as Brian Redman stormed to his third North American F5000 title driving the latest update of the evergreen Lola T332. Gethin confesses to having been disappointed with the Chevron. 'It was small and it looked lovely. But it was a bit crude. To be honest, my impressions today are that Derek had not advanced as much with his 5000 as other people had with their cars. But I'd got van der Straten to run the car for me and Derek Bennett to build it for me and I felt that I should persevere with it.'

Paul Owens defends Derek, saying that he was reluctant to put a lot of development work into a car that might not even be raced. Paul maintains that VDS were going to come down totally on the side of Chevron or Lola after the evaluation tests, and that Derek would have got involved in a full development programme if they had decided to concentrate on the B37. As it was, the team's efforts were split and the Chevron's potential was never discovered.

At the end of 1976 the Americans got rid of Formula 5000 as well, bringing back their beloved Can-Am for 1977. There was a winter Rothmans Formula 5000 series in Australia though, in February 1977, and Gethin gave the B37 its best showings as he took a couple of second places on his way to finishing second in the series to his team-mate Warwick Brown, in the VDS Lola T432. When Brown crashed the Lola on the warm-up lap at Sandown Park, Gethin looked like giving the B37 its first win, but he went out five laps from victory when his engine expired.

Bruce Allison in the unique Formula 5000 B37 holds off the March 751 of Guy Edwards at Snetterton on 2 October 1977. Allison went out while lying second. (*Photo Tim Tyler.*)

After the series, the B37 was sold to the Australian Bruce Allison, who brought it over to Britain for the 1977 Group 8 Championship. The 22-year-old proved a revelation and was frequently the fastest driver in the series. But bad luck, rooted in a shortage of finance, stopped him getting the wins he looked capable of. He came close at Brands Hatch, where he was leading until his suspension broke, and in the end two second places were his best results. Allison's efforts did earn him the top Grovewood Award, however, and he became the first Australian to win it since 1968 when it had gone to another Chevron driver, Tim Schenken, after his Formula 3 championship win in the B9.

As attention focused on Chevron's single-seaters, the factory had continued to make sports cars, but with the category in decline throughout the world they sold just six B31s in 1975 and eight B36s the following year. The B31 made its début at Mugello in March of 1975 in the second round of the World Championship for Makes with Ian Grob and John Hine finishing a fine fifth overall to win the 2-litre class in their KVG Racing example. They did even better at Dijon two weeks later, bringing the Hart-engined B31 into third place. The 2-litre class had been a close battle with the Alpine-Renault A441 of Lella Lombardi and Marie-Claude Beaumont. But when the Alpine blew its engine, the Chevron went on to win the class comfortably, finishing almost 100 miles ahead of the Lola T294 of Alan Jones and John Sheldon.

Chevrons scored in seven of the nine rounds, ending up fourth in the championship, which Alfa Romeo won. Hine and Grob's two early season results remained the best of the year and the only other points picked up by a B31 were at Enna, where a 1600cc version, driven by Gagliardi and 'Bramen', came in sixth overall after a tedious race which only 16 cars started. Chevron's other World Championship points were picked up by two privateer B23s. Pete Smith and John Turner took theirs to seventh place at the Osterreichring and 10th at Spa to collect five points, while Robin Smith and Richard Robarts contributed another four points by finishing eighth at Monza and 10th at the Nürburgring in their B23.

Meanwhile, the European 2-litre Sports Car Championship expired completely, with only two of the scheduled 12 races taking place in 1975 and the series being abandoned for 1976. Martin Raymond had the distinction of winning the last race for Chevron when he took his Fisons-backed B31 to victory at Hockenheim on 31 August.

Interest in sports car racing dwindled even further in 1976, although there was a British 2-litre championship with a healthy representation of Chevrons. Unfortunately the

FINDING A SUCCESSFUL FORMULA

Chevron drivers had to contend with John Lepp, who thought he had retired from racing at the end of 1974, but had been lured back to drive a works March. His March 75S won the championship, but Tony Charnell's B31 beat Lepp in the rain at Thruxton, and Iain McLaren won the final round at Mallory Park in his B26 to claim the runner-up position in the series.

John Blanckley put a DFV engine into his B31 and Martin Raymond tried some European Interserie races with the car. He was rewarded with a win at Zolder in June. Sadly, his win was overshadowed by the death of Richard Sutherland, who became only the third driver to be killed in a Chevron when he crashed his B23, bringing the race to a halt.

Trivellato gave the B36 its World Sports Car Championship début at Monza in April, but neither of their two cars achieved much in the way of results. The French ROC team also ran a couple of B36s and persisted with their 2-litre Chrysler engines. Their best showing was at the Dijon World Championship event when Jean-Louis Lafosse and Jean-Pierre Jaussaud won the 2-litre class and finished seventh overall. The best overall placing of the year, though, went to Anthony Cicale who took his Hart-engined B26 to sixth place in the Canadian Round of the World Championship at Mosport in August.

At the end of 1976 Chevron was firmly back on an even

Martin Raymond takes the chequered flag at Hockenheim on 31 August 1975 to win the last ever European 2-litre Championship race in his B31. (*Photo Jeff Hutchinson.*)

keel. The success of the B34 had made it the best selling model since the B19 and total production, at 55 cars, was the highest ever, narrowly beating the previous best year, 1973. With Chevron's worldwide profile higher than ever, there was no time for an off-season and at the beginning of November the works B35 went out to Japan for Jacques Laffite to race in the Suzuka Formula 2 race. In front of a huge crowd, Laffite led the race from start to finish, beating the Japanese challenge and the March of Hans Stuck, and giving Chevron their first Formula 2 win since Peter Gethin had won at Pau in 1972.

Back in Britain a few days later Chevron set up a test day at Silverstone for potential Formula 3 customers, using Geoff Lees' B34. The response was so great that a second day had to be scheduled the following week. Among those to try out the car that day was Derek Warwick, who had dominated Formula Ford during the year and was about to collect a Grovewood Award for his 31 victories. The first of the 1977 Chevrons also put in an appearance at Silverstone as Derek Bennett tried out the latest Formula Atlantic car, the B39, which would soon be on its way out to the South African Atlantic series. For the 1976 series Chevron had run a car for the Canadian champion, who was then Bill Brack. The Springbok organisers wanted the Canadian champion again for 1977, so Chevron were busy putting together a deal which would see Gilles Villeneuve give their new car its début.

CHAPTER 13

Famous victories in Formula 2

THE night before Christmas Eve 1976, Keke Rosberg got a phone call from Fred Opert asking how quickly he could get himself to New Zealand. 'I didn't even know where New Zealand was,' recalls Rosberg. 'But I tell you, I was there!' Rosberg knew Opert was planning to take a couple of his B34 Atlantic cars out to New Zealand for the Stuyvesant Series there, but he could not bring in enough money from his sponsor, Warsteiner, to pay for the trip and he thought his chance had gone. Meanwhile, Marlboro wanted Opert to run their driver, Mikko Kozarowitsky, to try and make up for the disappointing début season he had just had in Formula 2 with the ATS Lola.

Not only was Kozarowitsky a Finn, but he was the Finn who had beaten Rosberg to the European Super Vee title in 1975. When Opert broke the news to Keke, he cursed his luck and resigned himself to staying at home for the winter. But when his second driver could not put together a deal in time, Fred came up with a way to finance Rosberg in the second car and Keke was in after all.

The rivalry between Opert's two Finns was strong, but neither of them finished the opening race, at Bay Park on 3 January. Instead, Opert had to watch one of his Formula 2 B35s take the flag first, in the hands of its new owner, the New Zealander Steve Millen. Five days later, Rosberg won at Pukekohe as Kozarowitsky went out with a misfire after starting from pole. At Manfeild, Rosberg won again after getting the best of a dice with his team-mate and Tom Gloy's Tui. A runaway win over Kozarowitsky confirmed Rosberg as the Stuyvesant Champion at Teretonga with one race still to run. Four laps from the finish, Rosberg looked like winning that as well, but a puncture sent him into the pits and he had to settle for second place being Gloy.

While Rosberg was taking New Zealand by storm, Gilles Villeneuve was having a more difficult time in South Africa. A crash during testing meant that he had missed official practice for the opening round of the Philips Formula Atlantic series at Pietermaritzburg and his works B39 had started its

CHEVRON

first race from the back of the grid. As Ian Scheckter's March 77B won, Tony Martin finished second in his brand new B39, but Villeneuve came through the field to finish an encouraging third.

When the series moved to Kyalami a fortnight later, Scheckter won again, but Villeneuve could manage no better than fifth place, beaten by the B34 of the South African, Basil van Rooyen. Once Derek Bennett had produced a new car, Paul Owens was normally quite happy to be left to get on with developing and racing it. But as Villeneuve struggled with the B39, this was one of the few occasions when Paul needed his lifeline back to Derek. No matter what he did to the car they could not get it to grip enough at the back, so he got on the phone to Bolton for some advice from Derek. Derek's response was predictable. When he had tested the car in Britain it had been extremely quick and he was quite confident that there was nothing wrong with the design. 'Well, we're not winning out here,' replied Paul in desperation, 'so I suggest that you come out here and have a test in it yourself.'

Derek flew straight out before the next race, drove the car round Welkom for three laps and declared that it was not the car he had tested. Something had happened to change it. So he and Paul sat down and went through every component on the car, recalling every tiny alteration that had been made, either in testing or in rebuilding the car after Villeneuve's crash.

Gilles Villeneuve on his way to fifth place in the works B39 Formula Atlantic car at Kyalami on 29 January 1977. (*Photo Autosport.*)

Eventually Derek hit on a slight change to the construction of the chassis as the only thing that marked Villeneuve's production car out from his own prototype. He phoned the factory to prepare them, got straight onto the next plane home and built a new monocoque exactly to the original specification. A little over a week later, Derek was back in South Africa, having flown back with the new monocoque as his excess baggage.

They built up a new car in a day, ready for Villeneuve to race at Cape Town. Unfortunately, Villeneuve's confidence in the car had taken a knock and although it was much better in slower corners, he was still unhappy with its handling through the faster ones. Even so, he was dicing for third place in the race until he came round a corner to find Ian Scheckter's March broadside across the track. Leading comfortably, Scheckter had spun while trying to get past an unco-operative back marker, and Villeneuve ran straight into the side of him. The March did a somersault and landed upside down, leaving Scheckter with a broken ankle. The Chevron was badly damaged and so Villeneuve's fraught series of races came to an unsatisfactory end.

The disappointment of South Africa was hurriedly put behind them as Derek and Paul returned to Bolton where the company's busiest year to date was in full swing. Deposits on 45 new cars had been taken by mid-January and there was less than three weeks to go before the European Formula 2 Championship opened at Silverstone. One project was a particular focus of attention at the factory, and a great source of pride to the people who worked there because it brought together the names of Chevron and Ferrari.

Ferrari had decided that they wanted to supply a small number of V6 Dino engines to Formula 2 teams running Italian drivers. Trivellato were ready to move Riccardo Patrese into Formula 2 and so he was an obvious candidate for one of the engines. Seeing the drawings of the new engine Derek and Paul knew that it was unusually tall and would sit too high in the new B40 chassis. So when the V6 arrived in Bolton they set to work to lower it by $1\frac{1}{2}$ inches, so that the gearbox would come down to the right level and the driveshafts could be put on at a sensible angle. The only way to do this was to make a new, shallower sump. So Derek designed one, had it cast specially, and fitted it to the engine, along with a new oil pump.

After many long nights of hard work the car was completed shortly before the Silverstone race and rushed out to Maranello to be shown to Ferrari and tried out on their test track at Fiorano. The men from Ferrari were pleased with the appearance of the car, but threw their hands up in horror when they saw what had happened to their engine. In daring to alter a

Ferrari engine, Chevron had committed an act of absolute sacrilege and they were immediately forbidden to race the car. Paul Owens was taken into a meeting with Mauro Forghieri and Enzo Ferrari's son, Piero Lardi, and given a severe reprimand. After all the hard work that had gone into the car, Paul was rather taken aback by this reaction, but with Pino Trivellato interpreting for him, he got them to agree to test the engine as it had been modified.

They had to give Silverstone a miss while Ferrari got on with the tests, but Paul returned to Italy later in March, accompanied by Dave Wilson, who spoke reasonable Italian. The men from Ferrari told them that the engine had performed well on the dynamometer under static conditions, but when it was rotated through 45 degrees, in a technique they used to simulate cornering forces, there was a loss of power because the pumps were not scavenging properly.

Derek Bennett was not at the meeting, having entrusted the project to Paul, but his attitude was typically pragmatic. The car would not handle with the engine sitting up in the air. He had modified the engine. Now the car would work. As the parties involved sat round a table at Maranello, Paul got this point of view across forcefully. With equal force, Ferrari replied that they were not prepared to lower their engine, so Chevron must alter their car. The argument got more and more heated and after much shouting and thumping on the table, the meeting broke up acrimoniously, with Paul declaring that Chevron were no longer interested in pursuing the project because it would be detrimental to their reputation. Although that was exactly what he and Derek believed, it still felt extremely strange to be telling Ferrari that running their engine could be bad for Chevron.

The stalemate was eventually broken by Pino Trivellato, who carried on his own talks with Ferrari behind the scenes and came up with an apparent compromise in which Chevron agreed to build a car to run the engine in its original form, which would then be tested at Fiorano, back-to-back with a BMW-engined Chevron. In fact, rather than modify the B40 so that the engine could sit high in the car, they merely fitted the engine so that it protruded below the bottom of the chassis. 'You couldn't drive it very hard because the sump was always hitting the ground,' said Paul. As the sump distorted it would cause the pumps to seize and break up, acceleration would suffer and the lap times would get slower. The Ferrari car remained slower than the BMW car.

While all this was going on, the European Formula 2 season was well underway. With his B40-Ferrari unable to race, Patrese had made his Formula 2 début at Silverstone on 6 March in one of Trivellato's B35s from the previous season. Also on the grid in a B35 was Keke Rosberg, who had been a surprise last-minute addition to Fred Opert's line-up. After Rosberg had gone so well in New Zealand, Opert had talked to him about them doing Formula 2 together. Keke liked the idea, but as neither he nor Fred had any money, he failed to see how it could come about, so when Jorg Obermoser offered him a contract to race his Toj for another season, he signed. Six weeks later Rosberg was in Heidelberg, ready to test the Toj for the first time at nearby Hockenheim at nine o'clock the next morning. At around midnight, his phone rang. 'I'll never forget the night,' Rosberg recalls. 'It was Fred, and he says "I want to run you in F2". ' Keke reminded Fred of his contract with Toj, but Opert was insistent. He was so keen to run Keke that he had broken the golden rule and put his own money into a car for him. If Keke would do Atlantic for him in the States as well, he could juggle the budgets enough to make up what was still needed to go Formula 2. Rosberg told Opert he would think about it. 'At six o'clock that morning I was ready with my decision — I'm going to quit Toj.'

History has proved that Rosberg made the right decision, but it is one he still has a bad conscience about. Obermoser was a close personal friend and he was stunned and heartbroken when Rosberg broke the news to him that morning at Hockenheim. 'It was a terrible decision for me,' says Rosberg. 'But it really was a decision which I had to take: am I going to become an international racing driver, or am I going to go down the drain? The decision was correct, but it was a tough one. I sacrificed a friend on the way to becoming an international racing driver. The decision was correct, but you can never say it's worth it.'

The following week Rosberg put the year-old Chevron onto the third row of the grid at Silverstone. A confused start did not help his already slipping clutch and 10 laps into the race Rosberg went out as the clutch packed up altogether. But he had already done enough to mark himself out as a potential front runner — especially once his new car was delivered. One driver who did have a new B40 ready in time, complete with the latest version of Brian Hart's 420R engine, was Ray Mallock, who started Creighton Brown's Ardmore car from row two. After a couple of seasons struggling to make his mark in Formula 2, the Englishman surprised many with an impressive drive to second place as René Arnoux's Martini won the race. Also earning plenty of praise was Riccardo Patrese, who ended his Formula 2 début in sixth place in Trivellato's B35-BMW.

When the championship moved on to Thruxton in April Patrese was the sensation of the race as, with wheels locking and tyres smoking, he fought his way through from the third

Riccardo Patrese created a sensation when he led only his second Formula 2 race at Thruxton on 11 April 1977. His Trivellato B35-BMW finished fifth after a pit stop to replace a punctured tyre. (*Photo John Gaisford.*)

row of the grid to take the lead off Eddie Cheever's Ralt in the closing stages of the race. For eight laps Patrese hung on to his lead, but with only another eight to go the punishment became too much for one of his tyres and the Chevron dived into the pits with a puncture. As Brian Henton's Boxer beat Cheever to win the race, Patrese picked up fifth place.

It was a fine performance that had everybody talking about him, but Patrese's progress from Formula 3 début to Formula 2 race leader in just a year had not been as effortless as it might have seemed. Riccardo had been particularly daunted by Thruxton, a featureless airfield circuit with sweeping, fast corners and few landmarks. In the opening laps of practice he had struggled to learn the track and as the established stars flew past him through the fast corners he became a little demoralised. 'I said to myself, "Is it really what you want to do, to be a racing driver? Do you think you are in the right place? Or maybe it is better you go home". ' Fortunately, Riccardo persevered despite his astonishment at the speed of everybody else, and he eventually outqualified Keke Rosberg. Once he had led the race, any doubts Patrese had about his chosen career were banished for good. 'Since that moment, everything was much easier,' he recalls. 'But there was one moment when I was asking myself if really it was my job to be a racing driver.'

A week later at Hockenheim, Patrese took his best result so far. Jochen Mass's works March 772P won both parts of the race, but fourth place in the first part and second in the second gave Patrese third place on aggregate. Nürburgring was next on the itinerary, and Patrese put his BMW-engined B35 on pole position in one of those performances that marks a driver out as something special, and leaves those watching to gasp in awe. McLaren Formula 1 driver and acknowledged 'Ringmeister, Mass, was 1.8 seconds slower than Patrese as Riccardo put in a lap in 7 minutes 15.3 seconds. With Ensign Grand Prix driver Clay Regazzoni behind him on the grid as well, Patrese was suitably pleased with his own performance.

Unfortunately, he went off later in practice when he missed a gear trying to put in an even quicker lap, and Paul Owens was left with a lot of work to do trying to bash the monocoque back into something resembling its original shape in time for the race. Patrese led the whole of the first lap as Mass struggled to get past Regazzoni. But once through, Mass hounded Patrese relentlessly and the pressure told as the Chevron slid wide and deposited Patrese in the catch fencing. The Nürburgring race saw Alan Jones make his Formula 2 début in one of Fred Opert's B40s. But it was a disappointing race for the Australian as he ran without fourth gear and lost time in the pits when the rear wing worked loose. Jones had already moved into Formula 1, taking over Tom Pryce's drive at Shadow a few weeks earlier after Pryce had been killed in a horrifying collision with a marshal during the South African Grand Prix. Unhappy with the performance of Renzo Zorzi, Shadow were on the lookout for another driver, and Patrese's performance at the Nürburgring put him at the top of their shopping list.

Three weeks later he made his Grand Prix début at Monaco, finishing ninth in a Shadow. Patrese had to work hard on Pino Trivellato to get him to agree to his signing a two-year contract with Shadow, but he promised that winning the Formula 2 Championship would remain his top priority, and Formula 2 races to take precedence over Grands Prix where the dates clashed.

When the Formula 2 championship moved to Pau at the end of May, the Chevron line-up was its strongest yet, with four B40s in the first six places on the grid. On pole position was Patrick Tambay, making a surprise appearance in the Ardmore car. Guy Edwards had brought sponsorship from ICI and *Newsweek* magazine into the team and it was planned that he and Ray Mallock would share the driving. But since Mallock's second place at the opening race, little seemed to have gone right for the team and when Edwards failed to qualify at Vallelunga, he took the decision to stand down in favour of a star driver to improve coverage for the sponsors. As Tambay put the Hart-engined car on pole, with René Arnoux's Martini alongside him, two more Chevrons made up the second row — Jacques Laffite, back in one of Fred Opert's cars, and

Patrese. With Rosberg sitting right behind them in another of Opert's cars, Chevron looked poised for a good result.

Unfortunately, the race started and ended in chaos. Tambay jumped the start, hesitated and then stalled, which caused a pile-up on the grid. As Arnoux disappeared into the distance, Laffite found himself stuck behind Bruno Giacomelli's March and eventually went out when they tangled as he tried to take second place from him. That left Patrese holding third place when a thunderstorm flooded the track. The race was stopped and Patrese was classified third, even though his Chevron was in amongst a heap of cars piled up at the hairpin. Rosberg, meanwhile, was already out of the race, having lost fourth place when he hit a kerb and damaged a shock-absorber pick-up point.

Hitting kerbs was not an unusual occurrence for Keke Rosberg and his press-on driving style was beginning to attract criticism. The B40 had a tendency to understeer, which did not suit Rosberg's exuberant driving style at all, and Keke tended to really fling the car round to try and compensate. It had taken Fred Opert months to work out why the *insides* of the wheels in Keke's car were always bent. Hitting the kerbs and bending the *outsides* of the rims was understandable, but it took him some time to figure out that Rosberg was lifting front wheels so high in the air as he threw the car over the kerbs that it was the *inside* edge that was clipping the kerb as the wheel dropped back again. When he realised that driving with bent wheels did not seem to slow Rosberg down, Opert soon started putting three-piece wheels onto his car. If you hit a kerb — particularly on a street circuit, with a one-piece cast wheel — a piece would often chip out, sending the tyre flat and prompting a pit stop. But the three-piece wheels just bent and Keke carried on.

Although Opert's team was widely thought of as being works-supported, and he now based his cars at the Bolton factory, there was quite a lot of rivalry between his set-up and the works effort. Paul Owens engineered Patrese's car. He and Riccardo had become close friends and Opert would accuse him of favouring Patrese. Fred, meanwhile, was an unwavering fan of Rosberg and still rated Keke as the best, despite the attention being paid to Patrese. What Opert refers to as 'the Bolton way of doing things' often contrasted with his own approach and the two teams would set their cars up differently, particularly when Opert was trying to get American Goodyears to work on Rosberg's car in preference to the British ones. But Opert prided himself in being able to find the best mechanics in the world and with Dick Bennetts working on his car, Rosberg was not worried that he was losing out to Patrese.

In the meantime, Patrese carried on knocking at the door of that seemingly inevitable Formula 2 win, finishing second three times in a row. Patrese had continued to test the Ferrari-engined B40 at Fiorano, but with the project still in a stalemate, Paul Owens had put together a deal with Paul Rosche for him to run works BMW engines. Much as Riccardo would have liked to have raced with an Italian Ferrari engine behind him, he also wanted to win races and the BMW deal was too good an opportunity to miss. So he committed himself to completing the season with works BMW power in the works B40, which had been built up to replace the B35 he had crashed at the Nürburgring.

Patrese qualified the car on pole at Mugello, but was beaten into second place by Giacomelli in the works March 772P. At Rouen a week later, Patrese was further down the grid after delays in practice while they got a new narrow-track set-up, adapted from Geoff Lees' Formula 3 car, working properly. Meanwhile, Patrick Tambay was back in the ICI B40, and once again started from the front row. Again he made a slow start and Patrese's Chevron was one of three cars which pulled alongside him as they headed for the first corner. There was no way four cars were going to get through side-by-side. Tambay, on the inside, banged wheels with René Arnoux's Martini and as the Martini slewed across the track, the Chevron shot off up the banking and Tambay was out again.

Patrese slipped through unscathed and set off after Eddie Cheever's Ralt and Didier Pironi's Martini. He eventually passed Pironi in a breathtaking manoeuvre as they went flat-out through a sweeping, downhill, left-hand bend. But it was too late for him to do anything about Cheever, who crossed the line to become the youngest ever Formula 2 winner at 19 years old.

At Nogaro, Patrese was beaten into second place by Arnoux after a decidedly fraught weekend. With severe flooding in the area and the province of Armagnac declared a disaster zone, the race only just went ahead. Patrese barely made the circuit in time to qualify, after being trapped in the floods en route when Pino Trivellato drove his prized Mercedes 300 through what looked like a puddle but turned out to be a small river. In the race itself, Patrese survived a wheel-bumping session with Giacomelli and a dramatic spin in front of the pits on his way to second place, and he remained second in the championship, eight points behind Arnoux.

Two weeks later, at Enna, a Chevron finally won. But it was not Patrese's, it was Rosberg's. A week before, at Westwood in Canada, Keke had won his first Labatt's Atlantic Championship race in Opert's B39, and he came straight to Sicily with his enthusiasm renewed. After a string of disap-

Keke Rosberg on his way to victory at Enna in Fred Opert's B40 on 24 July 1977. (*Photo LAT.*)

pointments with engine failures, tyre problems and collapsing wings, everything came right at Enna. The new narrow-track rear end seemed to be working well with the American Goodyears and Keke put Fred Opert's Chevron on pole position for the first time, just 12 months after he had failed to qualify for the same race in the Toj.

The two-part race turned out to be far from straightforward, though, as Enna's notorious track surface played havoc with the cars. As Rosberg made a tentative getaway from pole position, Patrese dived through from the second row to lead the race, with Keke back in fifth place. But when the track surface began to break up, Patrese got caught out and lost the lead with a dramatic spin. The consequent puncture put him out of contention as Eddie Cheever's Ralt took over the lead, with Rosberg a distant second. As Cheever obeyed his pit signals to take it easy on the treacherous surface, Rosberg closed right up on him and he was only 0.3 seconds behind at the finish.

Rosberg made an even slower start to the second part of the race, and as he struggled through the first corner he came into contact with Freddy Kottulinsky's Ralt and his Chevron was pitched up into the air. Rosberg came down with a bump on the infield and by the time he could rejoin, he was way back in 13th place. Patrese soon made his way to the front again, but lost the lead for the second time when a suspension link pulled loose and he spun into retirement. With the track continuing to deteriorate, Cheever had been happy to let Patrese go, knowing that Rosberg was the only threat to his overall victory. After leading briefly, Cheever was equally content to let Arnoux take over the running.

But Rosberg was making spectacular progress, hurling the Chevron round in his usual fashion as he clawed his way back through the field. Cheever lost time with a spin, and suddenly Rosberg was in third place and catching him. With 12 laps to go, Keke charged past Cheever, and quickly pulled out the advantage he needed to claim the aggregate lead. Cheever fought desperately to get back on terms with him, and eventually spun into the catch-fencing in the attempt. Rosberg hung on to take second place behind Arnoux and the overall victory was his.

It was an emotional victory for everyone involved. For Rosberg it was the final vindication of his decision to join Opert's team and a powerful answer to those critics who argued that his driving style was too wild to win races. For Chevron it was a morale-boosting European Formula 2 victory after a five-year dry spell. For Brian Hart it was a welcome second win for his 420R engine. It was also the biggest day of Fred Opert's life as he proudly claimed the first Formula 2 victory for an American-owned team.

Overshadowed by Rosberg's triumph was the fact that another Chevron finished eighth at Enna — the B40-Ferrari, which had finally made its début, driven by Italian Lamberto Leoni. Leoni had driven a couple of races for the Minardi team, who had been running the Ferrari engine in their Ralts from the beginning of the year. Ralt had merely redesigned their chassis to fit the tall, V6 engine and the Minardi team had met with a singular lack of success, with Leoni even failing to qualify at Rouen. When Patrese signed his BMW engine deal, Leoni took over some of the testing of the Chevron-Ferrari at Fiorano, and midway through the summer the vital compromise was finally reached.

As Paul Owens kept the B40 scraping round the test track with Ferrari's original sump on, Mauro Forghieri and Piero Lardi Ferrari became increasingly frustrated at the lack of progress. There was some more thumping of tables and then they told Paul to go away and come back again in two weeks, when they would have solved the problem. 'Two weeks later, we arrived there to be greeted with a sump the same height as the one we had originally made, almost a copy of it,' says Owens. 'From then onwards we started to make progress.'

Ironically, Leoni was overshadowed during practice at Misano by the driver who had replaced him in Minardi's Ralt-Ferrari, 19-year-old Elio de Angelis. The young Italian was virtually unknown when he brought his Trivellato B38 into second place in the Monaco Formula 3 race in May of that year, beaten only by Didier Pironi, who stepped down from Formula 2 to take a win for Martini. De Angelis had later switched to a Ralt to win the Monza Lotteria European Championship round, and just six weeks later he was at Misano making his Formula 2 début. Running with the latest version of the Dino engine, the Ralt-Ferrari looked more promising than it had all year and de Angelis qualified fifth fastest, two rows ahead of Leoni.

But nobody was seriously looking at Leoni to continue Chevron's success. With Rosberg giving the race a miss to defend his Atlantic championship lead in Canada, Arturo Merzario put the Enna-winning B35 onto the front row of the grid, while Patrese lined up behind him in the works B35, still eager to claim that first Formula 2 win. Merzario led the first part of the race away, but ran wide at the first corner; Arnoux's Martini went out in a first corner tangle; Giacomelli's March got stuck in second gear; and the surprise leader at the end of the first lap was de Angelis. Merzario was soon challenging hard for the lead, with Patrese snapping at his heels. But de Angelis refused to be intimidated and blocked Merzario's overtaking attempts time and time again. Then Patrese decided he would try and pass both of them and dived for the inside, just as de Angelis moved across on Merzario again. Merzario moved across to avoid hitting de Angelis, and Patrese locked up and ran straight into him. Patrese bounced over the grass and back into the race, a few places down. But Merzario was out, and furious with the tactics of de Angelis.

Eventually Eddie Cheever was able to achieve what the others had not, and pressure de Angelis into making a mistake. As de Angelis left his braking too late and sailed straight on at a corner, Cheever took his Ralt through to win, while Leoni followed him through to finish second, 0.7 seconds behind.

Full of confidence after his first heat showing, Leoni shot straight into the lead of the second heat, revelling in the apparent power advantage of his Ferrari engine. As Cheever struggled to stay with him, he missed a gearchange and ran wide, giving up seven seconds on Leoni. He fought hard to reduce the deficit, but Leoni was still well clear when the chequered flag came out and the Chevron-Ferrari took a totally unexpected aggregate victory. Coming just two weeks after Rosberg's win it was a great boost for Chevron, and it also justified their stand over the Ferrari engine. Ferrari themselves were delighted. They had achieved their objective sooner than they had dared to hope and, having succeeded, they could now end their time-consuming direct involvement in the project and bow

FAMOUS VICTORIES IN FORMULA 2

out gracefully. They continued to supply engines for another year, but their enthusiasm seemed to have waned and Paul Owens reckons they never produced an engine as good as the one Leoni won with at Misano.

Unhappy with their Ralts, Minardi persuaded Trivellato to loan them Leoni's B40-Ferrari for de Angelis to drive in the final race at Donington. But de Angelis badly damaged the car there in testing when he hit a concrete retaining wall after the car jumped out of gear. The team worked day and night at the Chevron factory to rebuild the car in time for the race, but it did not run as well as it had before the crash and a subdued de Angelis could only manage sixth place in the race.

Chevron's best showing in the last two races came from Rosberg, who came in second to Giacomelli at Donington. Patrese drove a new works development chassis at Donington as his regular car was on its way to Japan for the Suzuka Formula 2 race. His European season ended on a disappointing note as the new B42 went out with gearbox problems. But a week later he made up for it by winning the Suzuka race.

With that elusive win finally in the bag, Patrese went on to Macau to meet up with the development car which had been shipped out with a Hart-BDA engine for him to race in the Formula Pacific Macau Grand Prix for Bob Harper's team. Starting from pole, he was beaten away by Alan Jones in Teddy Yip's Ralt. But Jones' engine cut out briefly halfway round the lap and, as the Ralt slewed round, Patrese's Chevron clipped it. With Jones out of the race, Patrese struggled back to the pits and rejoined the race in 11th place. Ten laps later he was in the lead, and he went on to win comfortably from Steve Millen in his B35.

On the day the European Formula 2 Championship was coming to a close at Donington, the BP British Formula 3

Lamberto Leoni raises both arms in triumph as he takes the chequered flag in the B40-Ferrari to score a surprise win at Misano on 7 August 1977. (*Photo Jeff Hutchinson.*)

CHEVRON

Derek Daly won the 1977 BP Formula 3 Championship in Derek McMahon's B38. Here he bounces over the kerbs at Monaco. (*Photo Tim Tyler.*)

Championship was being decided at Thruxton, and once again it was a Chevron driver who came out on top as Derek Daly won the race in his B38 to take the title. The previous year in Formula Ford, the Dubliner had been dogged by ill luck as former stock car racer, Derek Warwick, stole the glory and won the European Formula Ford Championship. But everything came right for Daly in the Formula Ford Festival at Brands Hatch in November as he took his Hawke to a clean sweep, winning his heat, quarter-final, and semi-final, and then going on to beat Warwick in the final.

Daly had worked as a labourer in an iron ore mine in North West Australia to raise the money for his season of Formula Ford. But now he was in debt again and desperately in need of a backer if he was to graduate to Formula 3. He had already approached Irish motor sport enthusiast, Derek McMahon, a couple of years before, and been turned down. But after his success in the Formula Ford Festival, journalist Robert Fearnall thought it would be a good idea if Derek was reintroduced to 'The Big D'. So they met again in the congenial surroundings of the British Racing Drivers' Club's annual dinner, and McMahon agreed to run Daly in Formula 3. McMahon already knew Derek Bennett and had himself raced a Chevron GT (a fifth-hand B6 that had originally been Digby Martland's) in Ireland in 1970. Although he suspected that the new March might be potentially quicker than a B38, he was convinced that the Chevron would be far more 'user friendly' to a team with such limited experience, so they went to Bolton and bought a B38.

Daly found the process of learning to set up and drive a car with wings and slick tyres a daunting one, but midway through the season he felt he was on top of the learning process. Stephen South had established himself as the pacesetter with his March 763, and by the British Grand Prix meeting at Silverstone in July, Daly felt ready to take him on. For 15 dramatic laps of the final he held South at bay. Then the Chevron slid wide at Becketts and in an instant the March was alongside. They headed for the high-speed left-hander at Chapel side by side, with neither driver prepared to give way. When South tried to cut across to the apex of the curve, Daly refused to back off and the cars touched, sending South cartwheeling through the air.

Although he was rushed to hospital, South turned out to have only minor injuries, but Daly was widely accused of being responsible for what had looked a very serious accident. Although upset by the criticism, Derek refused to become dispirited. He had sensed for the first time that he could win and he was not prepared to give up now. So a week later, he took himself off to Croix-en-Ternois for a round of the European Championship — and won his first Formula 3 race. A few weeks later he did it again, this time at the Osterreichring where he outbraked Nelson Piquet's Ralt to snatch the lead halfway through the supporting race for the Austrian Grand Prix.

Back in Britain with a new confidence, Daly won his first BP Championship round at Brands Hatch in September. The championship was being led by Eje Elgh, a young Swedish protégé of Ronnie Peterson, who had won three races in a works B38 sponsored by Plastic Padding. But another win at Mallory Park brought Daly just two points behind Elgh. His third win in a row, at Donington, gave him the championship lead with only the Thruxton final to go. Elgh's chances evaporated in a first corner collision and Daly went on to beat Geoff Lees in the second works B38 to win the race and the championship.

Hindered by lack of finance, Lees had a disappointing year, only winning once, at Thruxton in June, where he headed Derek Warwick and Derek Daly in a Chevron clean sweep. Things had been equally disappointing for Warwick, who had taken a string of second places but could not find the extra straight line speed he needed to come up with a win. In desperation, he had switched to a Ralt late in the season, but a Formula 3 win continued to elude him.

In Europe, the 1977 season opened with a sensational victory in the opening round of the European series by 19 year-old Beppe Gabbiani in a Trivellato B38. It was only the

Eje Elgh (28) led the BP Formula 3 Championship for much of 1977 in his works B38. The Swede took the first of his three wins in the rain at Oulton Park on 26 March. A loose rear wing hampered Derek Warwick's challenge, but his B38 followed Elgh into second place as Geoff Lees made it a Chevron 1-2-3 in the other works car. (*Photo Eric Yuill.*)

Italian's second car race, after a successful career in karting. But as Trivellato's other teenager, Elio de Angelis, came to the fore, Gabbiani's season fell apart with a series of accidents that culminated in a dramatic exit from the championship final at Vallelunga. Gabbiani somersaulted out of the race at the very corner where his father was spectating. Beppe was unhurt, but his father had to be taken to hospital suffering from shock.

De Angelis followed in Patrese's footsteps by winning the Italian Championship and had already made his name in Formula 2 by the end of the season. Another Chevron driver who looked set to join him there for 1978 was Derek Daly, who had taken time off from his string of Formula 3 wins to make his Formula 2 début at Donington in October, finishing a highly impressive fifth in the ICI B40.

CHAPTER 14

'It's no more dangerous than driving a racing car'

CHEVRON'S success in 1977 confirmed Derek Bennett's company as one of the world's leading manufacturers of customer racing cars. It had recovered from the knocks of the oil crisis and the three-day week, production was back at record levels, and there was now more of an air of permanence about the company as it forged ahead into its second decade.

As the company had got bigger, many things had changed, but the essence of Chevron remained the same. The factory was still the place where Derek Bennett built his racing cars, and although he now had a workforce of around 30 people, they all knew that he would ask nothing of them that he was not prepared to do himself and their respect and admiration for him as a designer and a person remained undiminished.

In fact, Derek was probably the one thing about Chevron that had changed the least over the years. His success meant that he no longer had to worry about money, but he had no aspirations towards a lavish lifestyle. He had bought himself a BMW, and could be persuaded to buy his clothes from Kendal's, the more fashionable of Manchester's department stores, but these were his only concessions to the good life. He had moved house a couple of times, but he still lived with his mother in a semi in Whitefield.

When he made some money selling the first Chevrons he had immediately suggested that his parents should move to a more comfortable chalet bungalow in Simister. He put his money into it as well and moved there with them. Despite his lack of affinity with the work Derek did, his father followed the progress of Chevron closely and was tremendously proud of his son's achievement. But golf remained his first love and when his health began to deteriorate, they moved again to Ashbourne Grove, Whitefield, so that he could get to the golf course more easily. After Arthur Bennett died of pneumonia in 1973, Derek stayed at Whitefield with his mother.

He was still no closer to marriage than he had ever been, but he no longer felt the peer pressure to conform as his friends and family had got used to Derek's life being somewhat out of the ordinary. Despite his wariness of commitment, he had twice met people who he felt he wanted to marry. But ironically, they had been reluctant to commit themselves to his demanding lifestyle and had turned him down. Perhaps wary of becoming too dependent on one person, he had then let different girlfriends occupy different places in his life, and although he had an open-ended engagement to one of them, he continued to have close friendships with the others.

Just as Derek turned to different girlfriends in different circumstances, so he would spend time socially with a variety of people. On his regular outings to restaurants with John Bridges and his wife, he would go with a girlfriend. But often he would just call in on people alone whenever he was in need of company. The visits were never pre-arranged and whether the doorbell that rang belonged to Paul Owens, Derek's sister Wendy, or Derek Alderson, the greeting was always the same: 'Hello, I was just passing. Are you in?' They all knew that the route from Bolton to Whitefield did not pass anywhere near their front door, but Derek was always a welcome visitor. People who would have resented anyone else catching them unawares like that, would happily invite Derek in, knowing that he accepted them totally how he found them and would be glad of the company, as well as a share of whatever they were cooking.

Although he would drop in on people he worked with, Derek also needed the continuity of keeping in touch with old friends whose ideas he respected. People like Derek Alderson, whom he could use as a sounding board, revived the spirit of Jim's Snack Bar as they talked cars into the early hours of the morning. But even with people he knew so well, Derek seemed unable to relax. Through the most intense discussions he would be poised nervously on the Aldersons' settee, endlessly crossing and recrossing his feet in a curious shuffle that ground shoe polish into the flattened pile of the carpet.

If you were the person Derek came to when he wanted to talk about cars all night, you could be forgiven for thinking that cars were all he ever talked about. But other people would see a different side of him. He continued with his Sunday morning visits to Dave Willars' house, where he was regarded as a friend of the whole family. For a while, Dave's job took him abroad a lot, but Derek would still visit his mother for his customary Sunday morning chat. The one thing he never talked to Mrs Willars about was racing and she enjoyed the way he would talk animatedly about any subject that came up, often prompted by something in the Sunday newspaper. He still visited Jimmy Horrocks regularly as well, even though Jimmy had sold out his interest in the company back in 1968. There, too, racing was generally off the agenda and Jimmy's wife Maria enjoyed talking with Derek for hours about what

Jimmy referred to as 'all kinds of sensible topics.'

Derek was nothing like as single-minded about motor racing as people tended to assume. His fertile imagination and his prodigious work rate enabled him to achieve more than most people in half the time it would have taken them. As a compulsive thinker, he was still left with plenty of time to consider other things. He was always interested in hearing about Dave Willars' work overseas, and he was an avid reader of magazines like *Time* and the *National Geographic* when he had time to kill on foreign trips of his own. On the rare occasions when he had some spare time, or could be bullied by a girlfriend into taking some time off, he liked to go walking in the Pennines or the hills of the Lake District, climbing to where he could look out over a greater horizon and wonder at real perfection. But such moments of reflection were rare and closely guarded, and even in the calm of the Lake District his enquiring mind never stopped as he developed a fascination with the crash site of a World War Two aircraft, which he would visit to examine the remnants of the wreckage and speculate on the cause of the crash.

There were obviously times when Derek needed the company of people he felt close to and when he would have liked a family of his own. But he was honest enough to realise that he could never have committed enough of his time to making a successful family life and he steered clear of taking on a responsibility that he could not meet. Instead, Chevron became his family, and somewhat ironically he found himself coping with a much greater responsibility, with the families of everyone who worked for him dependent on him.

The financial worry of keeping the company successful

Derek created this setting-up rig for making the final, detailed adjustments to Chevrons before they left the factory. (*Photo Tim Tyler.*)

enough to be able to pay the wages made Derek uncomfortable, and he made no secret of his dislike of the growing pressure on him to be a businessman rather than a racing car designer. Although he was a man of particularly strong will, he still came under constant pressure from others to change things, or to expand, or to become involved in projects which did not instinctively appeal to him. Unwilling to let his own company slip too far out of his own control, he resisted most of the pressure, but some things he did let himself be talked into — like the ill-fated road car project.

From the moment the B16 first appeared, people used to talk about what a fabulous road car it would make, and indeed Jo Siffert did have a roadgoing one built for himself. But by 1972 the thinking was that they should not adapt a racing model but design their own road car from scratch. John Bridges had some industrial premises near Chorley, where the Red Rose sports car team was based, and the project was set up from there. Bob Faulkner was becoming increasingly disenchanted at Hawker Siddeley, and so Derek had suggested that he come and work full time on the road car. Denys Dobbie also had a stake in the project and when he wound up his DART sports car team, his team manager, Dave Wilson came temporarily back into the Chevron fold to work on the road car as well.

Like the B16, it was to be a mid-engined, two-seater with a central monocoque and tubular subframes. Jim Clark was brought in again to work on the body design, and a prototype body was completed. But the chassis took longer to get right and all the time there was uncertainty about exactly what market they were trying to produce the car for, whether it would be an out-and-out luxury sports car, or an affordable, lower specification one. With the initial choice of a BMW engine ruled out as too expensive, plans switched to a Ford unit. Meanwhile, Derek showed little interest in the project beyond producing the initial designs and as the indecision continued and the high cost of putting the finished car into production became apparent, the project foundered.

The other big question Derek was always being asked was 'When are you going to build a Formula 1 car?' After Peter Gethin won the Race of Champions in 1973 it seemed an obvious question to ask, and as the Chevron B24 was the only Formula 5000 car at the time with the new deformable structures that had been made mandatory in Formula 1, speculation grew that the chassis would be adapted for Formula 1. The stories began to link Gerry Birrell, and his strong Ford connections, with a Chevron Formula 1 project. Birrell's death brought any such plans to an end and the Chevron Formula 1 stories did not re-emerge until 1977, when Trivellato were said to be ready to commission a Grand Prix car and

Riccardo Patrese was being touted as the driver. Such rumours are often no more than people thinking out loud in the presence of journalists. Once in print they need neither be confirmed nor denied, but they do nothing to hurt the profile of the company and can easily become self-fulfilling.

Although Patrese does not remember any plans for a Trivellato Formula 1 Chevron, Derek was actually working on a Formula 1 design at that time. It was still the one big challenge in motor racing that he had not tackled, but he had fought shy of it for some time, not wanting to be involved in a Formula 1 project unless it could be on his terms. Through Formula 2 he had got a taste of the politics and the machinations of big-budget, corporate-sponsored, international motor racing, and he did not like it.

Grahame White had left Chevron during 1975 when they had come to the conclusion that he was a luxury they could not afford. He had fulfilled his initial purpose of raising the profile of the company and countering some of the effects of the North-South divide, but in the long-term he was not generating enough additional business to pay for himself. White in turn was frustrated at the company's inability to afford to do some of the things he would have liked it to have done and it was agreed that the company would continue to use him only on a freelance basis. His leaving removed a lot of tension at the factory, where there was a certain amount of resentment towards anyone who was paid a lot of money and never got their hands dirty, but it also put Derek back in the front line of dealing with teams and, increasingly, their sponsors.

Keeping sponsors happy was not something he felt able to cope with, and there would occasionally be awkward situations when a disgruntled team would demand his presence to solve problems that were often of their own making, and then get disappointed when his mere appearance at the race track did not work miracles. Derek was not prepared to work for people who wanted the impossible, so he resolved that he would only build a Formula 1 car on his own terms.

Brian Hart was among those encouraging him to look at

Chevron's North American agent, Fred Opert (right), was thought by many to be an obvious choice to run a Chevron Formula 1 team. Patrick Tambay was just one of the many top drivers he put into Chevrons in Formula 2 and Formula Atlantic.

Formula 1. Brian's links with Fred Opert and Fred's success in Formula 2 with Rosberg seemed to point towards a Chevron Formula 1 project with Hart engines and Opert as team manager. Fred now believes that the inherent conflicts between his methods and 'the Bolton way of doing things' would have made such a tie-up impossible. But it seemed a logical step to Hart and he discussed it at length with Derek. He and Opert were also united in their wish to see Chevron expand their operation, believing that Derek ought to be able to match March in terms of volume car sales. Dave Wilson held the same views and felt Chevron should be more heavily involved with full works teams to promote themselves. But Derek continued to be daunted by the enormous cost involved in running a works team along March lines, and at the end of the day he did not really want his company to become any bigger than it already was.

Eventually someone might well have come along with a pot of gold and given him the *carte blanche* that he wanted for his Formula 1 project. But in the meantime, he decided he would work away quietly on a low-budget prototype, which he could use to stimulate interest in a full-scale effort when it was completed. A separate room was set aside at one end of the mill, and Derek retreated from the factory floor as he went back to first principles, working once again on his own to produce a prototype for its own sake, with no thoughts of customers or production lines. But Derek's progress on his Formula 1 car was uncharacteristically slow because, for the first time in his working life, he had discovered an interest that had nothing to do with cars. It was hang gliding.

During 1976, a racing acquaintance who sold hang gliders had persuaded Derek to buy one. Hang gliding was still very new in Britain. It was barely two years since the first national hang-gliding competition had been held and the number of people involved was small. There was a pioneering spirit of adventure to it all. For his part, Derek had always wanted to fly. His childhood fascination with model aircraft had led him to dream of becoming an airline pilot. He soon came to realise that his poor health would make that impossible, but his interest did not wane and he took a few flying lessons with Derek Alderson. The concept of man-powered flight had always fascinated him too, so the chance to try a hang glider was something he could not resist.

Jim Crawford was back in the Chevron family at this point. His Lotus Formula 1 deal had turned sour and the only works drive he had been able to get was behind the wheel of one of Chevron's two Volkswagen vans (Derek's brother-in-law, Geoff Smith, drove the other), making a twice-weekly run to London and all points south to collect parts.

'IT'S NO MORE DANGEROUS THAN DRIVING A RACING CAR'

The first time Derek flew the hang glider was the only time Jim ever saw him excited. He and Neil Edwards went out from the factory with Derek to nearby Winter Hill, a moorland peak famed for its television transmitter mast. It was a comical sight as Derek, strapped to his hang glider, kept running down the hill, failing conspicuously to get off the ground, while Jim and Neil waited to help him haul the glider back up to the top for another attempt. Eventually they all ended up running down the hill together, Derek in the harness and Jim and Neil holding a wing-tip each. Finally his feet came a few feet off the ground and he 'flew' for a couple of hundred yards. 'All you could hear was "Yeeeaaaahhh!",' Crawford recalls. 'I'd never heard anything like it in my life!' They were just as bemused a couple of minutes later when the normally sullen Derek Bennett reappeared, walking back up towards them, beaming from ear to ear and laughing uproariously.

Derek's sense of humour was always something that those who knew him well valued tremendously. He had a keen eye for the ridiculous and was quick to point out the funny side of people's behaviour. The absurd notion of Derek Bennett flying through the air like a bird could not do anything but make him laugh.

Once he was off the ground there was no holding Derek back and he launched himself into hang gliding with an enthusiasm that he had not felt since his early days racing cars in the 1950s. Frustrated by the high cost of increasingly complex motor racing technology he had told me little more than a year earlier how he sometimes wished he could go back to the simplicity of spaceframes and the old way of doing things. 'My first enthusiasm came 20 years ago,' Derek said. 'But the world was a lot different. I don't think I've changed, but the world has changed around me. What seemed like a good idea than perhaps isn't such a good idea after all'. Motor racing

Tucked away in a small room of his own, Derek worked on his Formula 1 project, the B41. The new-found distractions of hang gliding meant that this was as far as he got with it. (*Photo Tim Tyler.*)

had moved away from the intuitive 'fix it as you go along' techniques which had suited him so well. He was talented enough to be able to build cars the new way, but it was not fun any more. Hang gliding enabled him to go back in time, working with simple constructions to tackle fundamental engineering problems — and this time there was the added bonus that he got to fly. It was as if he had found a way to ride in his old model aircraft.

Derek made no secret of this new-found enthusiasm and tried to talk a number of his friends and employees into going hang gliding. Dave Willars gave up when exhaustion set in before he could get out of the bushes, Paul Owens tried it once on a very shallow hill and did not think much of it, but Derek Faulkner and John Lewis, who was an assembler at the factory, bought Derek's first glider from him when he progressed to a newer model after a few months. Derek Faulkner crashed the glider and dislocated his shoulder; for about six months the shoulder was too weak for him to have contemplated hang gliding again. After that he decided it was all too dangerous, anyway, as the injury rate among the Chevron flyers had continued to mount.

John Lewis wound up unconscious in hospital after a crash. But before that, Derek Bennett had also crashed badly, injuring his back. There was something rather comical about Derek Faulkner and Derek Bennett hobbling off on their crutches to visit John Lewis in Bolton Royal Infirmary, just down the road from the factory. But they did not realise at the time how lucky they had been, especially Derek Bennett, whose accident was a chilling forewarning of his later crash. Flying off Winter Hill, he had turned towards the hillside and suddenly lost airspeed. The glider stalled, the sail collapsed under him, and he plummeted to the ground, hitting his head on the hillside. Tommy Humphreys and John Lewis were in a group of people who had gone up to watch Derek and there was an air of panic as they all ran down the hill, where they found Derek unconscious. To their relief he came round after about 10 minutes, but as they walked him back to the car he remained incoherent for some time.

As they all recovered from their various injuries, the others decided it was time to give hang gliding up, but Derek was undeterred. The exhilaration of flying and the intellectual lure of getting to grips with the evolving technology were too potent for him to give up now that he had tasted them. With his friends, literally, falling by the wayside, Derek looked for new companions to share his interest with. Graham Hobson had been hang gliding since 1973 and had set up a hang gliding school at Lobden. The person who had sold Derek his original glider had got in touch with him to explain who Derek

Bennett was and to ask him to keep an eye on him and see that he 'didn't do anything silly'. So he had arranged to meet Derek at Rivington Pike, a hilltop close to Winter Hill, just outside Bolton. Having satisfied himself that Derek seemed to know what he was doing, he did not see him again until some time later, when Derek joined the Pennine Hang Gliding Club, on the recommendation of a group of pilots whom he had met at Winter Hill.

One of those pilots was John Hudson, from Rochdale, who went on to become a pioneer of Microlite aircraft, and Derek quickly realised that he could learn an awful lot from the experience of people like him and Graham Hobson. Soon he was flying at every available opportunity, working normal hours so he could get away at five o'clock to go hang gliding, much to the astonishment of Chevron's staff, who had grown used to him all but living at the factory. Sometimes he would even pack up his hang glider and disappear during the day when a call came in from the gliding club grapevine to say the wind conditions were perfect on one local hill or other.

The experienced men came to be impressed by his enthusiasm and the speed at which he was developing into a good pilot, and in February 1978 Derek went away on a hang gliding holiday with a group of them to Las Palmas in the Canary Isles. He took a long-standing girlfriend with him and it was the only time anyone could remember when he had actually taken a holiday, going out and buying a plane ticket for something that was not a business trip.

Graham Hobson and John Hudson were both in the party and Hobson was impressed at how competent Derek had become, coping well with the difficult terrain around Gran Canaria, which had lots of cliffs and small landing areas. Derek seemed completely caught up in the excitement of the technical innovations that were sweeping through the hang gliding world, and was happy to have found something that took his mind away from the pressures of work. Paul Owens remembers Derek saying to him 'When you're up there, there's only you to worry about.' Derek had been famed over the years for disappearing when the pressures got too great, and 200 feet up in the air was the ultimate place to be able to disappear to when he wanted to be unavailable.

People close to Derek were becoming increasingly concerned about his hang gliding. George Walker was a motor trimmer who had known Derek since Chevron first set up in Bolton. He worked further up Chorley Old Road and Robert Ashcroft had asked him if he could come down to the factory and cover the seats and the dashboard on the Clubmans cars they were building. From then on he trimmed the seats of every Chevron that left the factory, at first fitting in the work in the evenings, and then, when the operation grew bigger, spending all day, every day from January to Easter down there. 'I probably lost a lot of my own business because of it, but I was happy doing it,' he says.

Soon after Derek returned from the Canaries, George got talking to him while he was working on his hang glider in the factory one evening. He was experimenting with a system of wires connected to a twist grip, which would enable him to stop the wing tips dropping in flight.

'Eee, Derek. I wish you'd leave this thing alone,' he told him.

'What do you mean?' came the reply.

'You've got so many people relying on you,' answered George.

'But I'm not married,' Derek came back.

'But you've got too many wives and families that rely on you,' said George.

Derek obviously resented the suggestion that he should feel any more responsible for his workforce than he already did, and he defended his valued escape fiercely. 'If you remember those early years,' he said. 'If I hurt myself driving a car, that was all right. Now, if I hurt myself enjoying myself — that's all wrong.'

To others who voiced their concern for his safety, rather than trying to appeal to his sense of responsibility, Derek offered reassurance. When Dave Willars' mother worried about him, he would shrug off the risk, saying hang gliding was no more dangerous than driving a racing car. He used exactly the same words to Paul Owens the day before his fatal accident. He had asked Paul if he wanted to come up on the moors with him, and Paul had replied that he thought it was about time he gave it up. 'Those words still stick in my mind,' says Paul, 'it's no more dangerous than driving a racing car. I said, "You must be crazy, Derek. Forget it." '

The next day, Sunday 12 March 1978, Derek was back at Lobden Moor, taking part in a competition organised by the Pennine Hang Gliding Club. Such competitions were held quite regularly and Derek, inevitably, would enjoy the extra element of competition. The pilots would have to complete various tasks and fly round marked courses. Graham Hobson was watching as Derek negotiated a slalom course, making tight turns only about 50 feet above the ground. After one turn he had let his airspeed fall too much and the hang glider stalled. One wing dropped and the hang glider went into a spin, turning back towards the hill as it fell. Hobson believes that Derek panicked and, instead of pulling back on the bar to try and increase his airspeed so that he could regain control, he swung out of his prone position and tried to prepare for a crash landing.

Out of control, the hang glider continued to fall, and Derek hit the hillside head first. He was immediately knocked out, but he came to as they took off his crash helmet and put him into the ambulance. 'Don't worry. I'll be all right,' was the last thing he said before they rushed him to hospital. But Derek had taken such a heavy knock that the bruising to his head continued to swell, restricting the oxygen supply to his brain and sending him into a coma. At the hospital in Rochdale the doctors carried out an exploratory operation and became worried about a blood clot on his brain. But they needed the permission of a relative before they could go any further.

They eventually found Derek's sister Wendy's phone number, but she was out, celebrating the birthday of June's son, Andrew, in Blackpool. When they found that number, the phone was out of order. It was only when Wendy returned in the early evening that the news of the accident could be broken to the family and permission granted for the operation. Wendy rushed straight to the hospital and told them she wanted Derek transferring to the neurological unit at North Manchester Hospital. Within half an hour everything was sorted out and she followed the flashing lights of the ambulance as it made the journey between the two hospitals. The surgeons began operating immediately. Wendy contacted Paul Owens, who rushed straight to the hospital. They waited together through much of the night as the surgery continued.

The next morning, Peter Gethin got a phone call from Paul Owens. Shocked by the news, Peter immediately phoned Jackie Stewart to ask if he could find him the name of a brain specialist. Stewart came back with the name and phone number of an expert surgeon, who Peter quickly contacted. The specialist contacted the hospital and spoke to the surgeons there. He reported back to Peter that they had done everything they could. There was nothing he would have done any differently.

Derek's sisters and Paul kept a constant vigil at his bedside, and the waiting area next door was constantly full of people. Few of them were allowed to see Derek, but they all wanted to be there, hoping against hope that their presence could help him. His sisters would ask Derek to squeeze their hand if he could hear them, and for the first few days he was able to respond with a gentle squeeze. But the coma deepened and soon even that basic contact was lost.

On 22 March, on his 11th day in hospital, at the age of 44, Derek Bennett died.

CHAPTER 15

Postponing the inevitable

THE news of Derek Bennett's death devastated his workforce in Bolton. Everyone felt it like a family bereavement. His accident had happened at the busiest time of the year for the factory as they rushed to get as many cars as possible ready for the imminent start of the new season. Work had to carry on as normal, but the death of their leader had extinguished a spark.

Derek had, of course, completed all the design work on the latest range of cars some time before his death, so his absence initially created few practical problems. But practice for the opening round of the European Formula 2 Championship at Thruxton began only a couple of days after Derek's death, and when he arrived there Paul Owens found his customers were not only mourning the death of Derek Bennett, but of Chevron Cars as well. Getting a record 10 new cars ready for the opening race would have been a difficult task under any circumstances, but now any delay or problem was treated as a sign that the company was in crisis.

Fred Opert was particularly worried when his new B42 for Keke Rosberg had not arrived a few days before the race. Over the winter Rosberg had been back to New Zealand where he had won the Peter Stuyvesant Formula Pacific Championship for the second year running in one of Opert's B39s. Opert had run a second car for Rosberg's North American Atlantic rival, Bobby Rahal, who took an aggregate victory in one of the two-part races and finished the series in third place.

Then, the week before Thruxton, Rosberg had been the shock winner of the non-championship International Trophy Formula 1 race at Silverstone, bringing the Theodore TR1 through to victory in appallingly wet conditions. Keke was becoming a hotter property by the minute, but Opert did not underestimate the scale of the task he faced if he was going to beat Bruno Giacomelli's works March to the championship. Chevron got their 10 B42s to the line in time, but March were already way ahead of them on development and Derek Daly was the best-placed Chevron driver finishing sixth in his ICI-backed B42-Hart as Marches took the first five places, led by Giacomelli's works 782-BMW. Seventh was Beppe Gabbiani, showing well on his Formula 2 début in a Trivellato B42-Ferrari. The media attention at Thruxton, though, was focused on another *débutant* as former world motorcycle champion Giacomo Agostini drove his very first car race in a Trivellato B42-BMW. He struggled to qualify and obviously had a lot to learn as he finished the race last. Rosberg, meanwhile, did not finish the race at all, going out with electrical problems.

Two weeks later, there were no Chevrons in the first six as Bruno Giacomelli and Marc Surer took the first two places at Hockenheim in their works Marches. Jochen Mass was seventh on aggregate in the ICI 'Star Car', with Rosberg eighth, delayed by a slow puncture, and Daly ninth after a pitstop with gearchange problems.

Rosberg had qualified his B42 on the front row at Hockenheim, but Mass and Daly had been well down the grid in both races and the team was openly expressing its concern about the handling of the Chevron and its apparent lack of straight-line speed. Daly had moved into Guy Edwards' ICI team with personal backing from Derek McMahon and a car provided by Chevron. Just before Derek Bennett was killed, he had been to Mugello for a test session with Daly and he had been concerned that the car was not performing as well as it had when he had it set up at Oulton Park. Paul Owens felt the ICI team was going in the wrong direction in its attempts to get the cars right, but without Derek Bennett to take over the development, Paul felt helpless to prevent the damage that Chevron's reputation was suffering. So he decided to put together a development car and he called up Riccardo Patrese to ask if he would do some testing in it.

Patrese had only met Derek Bennett on a handful of occasions and remembered him only as 'a quiet person'. But he and Paul had developed a close friendship and although Riccardo was heavily committed with Arrows in Formula 1, he could see that Paul was in trouble and he did not hesitate to offer him his help. Patrese tested the car at Donington and changing the rear shock-absorber pick-up points seemed to cure it of the handling problems which Derek Bennett had experienced at Mugello. Confident that the car was basically sound, Paul asked Patrese to race it at the Nürburgring in an effort to silence the doubters. Delayed by problems in practice, Patrese started the race from the sixth row, but he was challenging Eddie Cheever's March for fourth place when he spun. With all four-tyres flat-spotted he retired from the race.

Ironically the message that Chevron should not be written off came, not from Patrese, but from Rosberg. Fresh from winning the Westwood round of the Labatt's North American Atlantic Championship in one of Fred Opert's B45s, Keke had

CHEVRON

Opposite: Alain Prost made an impressive Formula 2 début at Pau on 15 May 1978, driving an Opert B40. Prost's only race in a Chevron came to an end when his Hart engine blew. (*Photo LAT.*)

stormed round the Nürburgring in 7 minutes 12.4 seconds to put his B42-Hart alongside Giacomelli's March-BMW on the front row. At the start his first gear proved to be too high as he was swamped by the field, only getting away in ninth place. But he fought his way back and crossed the line to start a thrilling last lap side by side with the Marches of Alex Ribeiro and Eddie Cheever. At the finish Ribeiro just snatched victory, but Rosberg was tucked right under his rear wing and Cheever flashed across the line only another half-a-second back. Meanwhile, a disgruntled Jochen Mass trailed in to finish in eighth place as the ICI team's problems continued.

For the next race, at Pau, Patrick Tambay took over the 'Star Car', bringing about an immediate change of fortunes as he put it onto the front row of the grid. Anxious to make up for his disastrous performances for the team the previous year, he muscled ahead of Brian Henton's March to take the lead at the first corner and soon had a commanding advantage. But halfway through the race his car began trailing a plume of smoke from an oil leak and as he nursed it across the line to start the last lap the engine let go with a bang and Tambay was out. It was a bitter disappointment for everyone, not least Brian Hart. 'That sticks in my mind as one we should have won,' he says. 'We broke a stud and we botched it up, and it wasn't good enough — but there weren't any spare engines.' Tambay was still classified sixth as Giacomelli won from Eje Elgh, taking his best result of the year in one of Opert's Chevrons.

The regular Chevron runners had been given quite a shock in practice by a 23 year-old Frenchman who had used some money from Elf to make his Formula 2 début in one of Opert's year-old B40s. His name was Alain Prost and both Fred Opert and Brian Hart had been eyeing his performances in a Formula 3 Martini and wondering how they could do a deal to get him in a Chevron-Hart. When the package came together for Pau, Prost astounded everyone by qualifying the B40 fifth fastest, ahead of Daly, Rosberg and Elgh. Unfortunately he only lasted a few laps into the race before he missed a gear and over-revved the Hart engine. Opert's beliefs about Prost's talent had been confirmed, but there was no money to even think about running him again and Opert reluctantly left him for someone else to discover. After all, he already had his own world champion to be!

Behind the scenes, Paul Owens had been involved in an enormous row with the ICI/Ardmore team, threatening to take back Daly's car if they did not stop their public criticism of it. At such a difficult time for Chevron, Owens was even more prone than usual to speak his mind, and his determined stand eventually brought about a reorganisation of the team as, with the

POSTPONING THE INEVITABLE

CHEVRON

Derek Daly won twice for Chevron in 1978. His B42-Hart is pictured at Donington, where he qualified faster than eventual winner Keke Rosberg, only to go out in one of a series of dramatic first lap pile-ups. (*Photo John Gaisford.*)

direct approval of ICI, he stepped in to take over the running of Daly's car himself. The results were immediately encouraging when Daly ran a good third at Pau until he hit a kerb and spun in the closing stages.

Daly's disappointment was short-lived because less than a fortnight later he was on the winner's rostrum at Mugello after a dream race that he still describes as the race of his life. Feeling confident at Mugello after his pre-season testing there, Daly led from start to finish, holding the works Marches of Surer and Giacomelli at bay. Both were within a second of him at the finish, and Surer hounded him throughout the race, pulling alongside on a couple of occasions and forcing Derek to use the kerbs, and occasionally the grass, to stay ahead of him. Paul Owens and Brian Hart joined Derek McMahon and Derek Daly for a night of fairly wild celebrations. For Daly it was the biggest day of his career so far, while for Owens it brought the welcome relief of success after two months of trauma since Derek Bennett's death.

Three days later, a Manchester jury returned a verdict of Accidental Death at Derek Bennett's inquest. Many of his friends, believing him infallible after so many years of wondering at his genius, refused to believe he could have done something so mortal as to have made a mistake. There was a widespread belief that he must have had a blackout or a heart attack, maybe connected with his earlier ill-health. But the pathologist said that there was no evidence of any heart condition, or other contributory medical condition, and Derek's fellow hang gliders insisted that the accident had happened because of his failure to correct a mistake.

Almost as if to prove that Derek Bennett's genius was not

dead, Chevron won again the following weekend as Derek Daly took his second victory in a week at Vallelunga. This time, the luck was running Daly's way as he lost the lead early on, under pressure from Giacomelli, but snatched it back in determined fashion on the last lap as the March slowed, overheating.

Giacomelli was back on top at Rouen, but Keke Rosberg took his turn to win for Chevron at Donington at the end of June, ensuring Chevron of their most successful Formula 2 season ever with three victories. Rosberg had started the first part of the race back on the fifth row of the grid, but by the end of 12 laps he had climbed up to second place, with only Brian Henton's March ahead of him. Then Henton began to slow as petrol from a leaking fuel gauge got into the cockpit, and Rosberg was through to win. Fourth place in the second part was enough to preserve his advantage and give him the win on aggregate. For Brian Hart, Rosberg's win was 'enormously satisfying' as it demonstrated, just as Daly's had done at Mugello, that his 420R engine was now a match for the works BMWs. The weight advantage of its light alloy block over the iron block of the BMW was now providing a significant performance advantage through certain corners, which could more than compensate for a slight disadvantage in straight-line speed at most circuits.

Little more than a month after Prost's Formula 2 début, Nigel Mansell had his first taste of the formula at Donington and demonstrated that having a Chevron did not always guarantee you a dream début. A scholarship instigated by Donington's owner, Tom Wheatcroft, had been set up to fund a one-off Formula 2 drive for an up-and-coming British driver. A panel of journalists had selected 24-year-old Mansell, who had recently run out of money to continue his efforts in Formula 3, and the award paid for him to make his F2 début in the second ICI Chevron B42.

Unfortunately Mansell ran straight into the organisational problems that continued to dog the team, and which were complicated at Donington by the appearance of Elio de Angelis in a third B42-Hart, the Italian having defected from the Minardi team after some dreadful performances in their B42-Ferrari. Mansell did not make matters any easier for the hard-pressed team when he crashed his car in testing during the week and by the time practice arrived the mechanics were tired from late nights rebuilding the car, and overstretched with three cars to look after, especially with Team Manager Pat Mackey away ill.

Minor problems with his car kept Mansell off the track for too long during practice and team boss, Guy Edwards, returned from winning a British Formula 1 Championship race at Oulton Park on the Saturday to find that Mansell had failed to qualify. It was a great embarrassment to all concerned. 'I suppose everyone will write me off now,' said a forlorn Mansell.

Most of the drivers had two weeks before they were due to race again at Nogaro. But Keke Rosberg was running to an altogether different schedule. From Donington he went straight to Paul Ricard to practice the ATS for the following weekend's French Grand Prix. After struggling with the uncompetitive car there, he dashed to catch Concorde so he could fly to the United States for a midweek 4 July Atlantic race at Lime Rock. He wrote off his Opert B45 in practice, took over his team-mate Eje Elgh's car for the race and finished sixth. With Lime Rock out of the way it was almost time to start practising for the Formula 2 race at Nogaro, and Rosberg arrived back in France, the personification of jet lag. Obviously suffering from the effects of his schedule, he was dicing for eighth place when his engine died a few laps from the finish.

The next two Formula 2 races clashed with North American Atlantic rounds, so it was decision time for Opert and Rosberg. Keke reckons he clocked up 450 flying hours commuting between his drives that season and says that if any of the young drivers he now manages came to him with a schedule like that he would tell them they were insane. But then, the enthusiasm for being able to race as much as he wanted had not worn off and he felt he owed it to Fred Opert to fit in as many races as he could alongside his ventures into Formula 1. Although Opert's team continued to be one of the very best prepared and presented on the Formula 2 scene — he had even flown his local sign writer, 'Hank the Brush', from Paramus,

Nigel Mansell should have made his Formula 2 début in an ICI B42 at Donington on 25 June 1978, but a string of practice problems meant that he failed to qualify. Mansell is pictured here during pre-race testing. (*Photo Geoff Werran.*)

CHEVRON

New Jersey, to Bolton for a weekend to paint the bodies of his 1978 cars because he did not think anyone in Europe could do them as well — it was still working miracles on a shoestring. Apart from some backing from Fred's longtime sponsor, Valvoline, Rosberg's car continued to be run on Fred's own money and the entire operation was a masterpiece of organisation as Opert worked out of hotel rooms and airport lounges. His travel arrangements were especially legendary. He always seemed to carry a wad of leftover airline tickets which he had obtained at virtually no cost. All you needed to be able to use them was an atlas, as Rosberg explains: 'From Frankfurt to Chicago, there's a non-stop flight. Except, when I went with Fred's ticket it took me 24 hours to get there. Fred was the most incredible travel organiser that anybody has ever seen in racing. He would get you at the cheapest rate from A to B, but mostly you had to go via Z and X.'

With Opert's funds rapidly reaching their limits and Rosberg wilting under the jet lag, they decided to concentrate on the Atlantic championship, which Keke still had a good chance of winning. Opert still thinks Rosberg would have been happier with the exposure staying in Formula 2 would have given him, but Rosberg believes he was not pressured into the decision and does not regret dropping out of Formula 2 at that point. Atlantic in the States was almost as competitive as Formula 2, and Rosberg would have to work just as hard to win. He also welcomed the chance to make up for the disappoint-

Keke Rosberg took Chevron's last Formula 2 win at Donington on 25 June 1978 in Fred Opert's Hart-engined B42. (*Photo John Gaisford.*)

ment of losing the previous year's championship to Gilles Villeneuve at the end of an increasingly fraught season. 'Between Gilles and me it was tough,' Rosberg recalls. 'I mean, it was knife between your teeth — and we weren't talking, either.'

Midway through the year he had been leading the series, but things started to go wrong when the throttle stuck open at St Felicien and he hit a concrete wall head on, putting himself in hospital with concussion and an injured foot. He still had a chance of winning the title at the final round on the Quebec City road circuit, but he lost time in the pits after a collision with Bobby Rahal's Ralt, and Villeneuve's March won the race and the Labatt's Canadian Championship.

Now, a year later, he was poised to win the extended Labatt's North American series, and as Arturo Merzario took over his Formula 2 car at Misano, Rosberg put himself firmly in the Atlantic championship lead with a win at Hamilton, Ontario. Sadly, it all fell apart in the final round again, held this time at Montreal's new Isle de Notre Dame circuit. A broken spark plug brought Keke's B45 into the pits and third place was enough to give Howdy Holmes the title in Doug Shierson's March.

With Rosberg away from the Formula 2 scene, Chevron's other winner, Derek Daly, was also having his concentration lured away from Formula 2 as he established a foothold in Grand Prix racing — first with Hesketh, and then with Mo Nunn's Ensign team, for whom he scored his first world championship point in the Canadian Grand Prix that October. Daly managed a couple of third places in his B42, at Nogaro and Enna, but the last four races were all won by Bruno Giacomelli, who won the European Championship easily after winning eight of the 12 rounds. Only March and Chevron scored points all year and Daly was the best-placed Chevron driver, in third place behind Giacomelli and his team-mate, Marc Surer. Rosberg was fifth, despite missing the last three races.

Only a handful of other Chevron runners picked up points. Eje Elgh never improved on his second place at Pau, while Elio de Angelis' best result of the year was a third at Misano in the ICI B42-Hart. Geoff Lees moved into Formula 2 late in the year with a B42-Hart bought for him by businessman Jack Kallay, and Misano was also his best showing as he followed de Angelis home in fourth place. Clay Regazzoni had taken over the Minardi team's BMW-engined B40 for that race and started ahead of all the Chevrons on the second row. But he failed to finish when the engine blew. Arturo Merzario picked up two points driving Opert's B42 in that race to add to the one he had scored for finishing sixth at Mugello in the second ICI B42-Hart.

CHEVRON

The Ferrari V6 engines supplied to Minardi for de Angelis, and Trivellato for Gabbiani, proved unreliable and Ferrari axed the project completely at the end of the year. Miguel Angel Guerra took over at Minardi when de Angelis walked out, and seventh at Donington was his best showing. Gabbiani persevered for the whole season and did little to dispel the wild reputation he had brought with him from Formula 3. He did manage to score a couple of points when he finished fifth at Vallelunga, although he had to elbow Rosberg off the track to do it.

Peter Gethin also made a return to Formula 2 in 1978, but as a team manager not a driver. Now retired from racing himself, he bought a clutch of B42s with Hart engines on behalf of wealthy young Americans, John David Briggs and Don Briedenbach, who had tried Can-Am and now wanted to learn the ropes in Formula 2. It was an experience Gethin did not get a lot out of as both drivers struggled to qualify for much of the season. 'They both tried very hard,' he said, 'but I didn't enjoy walking from the back of the grid as often as I did that year.'

Although the B42 was Chevron's best selling Formula 2 car and 21 were built, the Formula 3 market became more competitive as Ralt established themselves on the scene and sales of the B43 fell considerably behind those of the B38. Dave Wilson was keen for Chevron to run a works team in Europe and sponsorship from F & S Properties brought Dutchman Michael Bleekemolen the drive. The Frenchman Patrick Gaillard was added to the works team when he came up with some more sponsorship.

Bleekemolen was fifth in his first race at Silverstone's Inter-

Patrick Gaillard leads his Chevron teammate Michael Bleekemolen through the trackside snow at the Osterreichring on 16 April 1978. The race was eventually won by Anders Olofsson's Ralt, but Gaillard won two European Formula 3 rounds later in the season with his B43, and Bleekemolen took one victory.
(*Photo Tim Tyler.*)

Elio de Angelis was a controversial winner of the 1978 Monaco Formula 3 race. Here his B38 leads the March 783 of Teo Fabi. (*Photo Tim Tyler.*)

national Trophy meeting in March, but that same day the B43 was being given its first win at Misano, where Trivellato had done it again and produced a race-winning young Italian for the third year in a row. This time the driver was Siegfried Stohr and the win came in only his second Formula 3 race.

The next Chevron win was not by a B43, but by a B38, which was driven by no less a personage than Elio de Angelis to a controversial victory at the Monaco Formula 3 race. De Angelis decided to try and do what Didier Pironi had done the year before and revive his flagging fortunes in Formula 2 by winning the glamorous Monaco Formula 3 race. Driving the same car which he had driven to second place for Trivellato in the 1977 race, de Angelis chased Gaillard's works B43 for the lead in the final until, with seven laps to go, he made a rash overtaking move on the inside at the Station Hairpin and bumped wheels with Gaillard. The works car reared up drunkenly on two wheels before crashing into the armco, while de Angelis darted through to win. Stohr brought his B43 in second and Jean-Louis Schlesser was sixth in Gaillard's B38 from the previous year.

Robbed of the glory of taking his first Formula 3 win at Monaco, Gaillard came right back and won the following weekend at Imola instead. Two weeks later he won again at the Nürburgring, but in the second half of the season the Ralt of Jan Lammers developed an advantage and Gaillard had to be content with a string of second places. Towards the end of the year Gaillard met with more opposition from the likes of Alain Prost and Anders Olofsson and, as Lammers won the European Championship, Gaillard slipped back to third. Bleekemolen, meanwhile, only won once, at Enna, where he beat his team-mate to head a Chevron 1-2.

Although moving the works Formula 3 team into Europe was potentially good for export sales, Chevron suffered by not having a works driver in the British Championship, which remained a vitally important showcase. After winning the BP series two years in a row, Chevron had no-one who could answer the two Brazilian discoveries, Nelson Piquet and Chico Serra, who made it a contest between Ralt and March. Derek Warwick was the only driver who could run with them consistently, and he won the Vandervell series in his Ralt as Piquet made it a clean sweep for Ron Tauranac's company by taking the BP title.

Jim Crawford had spent the previous year in Switzerland, working for Chevron's agent there Freddy Kessler, who ran Toyota Switzerland. He came back with enough money to buy a second-hand B38 and planned a comeback in Formula 3. In only the second race of the year, Crawford was lying third at Thruxton, sandwiched between Piquet's Ralt and Serra's March, when he got a wheel off the dry line on one of the high-speed corners and rolled spectacularly out of the race. The first racing car he had ever been able to buy himself was destroyed, but Kessler stepped in with a new B43 for him. However, Kessler had started building his own Toyota engines and Jim's was never a match for the Novamotor units. A third place at Oulton Park was the best Crawford managed and his effort petered out before the end of the season. Chevron ended the year without a single Formula 3 win in Britain. Only the under-financed Philip Bullman came close, being disqualified from victory at Oulton Park for overtaking under a yellow flag, and finishing second to Piquet at Donington in his Alan Docking B38 before his money ran out.

During 1978 sales of Formula Atlantic cars also continued to fall back. For the second year running there was no Atlantic series in Britain, but Chevrons continued to dominate the scene in Ireland. Patsy McGarrity had won the 1977 Championship in a new B39, but the 1978 series was dominated by newcomer Eddie Jordan, who left his job at the Bank of Ireland to concentrate on becoming a racing driver, and won eight championship rounds in the three-year-old B29 originally driven by Richard Morgan.

Chevron's sports car market also continued to decline in 1978. The two-year-old B36 design was still being made to order, but only four were sold in 1978, compared to nine the year before. As the World Championship continued to sink into insignificance, only the French ROC team kept up a serious Chevron challenge, winning the 2-litre class at Le Mans in 1977 and 1978. Their 1977 performance was Chevron's best showing at Le Mans as Michel Pignard, Jacques Henry and Albert Dufresne finished sixth overall.

With Formula 2 the only area in which sales were still buoyant, and Ralt waiting in the wings to move in on that territory too, the people who made up Chevron after Derek Bennett had to work hard and fast to come up with a plan that would secure the company's future. Derek had not left a will, so what he would have wished could only be guessed at. His controlling interest in Chevron passed to his mother, who in turn handed it over to his sisters. Many people thought of June and Wendy as complete outsiders who had no previous interest in the company. But June knew a fair bit about the running of Chevron from her days working in the office, and Wendy had been constantly aware of Chevron through her husband Geoff's work there. They knew enough to know that it was going to be a tremendous struggle to keep the company viable without Derek as its kingpin. But they also felt that they owed it to him to try and do just that, and so they sat down with the senior men at Chevron to thrash out a plan of action.

By August they were ready to announce the structure of the new Chevron Cars. Dave Wilson was to be Managing Director, taking over from John Bridges, who had assumed the role on Derek's death, while Bridges himself would become Chairman. Paul Owens was made Racing and Development Director, and Nigel Dickson was given the title of Finance and Production Director. Nigel had first worked at the factory in the days of the B8 when he had persuaded Bromsgrove College of Further Education that it was a legitimate place for him to carry out the work experience part of his sandwich course for a Higher National Diploma in Automotive Engineering. After completing the course he had worked as a mechanic, first for Jürg Dubler on his Formula 3 Chevron B15, and then with the DART and Red Rose sports car teams. He eventually came to work full time at the factory in 1973, and after a year building B23s he was drawn into trying to unravel Chevron's tangled accounts. He ended up becoming Company Secretary, taking over much of the administrative and financial work that had been done previously by Doug Linton.

But the headline news in the package was that Arrows' Formula 1 designer, Tony Southgate, had been appointed Chevron's consultant designer. The calm of the announcement hid the turmoil that had been gone through before it could be made. When Derek's sisters, as majority shareholders, supported by John Bridges, had made Dave Wilson Managing

CHEVRON

Director, Paul Owens had resigned. Unlike Dave's, his association with Derek went back virtually into his childhood, and he felt that this enormous personal investment in the company had been overlooked. For so long, the embryonic Chevron had been just him and Derek and he felt that those long years of virtually unrewarded labour deserved greater recognition. And underneath all that, he could not believe that Dave Wilson could have Chevron 100 per-cent at heart in the way that he did. Paul accepts that he would probably not have been the right person to run the company in the long term. But in the short term, it hurt not to be asked, or even to have a say in who was asked. Paul withdrew his resignation when Dave Wilson appealed to him not to go, and he was touched when Dave argued that this was not what Derek would have wanted, and told him how much the company still needed him.

One area where Paul's view did carry some weight was in the appointment of Tony Southgate. While the friction in Bolton grew, Paul had carried on with his own development programme for the B42, acutely aware that Chevron had to start thinking of keeping their customers into 1979, when there would no longer be any new Derek Bennett designs to reassure them. Ground effect was finding its way from Formula 1 into Formula 2 much faster than anybody had expected and Paul designed some ground effect side pods with skirts to put on

Dave Wilson on the factory floor in 1978 in his new role as Chevron's Managing Director. (*Photo Tim Tyler.*)

Tony Southgate (left) and Paul Owens confer with Riccardo Patrese during tests of the new B48 Formula 2 car at Donington in October 1978. (*Photo Tim Tyler.*)

a development B42. Although he was pleased with his own developments, he felt that ultimately he was a development engineer and not a designer and Southgate's appointment was announced practically on the same day that Derek Daly tested Paul's new-look B42 at Silverstone.

Paul believed that a 'name' designer was vital to maintain customer confidence in Chevron, and Southgate took over the brief to produce a 'wing car' version of the B42 for the following season. In retrospect it might have been better for Southgate to have designed a complete car from scratch. But at the time Southgate's commitment to Arrows meant that the time he had available for Chevron was limited, while Chevron could not afford to use him full-time or to scrap the B42 and retool for an entirely new car. So a brand new design remained the plan for 1980 if Southgate's interim Formula 2 car could get them through 1979.

When the B48 appeared for the first time, being tested by Riccardo Patrese at Donington in October, it bore little outward resemblance to the B42 on which it was based, thanks largely to Southgate's Arrows-inspired bodywork, which replaced the distinctive Chevron full-width nose with a narrower snub nose containing the radiator, and front wings. The front suspension had also been moved inboard to give a better airflow to the flared side pods. Patrese gave the car its début at Suzuka on 5 November and finished an encouraging third.

Dave Wilson came up with a deal to run Bobby Rahal in a works B48 the following season, and Pino Trivellato stuck with Chevron, putting Siegfried Stohr into a B48. Patrick Gaillard raced a second works car on occasions and Alan Docking ran Huub Rothengatter in another B48, but other customers

241

were hard to find, particularly since Fred Opert had parted company with Chevron. Opert did not see how Chevron could deliver the goods without Derek Bennett, and so he opted out of Formula 2 to take up the job of Team Manager for the ATS Formula 1 team, on the recommendation of Keke Rosberg. Despite all the hopes that were pinned on it, the B48 proved to be a disappointment and Paul Owens struggled to get to grips with its shortcomings throughout the season. Rahal's fourth position in the opening race at Silverstone was only matched once all year. Stohr fared better and managed a couple of second places before switching to a March midway through the season.

The story was pretty much the same in Formula 3, where Derek McMahon ran a couple of works B47s for Bernard Devaney and Stefan Johansson, backed up by private entries for Michael Roe and Eddie Jordan. The car was only ever competitive in the rain and Devaney gave it its only win at a very wet Silverstone in May. Radical modifications were tried to improve the car, but the drivers had all lost faith and only Devaney was still racing a Chevron at the end of the year. Jac Nellemann raised hopes for the B50 Super Vee version of the car when he won at Donington in May, but again that failed to be translated into sales. Motor racing is a precarious business in which a manufacturer is only as good as his last car, and Chevron's reputation had crumbled in less than a season.

Faced with poor sales of the B47 and B48, Chevron had looked around for other markets and throughout the year various projects got under way. There was talk of a Formula Ford chassis, Paul Brown and Nigel Dickson worked on a car for the new Sports 2000 category, and by September hopes were

Derek Bennett always had a soft spot for animals. As a child he once brought home a stray dog, and at the factory in Bolton he adopted a stray cat. The cat had its own cat door to enable it to come and go as it pleased and Derek's staff joked that he gave it better food than they got in the works canteen. Three days before the factory closed its doors for the last time the Chevron cat left, never to be seen again. (*Photo Tim Tyler.*)

POSTPONING THE INEVITABLE

Derek Faulkner (left) and John Lewis at work on the B51 Can-Am car on which Chevron's hopes of survival were pinned. (*Photo Bolton Evening News.*)

being pinned on a Can-Am car as Chevron's predicament became increasingly dire. When the order books dried up, some of the workforce were kept busy fabricating parts for Formula 1 teams, but it seemed that the variety of plans that were put into action were concerned more with finding a use for existing equipment and labour than with making a concentrated effort to secure Chevron's future.

Commissioning an outside designer to produce a car was now financially out of the question, so Paul Brown and Nigel Dickson emerged as Chevron's own in-house design team. Brown had joined Chevron as a fabricator at around the same time as Dickson, but had progressed to the drawing office where he had worked closely with Derek Bennett, helping to put his concepts and designs onto paper. Dickson had no design experience but welcomed the opportunity to put his HND to practical use.

While they got their heads together to design a simple, cost-effective Sports 2000 car, Dave Wilson went to America, still intent on finding the 'big deal' that would rescue the company. His initial idea was to look at the potential in USAC oval racing, but just before leaving he called in on a Formula 1 test session at Silverstone and met up with Keke Rosberg, who was driving in Can-Am for Paul Newman and Bill Freeman's team. Keke suggested that he take a look at Can-Am as well while he was over there. So, after a largely unproductive look at the USAC racing, Dave went on to a Can-Am race and met Bill Freeman and his Team Manager, Peter Hemming. They were interested in what Chevron might have to offer, so Dave agreed to come back to the next Can-Am race, three weeks later, with the layout of a Can-Am car on paper. He went back to Bolton and presented fledgeling designers Brown and Dickson with the brief.

243

Three weeks later, he was back in America with some basic sketches of the new car. Freeman was sufficiently impressed to arrange a meeting with Paul Newman and they sat in the airport at New York and hammered out a deal. With the B51 Can-Am car about to become a reality, Wilson got in touch with Count van der Straten, whose team was also in Can-Am, and by the end of July he had an agreement with Newman/Freeman for Chevron to produce a prototype and a production run of six cars — four of which would go to the Newman/Freeman team and be known as Budweiser Spyders, and two of which could be supplied, as Chevrons, to VDS. With a cash deposit from Newman they were able to finance the building of the prototype and Brown and Dickson got to work to combine a new honeycomb monocoque with as many of the components as they could use, or modify, from Derek Bennett's unfinished Formula 1 project.

Although Wilson believed he had done the 'big deal' that would save Chevron, time was ticking away as the company's financial resources ran out, and potential buyers were being courted, with the Can-Am orders providing a useful incentive for the company to be bought as a going concern. Sadly, mutual distrust among those running the company was now so rife that no potential deals came to fruition. American Peter Gregg had plans to use Chevron's resources for a USAC project and he came the closest to buying them out, but agreeing on a price proved impossible. Derek's sister June was taking a Master's Degree in management at Lancaster University but she still felt ill-equipped to untangle the complexities of Chevron's situation.

The Can-Am prototype was ready for Geoff Lees to give a quick shakedown at Silverstone at the beginning of November before it was flown to California for its official trials with Newman's team. But the financial pressures continued to close in. A week before Christmas the two dozen staff were put on temporary lay-off until 2 January. But when the New Year arrived the production line remained at a standstill. John Bridges had put up his home as collateral against some of Chevron's debts, and when the bank decided to call in its loan, he was forced to put his farm house up for sale. Then on 30 January 1980, the bank pulled the plug completely and Chevron had to call in the liquidator.

Dave Wilson continued his frantic trips across the Atlantic, securing a promise from Paul Newman that he would pay half the total cost of his cars immediately if the company was bought as a going concern. But two weeks later no buyer had been found and Newman took his deal off the table as Chevron's creditors filed into a meeting with the liquidator.

CHAPTER 16

The Chevron tradition lives on

CHEVRON Cars was eventually bought from the liquidator in May 1980 by the consortium of Robin Smith, Laurence Jacobsen and Les Cuthbertson, who moved its assets to premises on Smith's farm near Glasgow. Smith and Jacobsen had raced Chevrons themselves for a number of years, but many people were keen to see the company remain in Lancashire, close to its roots. But in the end, only Manchester-based Bob Howlings put in a bid, and this was beaten by the Scots' offer. They confined themselves mainly to producing the B52 Sports 2000 car and selling spares, and in October 1983 they, too, were bought out, by Chevron's present owner, Roger Andreason, who moved the company to his premises in Winchester.

The most recent new cars to carry the Chevron badge have been Sports 2000s and Formula Fords, but the company has become increasingly involved in rebuilding and supplying parts for older Chevrons as more and more of them resurface in historic racing. Indeed Derek Bennett's Chevrons have continued to thrive since the death of their designer, producing racing successes that none of the new Chevrons have been able to match.

When Derek died, his B41 Formula 1 project was sold to Graham Eden, who completed the car for the 1979 British Formula 1 Championship. With sponsorship from Durex, Eden announced an award scheme for several British drivers, who would each drive the car in a number of races. Tiff Needell was the first driver and he gave the B41 a promising début at Zolder in April, finishing second, only 0.2 seconds behind David Kennedy's Wolf WR4 after an exciting four-car tussle for the lead. Unfortunately, the conventional Chevron was always going to be at a disadvantage against more modern ground-effect cars, and as these started to filter into the series, so the B41 slipped back.

Changing drivers every few weeks interrupted what was in any case a limited test programme and the project fell apart as Ray Mallock, David Leslie and Kim Mather tried in turn to get to grips with the car. In the end, Needell returned to

CHEVRON

Graham Eden bought Derek Bennett's B41 Formula 1 project and completed the car in time for the 1979 British Formula 1 Championship. Here the car, with Tiff Needell at the wheel, leads Hervé Regout's B42 at Zandvoort on 4 June. (*Photo Tim Tyler.*)

take sixth place in the final race. Then a year later Mike Wilds gave the car one final outing before Eden sold it, finishing fourth at Silverstone.

On a more successful note, Formula Atlantic had returned to Britain in 1979, and with it came Jim Crawford, engaged in another comeback mission. Returning to Bolton from Switzerland at the end of his salaried job as Freddy Kessler's racing consultant, he was led inevitably to the Chevron factory and went back to driving their van for a while. Sitting in the back of the workshop there was Keke Rosberg's North American Atlantic B45, and when Fred Opert turned up, Jim offered him a shoebox of Swiss francs for it. Fred accepted the offer, and Jim borrowed an engine to make a slightly late start to the Hitachi Atlantic Championship. It took Jim until the end of May to get the car set up well enough to beat Ray Mallock's Ralt. But although he won another seven races after that, Mallock's lead in the championship was unassailable and Crawford came in the bridesmaid once again.

The following year Crawford put a 2-litre Swindon BDX into the B45 to contest the Formula 2 category of the British Formula 1 series, which he won comfortably. His seven Formula 2 wins also included an overall victory in a wet race at Oulton Park in September. Chevrons were a popular choice for the Formula 2 class and Crawford led home a string of five of them at Mallory Park in May. With the help of his sponsor, Plygrange Racing, Crawford also put Chevron briefly back into Formula 2 during 1980, when he took in a couple of European Championship rounds in June.

Outclassed by the newer ground-effect cars, Crawford flung his B45 round Silverstone in spectacular fashion and was trying to wrestle ninth place from Manfred Winkelhock's March 802 when he damaged the car's nose in a slightly overambitious attempt to pass. Two weeks later he finished 10th at Zolder.

In sports car racing, Scottish garage owner Tony Charnell was talked into racing his updated B31 at Le Mans by Ian

THE CHEVRON TRADITION LIVES ON

Bracey. They did not finish the race but Charnell found he had been bitten by the Le Mans bug and he went back a year later, with Robin Smith co-driving for the second time, along with Richard Jones and Frederic Alliot. The Hart-engined car was running well at dawn on the Sunday morning when something broke as Charnell was travelling down the Mulsanne Straight at maximum speed. It bounced off the barriers and flew into the trees, but somehow Charnell stepped from the wreckage unhurt. The following year, Charnell, Smith and Jones were back with the car rebuilt around a new B36 monocoque. This time they finished the race, in 17th place, and won their class.

Later in 1979 Charnell teamed up with Martin Raymond for the Brands Hatch round of the World Championship for Makes, the Rivet Supply Six Hours, winning his class again from a fine third place overall. When Brands Hatch hosted the second round of the championship early the next year, Charnell entered the car again for himself and Raymond. Another good result looked on the cards as Raymond challenged the Lancia Montecarlo turbo of eventual winner Riccardo Patrese for second place. But then Raymond spun at Westfield and stalled the car. Unable to restart it, he climbed out and had just begun to walk away when two other cars touched at speed. One of them hit the abandoned Chevron and bounced off it into Raymond. He was thrown through the air and killed instantly.

Charnell had planned to do a full World Championship season with Raymond but, devastated by the freak accident, he gave up racing immediately. However, there was still a Chevron win in the 2-litre Group 6 class at Le Mans that year, taken by the ROC Simca-powered B36 of Sotty, Hesnault and

Chevrons won the 2-litre class at Le Mans four years running, from 1977 to 1980. Tony Charnell won the class on his third attempt, in 1979, sharing his updated B31 with Robin Smith and Richard Jones. (*Photo LAT.*)

Derek Bennett's Chevrons kept winning through the 1980s. Here Mike Wilds heads for victory in the Thundersports race at Thruxton on 8 July 1984 in the 2-litre B36 he shared with Ray Bellm. (*Photo John Gaisford.*)

Laurent, which came in 17th overall.

On Easter Monday 1983, a new British national sports car formula, Thundersports, began at Brands Hatch and many of Derek Bennett's Chevrons were given a new lease of life. Four Chevrons took part in that first race and two successful drivers from Chevron's early days, cousins Steve Thompson and Alan Rollinson, co-drove a B19 to fourth place overall and a class win. In June, Oulton Park's famous Gold Cup race was run for the new Thundersports cars, and 10 years after Peter Gethin had won the race in his Formula 5000 B24, a Chevron won again as the bigger cars fell by the wayside and the 2-litre B19 of Vin Malkie and Richard Budge came through to win. For Vin, who had helped build B19s when he worked at the Chevron factory, winning the Gold Cup was a dream come true and a success in the best tradition of Derek Bennett's cars. Chevron's other outright win in Thundersports that year went to James Weaver and Edward Arundel, who took their 2-litre BDX-engined B36 to victory at Thruxton.

As the big Can-Am cars in the series found their reliability, the chances of outright victories for the Chevrons diminished, but Mike Wilds and Ray Bellm led home a Chevron 1-2 at Thruxton in July 1984 as their Hart 420R-engined B36 beat the similarly powered B26/36 of Richard Piper and Tiff Needell. Piper put a 3-litre Cosworth DFV into his car for the following year, and he and Needell won again at Brands Hatch in April.

THE CHEVRON TRADITION LIVES ON

The early 1980s also saw the return of increasing numbers of Derek Bennett's first sports and GT cars to the tracks as historic racing continued to grow. Through much of the 1970s, Chevron B8s had languished in garages and barns as examples of that unsaleable commodity — the obsolete racing car. Some were converted to open 'spyder' form in an attempt to prolong their competitive life, some were sold at giveaway prices, and others were left with racing car dealers in part-exchange for more valuable machinery. Many drivers lived to regret these transactions at the start of the 1990s as the price tag of restored B8s stood at around £80,000 and rising!

When Tom Wheatcroft re-opened the Donington Park circuit in May 1977, John Beasley won his class and finished third overall in a historic sports car race driving a B8. Back at Donington almost two years later, the Historic Sports Car Club organised its first race meeting and Chevron B8s had become the most popular choice in the 2-litre class of the Historic Special GT category. Winning the class that day was none other than John Lepp, reliving some of his triumphs of a decade earlier, in a B8. The next car across the line was also a B8, driven by another name from Chevron's past, Rodney Bloor.

Chevrons soon formed the mainstay of a Championship for 2-litre cars and the growing popularity of historic racing brought work to a number of Chevron's former employees, who were able to use the knowledge gained when they worked at the factory to rebuild, restore and repair cars in small workshops reminiscent of the earlier days of Chevron itself. Neil Bailey and Steve Sheldon operated from part of the old factory itself, while Vin Malkie set up premises on a farm in Cheshire to handle some of the increasing business from Chevron owners throughout Europe.

The appeal of Chevrons seemed to go beyond nostalgia and their new owners frequently had no previous connection with the marque at all. It seemed that watching B8s or B16s in historic events kindled the same enthusiasm for Chevrons in a new generation of drivers that the cars had done in their predecessors when they were new. Former drivers whose own careers had pre-dated Chevrons also found themselves attracted to the Bolton-made cars in historic events.

At the end of 1972, 10 years after the crash at Goodwood which ended his Grand Prix career and almost took his life, Stirling Moss arranged to try one of John Bridges' Red Rose/Tergal B21s at Silverstone. He had never driven a modern racing car on wide racing tyres and he was keen to see how he would take to it. Brian Redman was brought in to set some times that Moss could use as a comparison, but the track was slippery and, disconcerted by the car's unfamiliar handling, Moss was considerably slower than Redman. He later denied

CHEVRON

Stirling Moss sits in his B8 awaiting his encounter with Richard Attwood's Porsche 917 at Phoenix Park on 29 August 1982. (*Photo Ian Lynas.*)

that he had been thinking of coming back into racing, but those who were at the secret test day felt that he had hoped to be competitive and believed that he had been too easily discouraged in the difficult conditions.

Eventually Moss made his racing comeback driving a saloon car, but the wheel turned full circle in 1982 when he tried out a B8 belonging to his friend Michael Campbell-Bowling. 'I think it was probably the best-handling car I'd driven. It was absolutely stunning,' says Moss. So he bought the car to contest the historic Super Sports series in Europe. One of the highlights of that year came at Dublin's Phoenix Park when Moss delighted the crowd as he took the Hart-engined B8 to victory after a spirited dice with Richard Attwood's Porsche 917 on a damp track. Earlier that year Moss had taken another popular victory in a Chevron when he shared Tony Gordon's B19 to win a 90-minute Historic Endurance race at Snetterton. Moss later bought and raced a B16, as did rock drummer and avid historic racing car collector, Nick Mason of Pink Floyd.

One of the astonishing things about the new Chevron owners

THE CHEVRON TRADITION LIVES ON

is the way they, too, feel the tremendous loyalty to the marque which was such a hallmark of the company's customers in Derek Bennett's day. Because, in so many ways, Derek Bennett was Chevron, many people felt at the time that their loyalty to Chevron was really a loyalty to, and a respect for, Derek himself. But it seems that Derek put something of himself into the cars he made that is still able to fascinate people today who never met him, or even saw his cars race while he was alive. Kent Abrahamsson and Richard Budge are two examples of this phenomenon among the many people who continue to keep the Chevron tradition alive.

Abrahamsson is a leading Super Sports competitor who had never seen a Chevron until 1986 and began racing in local Swedish events in 1987 with the B8 he bought from Stirling Moss. Since then he has switched to racing a B16 — the Chevron he first fell for — and has added a number of other sports cars to his Chevron collection. In Britain, Richard Budge discovered historic racing in 1980 as an escape from running

Rob Moores became Chevron's first champion of the 1990s when he won the 1990 Toyota Formula 3 Championship in his B38 – the same car that had taken Derek Daly to the BP Championship title 13 years before. (*Photo John Gaisford.*)

his construction company. Vin Malkie prepared his first B8, with which he won the 2-litre Championship, and Richard has gone on to assemble a comprehensive collection of Chevron sports cars and single-seaters, which Vin has restored.

It is not only Chevron sports cars which have had their active lives prolonged through other forms of racing. Many of the Formula 3 cars reappeared in other formulae over the years, such as the budget Formula 4 and Monoposto categories. In 1972 Nick Crossley won the British Formula 4 Championship in an updated B9, and Fergus Tait took the title the following year with a string of wins in another Chevron from the 1-litre Formula 3 era. In 1977 Alex Lowe dominated the same championship in the B20 works Formula 3 car which Chris Skeaping had first raced in 1972. Then when the car became eligible for Monoposto racing, he won that championship in 1980.

Rob Moores was another driver who went into Formula 4, driving the B38 in which Derek Daly won the BP Formula 3 Championship in 1977. Rob won the championship in 1986 with a virtually unbeaten record. In 1987 Toyota GB backed the introduction of Toyota Formula 3, which revived the 2-litre Formula 3 of 1974-80 and brought back numerous B34s, B38s and B43s to join Moores' car round the British circuits.

In the midst of this continuing interest in original Chevrons, the marque's Silver Jubilee was celebrated in a remarkable event at Donington in July 1990. Almost 25 years after Derek Bennett raced the first Clubmans Chevron at Kirkistown, and 12 years after his death, two races solely for Chevrons formed the centrepiece of a weekend of international historic racing. The races, a parade of Chevrons, and a reunion party, brought together family and friends of Derek Bennett, past employees of Chevron, and drivers past and present in an emotional tribute to Derek's memory.

The highlight of the meeting was the return from America of Brian Redman, who brought with him the B19 which he races regularly in historic events in the States, and won the Chevron sports car race in an evocative demonstration of his driving talents. Twenty years after his sensational, championship-winning victory at Spa in the prototype of the B19, there could have been no more fitting a winner than Brian Redman. Chevron's fairy tale scriptwriter seems to be still in business and Derek Bennett's cars continue to provide a living tribute to his genius.

APPENDIX 1

Chevron Type Numbers

THE quantity given for the production of each model is based on the chassis numbers allocated. In some cases damaged cars were rebuilt and given new chassis numbers, while in others customers were supplied with replacement chassis, or monocoques, with no new chassis number being allocated. New chassis numbers were also allocated in some instances when cars were updated, most notably when B16s were converted to B19s or B21s. The engines referred to are those originally supplied with the cars.

B1
Clubmans Formula
Year of Manufacture: 1965
Number built: 2
Engine: 1500cc Ford
Race début: 3 July 1965, Kirkistown, Derek Bennett
First win: 3 July 1965, Kirkistown, 1st overall and in class, Derek Bennett

B2
Clubmans Formula
Year of Manufacture: 1966
Number built: 4
Engines: 1500cc Ford (3)
         1000cc BMC (1)

B3
GT
Year of Manufacture: 1966
Number built: 2
Engine: 1598cc Ford twin-cam
Race début: 23 July 1966, Oulton Park, Digby Martland
First win: 23 July 1966, Oulton Park, 1st overall Sports and GT race, Digby Martland

B4
GT
Year of Manufacture: 1966
Number built: 1
Engine: 1991cc BMW
Race début: 6 August 1966, Crystal Palace, Derek Bennett
First win: 6 August 1966, Crystal Palace, 1st class GT race, Derek Bennett

B5
GT
Year of Manufacture: 1967
Number built: 1
Engine: 1938cc BRM V8
Race début: 1 April 1967, Oulton Park, Brian Redman
First win: 1 April 1967, Oulton Park, 1st class *Formule Libre* race, Brian Redman

B6
GT
Year of Manufacture: 1967
Number built: 7
Engines: 1598cc Ford twin-cam (1)
         1991cc BMW (6)
Race début: 16 April 1967, Brands Hatch, Digby Martland (BMW) and Peter Taggart (Ford)
First win: 16 April 1967, Brands Hatch, 1st overall GT race, Digby Martland

B7
Formula 3
Year of Manufacture: 1967
Number built: 1
Engine: 1000cc Lucas
Race début: 8 October 1967, Brands Hatch, Peter Gethin
Best result: 4th, 29 October 1967, Brands Hatch, Peter Gethin

CHEVRON

B8
GT/Group 4 Sports Car
Year of Manufacture: 1968-1970
Number built: 44
Engines: 1991cc BMW (34)
 1598cc Cosworth FVA (5)
 1598cc Ford twin-cam (1)
 1600cc BMW (1)
 1998cc Climax (1)
 2700cc Climax (1)
 1790cc Cosworth FVC (1)
Race début: 3 March 1968, Cadwell Park, John Bridges
First win: 30 March 1968, Silverstone, 1st overall GT race, Phil Silverston

B9
Formula 3
Year of Manufacture: 1968
Number built: 8
Engine: 1000cc
Race début: 31 March 1968, Barcelona, Chris Williams
First win: 2 June 1968, Brands Hatch, Tim Schenken

B9B
Formula 3
Year of Manufacture: 1968
Number built: 1
Engine: 1000cc
Race début: 2 September 1968, Brands Hatch, Peter Gethin
First win: 2 September 1968, Brands Hatch, Peter Gethin

B10
Formula 2/Libre
Year of Manufacture: 1968
Number built: 2
Engine: 1598cc Cosworth FVA
Race début: 7 April 1968, Hockenheim, Peter Gethin
Best F2 result: 4th, Pau, 21 April 1968, Peter Gethin
First win: 25 May 1969, Silverstone, Single-Seater race, Graham Eden

B12
GT
Year of Manufacture: 1968
Number built: 1
Engine: 2996cc Repco 640 V8
Race début: 4 May 1968, Silverstone, John Woolfe
First win: 4 May 1968, Silverstone, 1st overall Sports and GT race, John Woolfe

B14
Formula B
Year of Manufacture: 1968
Number built: 3
Engine: 1598cc Ford twin-cam

B15
Formula 3
Year of Manufacture: 1969
Number built: 14
Engine: 1000cc
Race début: 4 April 1969, Snetterton, Reine Wisell, Peter Hanson, René Ligonnet
First win: 4 April 1969, Snetterton, Reine Wisell

B15B
Formula B/Libre
Year of Manufacture: 1969
Number built: 7
Engine: 1598cc Ford twin-cam (6)
 1598cc Cosworth FVA (1)

B15C
Formula 3
Year of Manufacture: 1970
Number built: 1
Engine: 1000cc
Race début: 26 April 1970, Silverstone, John Ralph
This was the last B15 to be built and was given a 'C' suffix to denote its modified suspension pick-up points and Lockheed brakes)

B16
Group 6/Group 5 Sports Car
Year of Manufacture: 1969-1970
Number built: 23
Engines: 1790cc FVC (18)
 1598cc Cosworth FVA (2)
 2000cc BMW (2)
 2000cc Mazda (1)
Race début: 7 September 1969, Nürburgring 500km, Brian Redman, John Bridges
First win: 7 September 1969, Nürburgring 500km, Brian Redman

B16-Spyder
Group 6 Sports Car
Year of Manufacture: 1970
Number built: 1
Engine: 1790cc Cosworth FVC
Race début: 6 September 1970, Nürburgring 500km, Brian Redman
First win: 20 September 1970, Spa European 2-litre Championship race, Brian Redman

B17
Formula 3
Year of Manufacture: 1970
Number built: 9
Engine: 1000cc
Race début: 27 March 1970, Snetterton, Bert Hawthorne, Norman Foulds
First win: 26 April 1970, Barcelona, Jürg Dubler

B17B
Formula B/Libre
Year of Manufacture: 1970
Number built: 5
Engine: 1598cc Ford twin-cam (4)
1598cc Cosworth FVA (1)
Race début: 19 April 1970, Riverside, Mike Eyerly
First win: 19 April 1970, Riverside, Mike Eyerly

B17C
Formula 2/Libre
Year of Manufacture: 1970
Number built: 2
Engine: 1598cc Cosworth FVA
Race début: 30 March 1970, Thruxton, Reine Wisell
Best F2 result: 14th, 3 May 1970, Nürburgring, Reine Wisell
First win: 13 June 1970, Castle Combe Single-Seater and Sports Car race, Steve Thompson

B18
Formula 2/Atlantic/B/3
Year of Manufacture: 1970-1971
Number built: 13
Engines: 1598cc Cosworth FVA (4)
1790cc Cosworth FVC (1)
1598cc Ford twin-cam (6)
1600cc Cosworth BDA (1)
1600cc BRM twin-cam (1)
Race début: 30 August 1970, Mantorp Park F2, Reine Wisell
First F2 win: 7 February 1971, Bogota, Jo Siffert
First Atlantic win: 20 June 1971, Brands Hatch, Cyd Williams. (The Formula Atlantic car was known as a B18C although there is some doubt as to whether the 'C' suffix appeared on the chassis plates)
Best F3 result: 2nd, 3 October 1971, Snetterton, Barrie Maskell

B19
Sports Car
Year of Manufacture: 1971
Number built: 35
Engines: 1790cc Cosworth FVC (32)
2000cc Abarth (1)
3000cc BMW Alpina (1)
Race début: 20 March 1971, Oulton Park, John Bridges
First win: 20 March 1971, 1st class Oulton Park Sports, GT and Clubmans race, John Bridges

B20
Formula 2/Atlantic/B/3
Year of Manufacture: 1971-1972
Number built: 9
Engines: 1900cc Cosworth BDA-Smith (1)
1930cc Cosworth BDA-RES (1)
2000cc BDA-Hart (1)
1598cc Ford twin-cam (5)
1600cc Cosworth BDA-Richardson (1)
Race début: 20 February 1972, Bogota Formula B, Bobby Brown, Jim Grob
First F2 win: 7 May 1972, Pau, Peter Gethin
First Atlantic win: 6 August 1972, Croft, John Lepp
First Formula B win: 27 February 1972, Bogota, Bobby Brown
Best F3 result: 3rd, 14 May 1972, Silverstone, Chris Skeaping

B21
Sports Car
Year of Manufacture: 1972
Number built: 28
Engines: 1790cc Cosworth FVC (20)
2000cc Cosworth BDA-Hart (2)
2000cc BMW (1)
1300cc BDA (1)
1995cc Cosworth Vega EA (2)
2000cc Hart alloy BDA (1)
Race début: 25 March 1972, Sebring 12-Hours, Hugh Kleinpeter/Tony Belcher
First win: 21 May 1972, Salzburgring, Dieter Quester

B23
Sports Car
Year of Manufacture: 1973
Number built: 26
Engines: 1900cc Smith BDA
1930cc Smith FVC
2000cc Smith FVC
2000cc Schnitzer BMW
2000cc Tecno
2000cc Alfa
2000cc Hart alloy BDA
Race début: 25 March 1973, Vallelunga 6-Hours, 'Amphicar'/Ignazio Capuano
First win: 8 April 1973, Paul Ricard, John Lepp

CHEVRON

B24
Formula 5000
Year of Manufacture: 1972-1973
Number built: 10
Engine: 5000cc Chevrolet
Race début: 29 May 1972, Oulton Park, Brian Redman
First win: 29 May 1972, Oulton Park, Brian Redman

B25
Formula 2/Atlantic
Year of Manufacture: 1973
Number built: 16
Engines: 1600cc BDA
2000cc Smith FVI
1930cc Smith FVC
Race début: 6 January 1973, Cape Town, Peter Gethin, Ian Scheckter, John Love
First win: 8 April 1973, Cadwell Park *Formula Libre* race, Martin Webb
First Atlantic win: 13 May 1973, Oulton Park (non-championship), John Lepp
Best F2 result: 2nd, 12 August 1973, Karlskoga, Peter Gethin

B26
Sports Car
Year of Manufacture: 1973-1974
Number built: 9
Engines: 2000cc Hart alloy BDA
1900cc Richardson-FVD
2000cc Hart 420
1300cc FVC
2000cc BDA
Race début: 3 November 1973, Kyalami 9-Hours, John Watson/Ian Scheckter
First win: 17 November 1973, Cape Town 3-Hours, John Watson/Ian Scheckter

B27
Formula 2/Atlantic
Year of Manufacture: 1974
Number built: 16
Engines: 1600cc BDA
2000cc BMW
2000cc Hart BDA
2000cc Schnitzer BMW
Race début: 10 March 1974, Mallory Park, James King, Chip Mead, wink Bancroft
First Atlantic win: 18 August 1974, Halifax Nova Scotia, Bill Brack
Best F2 result: 2nd, 2 June 1974, Salzburgring, David Purley. (Purley was also 2nd at Enna on 25 August 1974 and at Rouen in a non-championship race on 30 June 1974)

B28
Formula 5000
Year of Manufacture: 1974
Number built: 2
Engine: 5000cc Chevrolet
Race début: 16 March 1974, Brands Hatch, Peter Gethin
First win: 16 March 1974, Brands Hatch, Peter Gethin

B29
Formula 2/Atlantic
Year of Manufacture: 1975
Number built: 27
Engines: 1600cc BDA
1600cc twin-cam
2000cc Chrysler
2000cc Hart BDA
2000cc BMW
Race début: 2 March 1975, Brands Hatch (Atlantic), Alo Lawler, Richard Morgan
First Atlantic win: 9 March 1975, Mallory Park, Richard Morgan
Best F2 result: 4th, 31 March 1975, Thruxton, Hector Rebaque; 14 September 1975, Zolder, Hans Binder

B30
Formula 5000
Year of Manufacture: 1975
Number built: 1
Engine: 3412cc Cosworth Ford V6
Race début: 15 March 1975, Brands Hatch, David Purley
First win: 31 March 1975, Brands Hatch, David Purley

B31
Sports Car
Year of Manufacture: 1975
Number built: 6
Engines: 2000cc Hart 420R
1600cc Ford
Race début: 23 March 1975, Mugello WCM, John Hine/Ian Grob
First win: 23 March 1975, 1st class Mugello WCM, John Hine/Ian Grob

B32
Hillclimb
Year of Manufacture: 1975
Number built: 1
Engine: 5700cc Chevrolet

TYPE NUMBERS

The one-off B32 was originally built as a hillclimb car in 1975 for John Cussins. In September 1979 Brian Redman drove it on the closed public roads of the Isle of Man in a match race against the 750 Yamaha of former World Motorcycle Champion, Phil Read. Here Redman brings the car through Creg-ny-Baa on his way up to the finish at Kate's Cottage. (*Photo Frank Hall.*)

B34
Formula 3/Atlantic
Year of Manufacture: 1976
Number built: 33
Engines: 1600cc BDA
　　　　　2000cc Toyota
Race début: 24 January 1976, Cape Town Formula Atlantic, Tony Martin, Bill Brack
First Atlantic win: 22 February 1976, West Palm Beach Florida, Bobby Brown
First F3 win: 19 April 1976, Zandvoort, Riccardo Patrese

B35
Formula 2
Year of Manufacture: 1976
Number built: 8
Engines: 2000cc BMW
　　　　　2000cc Chrysler
　　　　　2000cc Hart 420R
　　　　　2000cc Swindon BDX
Race début: 11 April 1976, Hockenheim, Willi Lovato, Roberto Marazzi, Jean-Pierre Jaussaud, Juan Cochesa, José Dolhem
First win: 7 November 1976, Suzuka, Jacques Laffite.

(Kim Mather raced a chassis known as a B35D in Britain during 1977 and 1978, which was said to have been built up to Formula 2 specification from the remnants of the prototype B39 Atlantic car which Gilles Villeneuve raced in South Africa at the start of 1977)

B36
Sports Car
Year of Manufacture: 1976-1978
Number built: 21
Engines: 2000cc BMW
　　　　　1598cc FVA
　　　　　2000cc Chrysler
　　　　　2000cc BDG
Race début: 25 April 1976, Monza 4-Hours WSC,

257

CHEVRON

François Servanin/Laurent Ferrier, Piazzi/Cinotti
First win: 5 September 1976, 1st class Dijon WSC, Jean-Louis Lafosse/Jean-Pierre Jaussaud

B37
Formula 5000
Year of Manufacture: 1976
Number built: 1
Engine: 5000cc Chevrolet
Race début: 9 May 1976, Pocono, Peter Gethin
Best result: 2nd, 6 February 1977, Australian GP Oran Park, Peter Gethin. (Gethin was also 2nd at Surfers Paradise on 13 February 1977)

B38
Formula 3
Year of Manufacture: 1977
Number built: 28
Engine: 2000cc Toyota
Race début: 6 March 1977, Silverstone, Beppe Gabbiani, Derek Warwick, Derek Daly, Eje Elgh, Geoff Lees
First win: 20 March 1977, Paul Ricard, Beppe Gabbiani

B39
Formula Atlantic
Year of Manufacture: 1977
Number built: 11
Engine: 1600cc BDA
Race début: 15 January 1977, Pietermaritzburg, Gilles Villeneuve, Tony Martin
First win: 26 June 1977, Donnybrook Rhodesia, Tony Martin

B40
Formula 2
Year of Manufacture: 1977
Number built: 11
Engines: 2000cc BMW
2000cc Chrysler
2000cc Hart 420R
2000cc Ferrari V6
2000cc Swindon BDX
Race début: 6 March 1977, Silverstone, Ray Mallock, wink Bancroft
First win: 24 July 1977, Enna, Keke Rosberg

B41
Formula 1
Year of Manufacture: 1978-1979
Number built: 1
Engine: 2993cc Cosworth DFV
Race début: 1 April 1979, Zolder, Tiff Needell
Best result: 2nd, 1 April 1979, Zolder British F1, Tiff Needell

B42
Formula 2
Year of Manufacture: 1978
Number built: 21
Engines: 2000cc BMW
2000cc Chrysler
2000cc Hart 420R
2000cc Ferrari V6
Race début: 27 March 1978, Thruxton, Beppe Gabbiani, John David Briggs, Boy Hayje, Elio de Angelis, Derek Daly, Jochen Mass, Don Briedenbach, Giacomo Agostini, Keke Rosberg
First win: 28 May 1978, Mugello, Derek Daly

B43
Formula 3
Year of Manufacture: 1978
Number built: 16
Engine: 2000cc Toyota
Race début: 19 March 1978, Misano, Siegfried Stohr; Silverstone, Michael Bleekemolen
First win: 19 March 1978, Misano, Siegfried Stohr

B45
Formula Atlantic
Year of Manufacture: 1978
Number built: 4
Engine: 1600cc BDA
Race début: 4 February 1978, Kyalami, Tony Martin
First win: 23 April 1978, Westwood, Keke Rosberg

B46
Formula Super Vee
Year of Manufacture: 1978
Number built: 1

APPENDIX 2

Major Chevron Successes

The following table lists outright wins and class wins in international championship events, and outright wins only in non-championship international and major national championship events.

Date	Venue	Driver	Car/Engine	Result/Event
GT and Sports Cars				
24 Mar 1967	Oulton Park	John Lepp	1.6 B3-Ford	1st overall, MN GT
27 Mar 1967	Mallory Park	John Lepp	1.6 B3-Ford	1st overall, MN GT
1 Apr 1967	Oulton Park	Phil Silverston	1.6 B3-Ford	1st overall, MN GT
16 Apr 1967	Brands Hatch	Digby Martland	2.0 B6-BMW	1st overall, MN GT
23 Apr 1967	Snetterton	Digby Martland	2.0 B6-BMW	1st overall, MN GT
13 May 1967	Oulton Park	Digby Martland	2.0 B6-BMW	1st overall, MN GT
20 May 1967	Castle Combe	Digby Martland	2.0 B6-BMW	1st overall, MN GT
28 May 1967	Brands Hatch	Derek Bennett	2.0 B6-BMW	1st overall, MN GT
29 May 1967	Crystal Palace	Brian Redman	2.0 B5-BRM	1st overall, Gp6 International
2 Jul 1967	Brands Hatch	Derek Bennett	2.0 B6-BMW	1st overall, MN GT
30 Jul 1967	Silverstone	John Lepp	1.6 B3-Ford	1st overall, MN GT
13 Aug 1967	Snetterton	John Lepp	1.6 B3-Ford	1st overall, MN GT
26 Aug 1967	Oulton Park	Digby Martland	2.0 B6-BMW	1st overall, MN GT
10 Sep 1967	Brands Hatch	Derek Bennett	2.0 B6-BMW	1st overall, MN GT
24 Sep 1967	Silverstone	John Lepp	1.6 B3-Ford	1st overall (1600 race) MN GT
25 Aug 1968	Jyllandsring (DK)	Barrie Smith	1.6 B8-Ford	1st aggregate, Ford Grand Prix
2 Feb 1969	Daytona (USA) 24-Hours	John Gunn/Hugh Kleinpeter/Bob Beatty	2.0 B8-BMW	1st class, 6th overall
13 Apr 1969	Brands Hatch BOAC 500	Reine Wisell/ John Hine	2.0 B8-BMW	1st class, 7th overall, WSC
17 May 1969	Silverstone	Chris Skeaping	2.0 B6-BMW	1st class, 5th overall, Martini International
26 May 1969	Oulton Park	John Lepp	2.0 B8-BMW	1st class, 4th overall, Tourist Trophy
29 Jun 1969	Mallory Park	John Lepp	2.0 B8-BMW	1st overall, Gp4 International
17 Aug 1969	Wunstorf (D)	Barrie Smith	1.6 B8-FVA	1st overall (2-litre race)
24 Aug 1969	Jyllandsring (DK)	Barrie Smith	1.6 B8-FVA	1st aggregate, Ford Grand Prix
7 Sep 1969	Nürburgring (D) 500km	Brian Redman	1.6 B16-FVA	1st overall
5 Oct 1969	Barcelona (E) 12-Hours	Guy Edwards/ Mike Franey	2.0 B8-BMW	1st class, 4th overall

259

CHEVRON

Date	Event	Driver(s)	Car	Result
22 Nov 1969	Cape Town (ZA) 3-Hours	Jack Holme	2.0 B8-BMW	1st class, 4th overall, Springbok
6 Dec 1969	Lourenco Marques (Mozambique)	Digby Martland	1.8 B16-FVC	1st class, 5th overall, Springbok
14 Dec 1969	Bulawayo 3-Hours (Rhodesia)	Peter Gough/ Clarrie Taylor	2.0 B8-BMW	1st class, 3rd overall, Springbok
27 Dec 1969	Pietermaritzburg (ZA) 3-Hours	Denis Joubert/ Clarrie Taylor	2.0 B8-BMW	1st class, 2nd overall, Springbok
27 Mar 1970	Snetterton	John Burton	1.8 B16-FVC	1st overall, RAC
30 Mar 1970	Thruxton	Brian Redman	1.8 B16-FVC	1st class, 2nd overall, RAC, International
12 Apr 1970	Brands Hatch 1,000km	Andy Mylius/ Gerry Birrell	1.8 Gropa-FVC	1st class, 15th overall
19 Apr 1970	Paul Ricard (F)	Brian Redman	1.8 B16-FVC	1st overall, Euro 2-litre
3 May 1970	Hameenlinna (SF)	John Burton	1.8 B16-FVC	1st overall, Euro 2-litre
31 May 1970	Nürburgring (D) 1,000km	Roger Heavens/ Mike Garton	2.0 B8-BMW	1st class, 17th overall
5 Jul 1970	Vila Real (P) 500km	John Bamford	2.0 B6-BMW	1st class, 2nd overall
15 Aug 1970	Enna(I)	Brian Redman	1.8 B16-FVC	1st Gp5, 3rd overall, Euro 2-litre
6 Sep 1970	Nürburgring (D) 500km	Vic Elford	1.8 B16-FVC	1st overall, Euro 2-litre
20 Sep 1970	Spa (B)	Brian Redman	1.8 B16S-FVC	1st overall, Euro 2-litre
7 Nov 1970	Kyalami (ZA) 9-Hours	Brian Redman/ John Hine	1.8 B16S-FVC	1st class, 5th overall
21 Nov 1970	Killarney (ZA) Cape Town 3-Hours	Brian Redman/ Richard Attwood	1.8 B16S-FVC	1st overall, Springbok
29 Nov 1970	Lourenco Marques (Mozambique)	Brian Redman	1.8 B16S-FVC	1st overall, Springbok
6 Dec 1970	Bulawayo 3-Hours (Rhodesia)	Brian Redman/ John Love	1.8 B16S-FVC	1st overall, Springbok
27 Dec 1970	Pietermaritzburg (ZA)	Brian Redman	1.8 B16S-FVC	1st overall, Springbok
2 Jan 1971	Welkom (ZA) 3-Hours	Brian Redman/ Richard Attwood	1.8 B16S-FVC	1st overall, Springbok
4 Apr 1971	Brands Hatch 1,000km	·John Miles/ Graham Birrell	1.8 B19-FVC	1st class, 7th overall
4 Apr 1971	Brands Hatch 1,000km	Andrew Fletcher/ Bill Tuckett	1.8 B16-FVC	1st class, 12th overall
9 Apr 1971	Oulton Park	Chris Craft	1.8 B19-FVC	1st overall, RAC
18 Apr 1971	Paul Ricard (F)	Andrew Fletcher	1.8 B16-FVC	1st Gp5, 13th overall, Euro 2-litre
8 May 1971	Silverstone	John Miles	1.8 B19-FVC	1st overall, RAC
9 May 1971	Spa (B) 1,000km	Tony Birchenhough /Brian Joscelyne	2.0 B8-BMW	1st class, 12th overall, WCM
16 May 1971	Targa Florio (I)	Mike Knight/ Richard Knight	2.0 B8-BMW	1st class
23 May 1971	Salzburgring (A)	Niki Lauda	1.8 B19-FVC	1st overall, Euro 2-litre
30 May 1971	Nürburgring (D) 1,000km	Tony Goodwin/ Ray Nash	2.0 B6-BMW (Redex-RPA)	1st class, 22nd overall
5 Jun 1971	Silverstone	Toine Hezemans	1.8 B19-FVC	1st, Martini Euro 2-litre
5 Jun 1971	Silverstone	Andrew Fletcher	1.8 B16-FVC	1st class, 7th overall Martini, Euro 2-litre

SUCCESSES

Date	Circuit	Driver	Car	Result
10 Jul 1971	Croft	John Miles	2.0 B19 Hart-BDA	1st overall, RAC
11 Jul 1971	Norisring (D)	Clemens Schickentanz	1.8 B16-FVC	1st class, 10th overall, Interserie
15 Aug 1971	Wunstorf (D)	Ed Swart	1.8 B19-FVC	1st aggregate
30 Aug 1971	Brands Hatch	John Miles	1.8 B19-FVC	1st overall, RAC, International
5 Sep 1971	Nürburgring (D) 500km	Brian Robinson/José Dolhem	1.8 B16-FVC	1st Gp5, 9th overall, Euro 2-litre
19 Sep 1971	Thruxton	John Lepp	1.8 B19-FVC	1st overall, RAC
26 Sep 1971	Zandvoort (NL)	John Hine	1.8 B19-FVC	1st overall, Euro 2-litre
3 Oct 1971	Hockenheim (D)	Michel Dupont	1.8 B19-FVC	1st class, 11th overall, Interserie
6 Nov 1971	Kyalami (ZA) 9-Hours	Howden Ganley/Paddy Driver/Mike Hailwood	1.8 B19-FVC	1st class, 3rd overall
28 Nov 1971	Lourenco Marques (Mozambique) 3-Hours	Jody Scheckter/Ed Swart	1.8 B19-FVC	1st overall, Springbok
5 Dec 1971	Bulawayo 3-Hours (Rhodesia)	Mike Hailwood/Paddy Driver	1.8 B19-FVC	1st overall, Springbok
11 Dec 1971	Welkom (ZA) 3-Hours	John Hine/Dave Charlton	1.8 B19-FVC	1st overall, Springbok
9 Jan 1972	Buenos Aires (RA) 1,000km	John Hine/José Juncadella	1.8 B19-FVC	1st class, 5th overall WCM
16 Jan 1972	Balcarce (RA)	John Hine	1.8 B19-FVC	1st overall
7 May 1972	Spa (B) 1,000km	John Hine/John Bridges	1.9 B21-FVC	1st class, 3rd overall WCM
21 May 1972	Salzburgring (A)	Dieter Quester	2.0 B21-BMW	1st overall, Euro 2-litre
28 May 1972	Nürburgring (D) 1,000km	John Hine/John Bridges	1.9 B21-FVC	1st class, 5th overall WCM
25 Jun 1972	Osterreichring (A) 1,000km	Rolf Stommelen/Toine Hezemans	2.0 B21-BMW	1st class, 5th overall WCM
22 Jul 1972	Watkins Glen (USA) 6-Hours	Peter Schuster/Paul Perez Gama	1.8 B19-FVC	1st class, 9th overall WCM
6 Aug 1972	Angola 6-Hours	Roger Heavens/Carlos Santos	1.8 B16/21-FVC	1st overall
13 Aug 1972	Wunstorf (D)	Bob Wollek	1.9 B21-FVC	1st, non-championship
24 Sep 1972	Thruxton 100km	John Burton	1.9 B21-FVC	1st overall
1 Oct 1972	Nogaro (F)	Jean-Pierre Beltoise	1.9 B21-FVC	1st overall, 2-litre race
8 Oct 1972	Montjuich Park (E)	John Burton	1.9 B21-FVC	1st overall, Euro 2-litre
4 Nov 1972	Kyalami (ZA) 9-Hours	Gerry Birrell/Jochen Mass	2.0 B21/B23-Hart BDA	1st class, 2nd overall
18th Nov 1972	Killarney (ZA) Cape 3-Hours	Gerry Birrell/Jochen Mass	2.0 B21/23-Hart BDA	1st overall, Springbok
26 Nov 1972	Lourenco Marques (Mozambique) 3-Hours	Gerry Birrell/Jochen Mass	2.0 B21/B23-Hart BDA	1st overall, Springbok
2 Dec 1972	Welkom (ZA) 3-Hours	Gerry Birrell/Peter Gethin	2.0 B21/23-Hart BDA	1st overall, Springbok
17 Dec 1972	Pietermaritzburg (ZA) 3-Hours	Peter Gethin/Jochen Mass	2.0 B21-BDA	1st overall, Springbok
25 Mar 1973	Vallelunga (I) 6-Hours	G. Morelli/Mauro Nesti	1.6 B21-FVA	1st class, 10th overall, WCM
8 Apr 1973	Paul Ricard (F)	John Lepp	1.9 B23-FVC	1st overall, Euro 2-litre

261

CHEVRON

Date	Event	Drivers	Car	Result
13 May 1973	Targa Florio (I)	'Frank McBoden'/ Luigi Moreschi	1.8 B21-FVC	1st class, 4th overall, WCM
27 May 1973	Nürburgring (D) 1,000km	John Burton/ John Bridges	2.0 B23-FVC	1st class, 3rd overall, WCM
24 Jun 1973	Osterreichring (A) 1,000km	Michel Dupont/ Paul Blancpain	1.8 B23-FVC	1st class, 10th overall, WCM
7 Jul 1973	Estoril (P)	John Lepp	1.9 B23-FVC	1st overall
29 Jul 1973	Luanda 2-Hours (Angola)	Roger Heavens	1.8 B16/21-FVC	1st, Angolan Sports Car Series
3 Nov 1973	Kyalami (ZA) 9-Hours	John Hine/ Ian Grob	1.9 B23-FVC	1st class, 3rd overall
17 Nov 1973	Killarney (ZA) Cape 3-Hours	John Watson/ Ian Scheckter	2.0 B26-Hart BDA	1st overall, Springbok
25 Apr 1974	Monza (I) 1,000km	Pete Smith/ Paulo Monti	1.9 B16/23-FVC	1st class, 10th overall, WCM
25 Apr 1974	Monza (I) 1,000km	Eris Tondelli/ A. Soria	1.3 B26-FVC	1st class, 22nd overall, WCM
12 May 1974	Silverstone	Peter Gethin	2.0 B26-Hart	1st class, 5th overall, Interserie
19 May 1974	Nürburgring (D) 750km	John Hine/ Ian Grob	1.9 B23-FVC	1st class, 8th overall, WCM
17 Jun 1974	Nürburgring (D)	Rafael Barrios	1.9 B26-FVC	1st class, 4th overall, Interserie
30 Jun 1974	Osterreichring (A) 1,000km	Rafael Barrios/ Richard Scott	1.9 B26-FVC	1st class, 7th overall, WCM
1 Sep 1974	Avus (D)	Ian Grob	1.9 B23/26-FVC	1st overall
29 Sep 1974	Brands Hatch BA 1,000km	Peter Gethin/ Brian Redman	2.0 B26-Hart	1st class, 4th overall, WCM
9 Nov 1974	Kyalami (ZA) 6-Hours	John Lepp/ Guy Tunmer	2.0 B26-Hart BDA	1st class, 4th overall, WCM
23 Mar 1975	Mugello (I) 784km	John Hine/ Ian Grob	2.0 B31-Hart BDA	1st class, 5th overall, WCM
6 Apr 1975	Dijon (F) 806km	John Hine/ Ian Grob	2.0 B31-Hart BDA	1st class, 3rd overall, WCM
4 May 1975	Spa (B) 761km	Pete Smith/ John Turner	2.0 B16/23-FVC	1st class, 10th overall, WCM
18 May 1975	Enna (I) 1,000km	G. Gagliardi/ 'Bramen'	1.6 B31-FVC	1st class, 6th overall, WCM
31 Aug 1975	Hockenheim (D)	Martin Raymond	2.0 B31-Hart	1st overall, Euro 2-litre
13 Jun 1976	Zolder (B)	Martin Raymond	3.0 B31-DFV	1st overall, Interserie
15 Aug 1976	Zolder (B)	Martin Raymond	3.0 B31-DFV	1st overall, Gp6, non-championship
30 Aug 1976	Thruxton	Tony Charnell	2.0 B31-FVC	1st overall, RAC
5 Sep 1976	Dijon (F) 500km	Jean-Louis Lafosse/ Jean-Pierre Jaussaud	2.0 B36-Simca	1st class, 7th overall, WSC
10 Oct 1976	Mallory Park	Iain McLaren	2.0 B26-BDG	1st overall, RAC
24 Apr 1977	Monza (I)	Claudio Francisci/ G. Piaccadori	1.6 B26-FVC	1st class, 8th overall, WSC
22 May 1977	Targa Florio (I)	Restivo/'Apache'	2.0 B36-BMW	1st overall
12 Jun 1977	Le Mans (F) 24-Hours	Michel Pignard/ Jacques Henry/ Albert Dufresne	2.0 B36-Simca	1st class, 6th overall
24 Jul 1977	Paul Ricard (F)	Jean-Pierre Jaussaud/Jacques Henry	2.0 B36-Simca	1st class, 3rd overall, WCM

Date	Circuit	Drivers	Car	Result
11 Jun 1978	Le Mans (F) 24-Hours	Michel Pignard/ Laurent Ferrier/ Lucien Rossiaud	2.0 B36-Simca	1st class, 11th overall
10 Jun 1979	Le Mans (F) 24-Hours	Tony Charnell/ Robin Smith/ Richard Jones	2.0 B31/ 36-BDG	1st class, 17th overall, WCM
5 Aug 1979	Brands Hatch 6-Hours	Tony Charnell/ Martin Raymond	2.0 B31/ 36-BDX	1st class, 3rd overall, WCM
25 May 1980	Nürburgring (D) 1,000km	John Blanckley/ Rolf Goetz	2.0 B31-BMW	1st class, 15th overall, WCM
15 Jun 1980	Le Mans (F) 24-Hours	B. Sotty/ P. Hesnault/ Y. Laurent	2.0 B36-Simca	1st class, 17th overall, WCM
28 Sep 1980	Dijon (F) 1,000km	C. Justice/V. Cheli	2.0 B36-Ford	1st class, 3rd overall, WCM
25 Jun 1983	Oulton Park	Vin Malkie/ Richard Budge	2.0 B19	1st overall, Gold Cup, Thundersports
24 Jul 1983	Thruxton	Edward Arundel/ James Weaver	2.0 B36-BDX	1st overall, Thundersports
8 Jul 1984	Thruxton	Ray Bellm/ Mike Wilds	2.0 B36-Hart	1st overall, Thundersports
8 Apr 1985	Brands Hatch	Tiff Needell/ Richard Piper	3.0 B26/ 36-DFV	1st overall, Thundersports

Formula 3

Date	Circuit	Driver	Car	Result
2 Jun 1968	Brands Hatch	Tim Schenken	B9	Lombank
11 Aug 1968	Schleizer-Dreieck (GDR)	Alan Rollinson	B9	International
2 Sep 1968	Brands Hatch	Peter Gethin	B9B	International
14 Sep 1968	Oulton Park	Tim Schenken	B9	Lombank
28 Sep 1968	Oulton Park	Tim Schenken	B9	Lombank
29 Sep 1968	Brands Hatch	Tim Schenken	B9	Lombank
20 Oct 1968	Brands Hatch	Tim Schenken	B9	International
26 Oct 1968	Oulton Park	Tim Schenken	B9	Lombank
4 Apr 1969	Snetterton	Reine Wisell	B15	International
20 Apr 1969	Pau (F)	Reine Wisell	B15	International
8 Jun 1969	Montlhéry (F)	Reine Wisell	B15	1st Equal
13 Jul 1969	Hockenheim (D)	Peter Hanson	B15	1st aggregate
19 Jul 1969	Silverstone	Alan Rollinson	B15	British GP International
1 Sep 1969	Brands Hatch	Reine Wisell	B15	International
12 Oct 1969	Mallory Park	Barrie Maskell	B15	Lombank
19 Oct 1969	Brands Hatch	Reine Wisell	B15	International
26 Apr 1970	Montjuich Park (E)	Jürg Dubler	B17	International
3 May 1970	Brands Hatch	Bert Hawthorne	B17	Lombank
24 May 1970	Brno (CZ)	Jürg Dubler	B17	International
14 Jun 1970	Hameenlinna (SF)	Peter Hanson	B17	International
9 Aug 1970	Karlskoga (S)	Peter Hanson	B17	International
30 Aug 1970	Zandvoort (NL)	Jürg Dubler	B17	International
19 Sep 1970	Oulton Park	Barrie Maskell	B17	Lombank
19 Apr 1976	Zandvoort (NL)	Riccardo Patrese	B34	European F3
13 Jun 1976	Enna (I)	Riccardo Patrese	B34	European F3
27 Jun 1976	Monza (I)	Riccardo Patrese	B34	European F3
15 Aug 1976	Mallory Park	Rupert Keegan	B34	BP
22 Aug 1976	Kassel Kalden (D)	Riccardo Patrese	B34	European F3
30 Aug 1976	Silverstone	Rupert Keegan	B34	ShellSport

CHEVRON

5 Sep 1976	Casale (I)	Fernando Spreafico	B34	Italian F3
18 Sep 1976	Silverstone	Geoff Lees	B34	ShellSport
19 Sep 1976	Snetterton	Rupert Keegan	B34	BP
31 Oct 1976	Thruxton	Geoff Lees	B34	BP
7 Nov 1976	Magione (I)	Riccardo Patrese	B34	Italian F3
20 Mar 1977	Paul Ricard (F)	Beppe Gabbiani	B38	European F3
26 Mar 1977	Oulton Park	Eje Elgh	B38	BP
11 Apr 1977	Thruxton	Eje Elgh	B38	BP
19 Jun 1977	Thruxton	Geoff Lees	B38	BP
24 Jul 1977	Croix-en-Ternois (F)	Derek Daly	B38	European F3
31 Jul 1977	Donington	Eje Elgh	B38	BP
13 Aug 1977	Osterreichring (A)	Derek Daly	B38	Austrian GP F3
29 Aug 1977	Silverstone	Beppe Gabbiani	B38	Vandervell
11 Sep 1977	Brands Hatch	Derek Daly	B38	BP
25 Sep 1977	Mallory Park	Derek Daly	B38	BP
16 Oct 1977	Donington	Derek Daly	B38	BP
30 Oct 1977	Thruxton	Derek Daly	B38	BP
19 Mar 1978	Misano (I)	Siegfried Stohr	B43	Italian F3
6 May 1978	Monaco (MC)	Elio de Angelis	B38	Monaco GP F3
14 May 1978	Imola (I)	Patrick Gaillard	B43	European F3
28 May 1978	Nürburgring (D)	Patrick Gaillard	B43	European F3
2 Jul 1978	Enna (I)	Michael Bleekemolen	B43	European F3

Formula Atlantic

20 Jun 1971	Brands Hatch	Cyd Williams	B18C-Hart	Yellow Pages
4 Jul 1971	Brands Hatch	Cyd Williams	B18C-Hart	Yellow Pages
15 Aug 1971	Mallory Park	Cyd Williams	B18C-Hart	Yellow Pages
3 Oct 1971	Silverstone	Cyd Williams	B18C-Hart	Yellow Pages
9 Oct 1971	Castle Combe	Cyd Williams	B18C-Hart	Yellow Pages
10 Oct 1971	Snetterton	Cyd Williams	B18C-Hart	Yellow Pages
31 Oct 1971	Brands Hatch	Cyd Williams	B18C-Hart	Yellow Pages
18 Mar 1972	Oulton Park	Cyd Williams	B18C-Eden	Yellow Pages
19 Mar 1972	Silverstone	Cyd Williams	B18C-Eden	Yellow Pages
3 Apr 1972	Brands Hatch	Cyd Williams	B18C-Eden	Yellow Pages
6 Aug 1972	Croft	John Lepp	B20-Richardson	Yellow Pages
7 Jul 1974	Thruxton	Dave Morgan	B25-Nicholson	MCD
14 Jul 1974	Mondello Park (IRL)	Patsy McGarrity	B25-Smith	Leinster Trophy, Irish Atlantic
28 Jul 1974	Mondello Park (IRL)	Patsy McGarrity	B25-Smith	Irish Atlantic
10 Aug 1974	Kirkistown	Patsy McGarrity	B25-Smith	Irish Atlantic
18 Aug 1974	Halifax (CDN)	Bill Brack	B27	North American John Player
26 Aug 1974	Mallory Park	Dave Morgan	B25-Nicholson	John Player
8 Sep 1974	Phoenix Park (IRL)	Dave Morgan	B25-Nicholson	Dublin GP, John Player
27 Oct 1974	Snetterton	Jim Crawford	B27-Hart	Southern Organs
3 Nov 1974	Brands Hatch	Jim Crawford	B27-Hart	Southern Organs
9 Mar 1975	Mallory Park	Richard Morgan	B29-Nicholson	John Player
15 Jun 1975	Mallory Park	Jim Crawford	B29-Hart	John Player
17 Aug 1975	Halifax (CDN)	Bill Brack	B29-Hart	Player's Canadian
24 Aug 1975	Mallory Park	Jim Crawford	B29-Hart	John Player
14 Sep 1975	Brands Hatch	Gunnar Nilsson	B29-Hart	John Player

SUCCESSES

Date	Circuit	Driver	Car	Race
21 Sep 1975	Brands Hatch	Gunnar Nilsson	B29-Hart	Southern Organs
4 Oct 1975	Oulton Park	Gunnar Nilsson	B29-Hart	Southern Organs
12 Oct 1975	Thruxton	Gunnar Nilsson	B29-Hart	Southern Organs
19 Oct 1975	Brands Hatch	Gunnar Nilsson	B29-Hart	MCD
27 Mar 1976	Kirkistown	Patsy McGarrity	B29	Irish Atlantic
8 Aug 1976	Thruxton	Phil Dowsett	B29-Swindon	Indylantic
12 Sep 1976	Mondello Park (IRL)	Patsy McGarrity	B29	Leinster Trophy
3 Jan 1977	Bay Park (NZ)	Steve Millen	B35	New Zealand Atlantic
8 Jan 1977	Pukekohe (NZ)	Keke Rosberg	B34-Hart	New Zealand GP Atlantic
16 Jan 1977	Manfeild (NZ)	Keke Rosberg	B34-Hart	New Zealand Atlantic
23 Jan 1977	Teretonga (NZ)	Keke Rosberg	B34-Hart	New Zealand Atlantic
26 Jun 1977	Donnybrook, Rhodesia	Tony Martin	B39	Philips Atlantic
16 Jul 1977	Westwood (CDN)	Keke Rosberg	B39-Hart	Canadian Atlantic
25 Sep 1977	Phoenix Park (IRL)	Patsy McGarrity	B39	John Player
20 Nov 1977	Macau GP	Riccardo Patrese	B42	Formula Pacific
2 Jan 1978	Bay Park (NZ)	Keke Rosberg	B39-Hart	Stuyvesant Pacific
8 Jan 1978	Pukekohe (NZ)	Keke Rosberg	B39-Hart	New Zealand GP, Stuyvesant Pacific
15 Jan 1978	Manfeild (NZ)	Bobby Rahal	B39-Hart	Stuyvesant Pacific
12 Mar 1978	Mondello Park (IRL)	Harold McGarrity	B39	Irish Atlantic
26 Mar 1978	Bay Park (NZ)	Steve Millen	B42	New Zealand Pacific
9 Apr 1978	Pukekohe (NZ)	David Oxton	B34	New Zealand Pacific
23 Apr 1978	Donington	Eddie Jordan	B29-Smith	Irish Atlantic
23 Apr 1978	Westwood (CDN)	Keke Rosberg	B45-Hart	Labatt's North American Atlantic
14 May 1978	Mondello Park (IRL)	Eddie Jordan	B29-Smith	Irish Atlantic
11 Jun 1978	Quebec City (CDN)	Keke Rosberg	B45-Hart	Labatt's North American Atlantic
24 June 1978	Kirkistown	Eddie Jordan	B29-Smith	Irish Atlantic
7 Aug 1978	Hamilton (CDN)	Keke Rosberg	B45-Hart	Labatt's North American Atlantic
7 Aug 1978	Mondello Park (IRL)	Eddie Jordan	B29-Smith	Irish Atlantic
20 Aug 1978	Mondello Park (IRL)	Eddie Jordan	B29-Smith	Irish Atlantic
26 Aug 1978	Kirkistown	Eddie Jordan	B29-Smith	Irish Atlantic
10 Sep 1978	Mondello Park (IRL)	Eddie Jordan	B29	Leinster Trophy, Irish Atlantic
17 Sep 1978	Phoenix Park (IRL)	Harold McGarrity	B39	Irish Atlantic
22 Oct 1978	Mondello Park (IRL)	Vivian Candy	B29	Irish Atlantic
19 Nov 1978	Macau GP	Riccardo Patrese	B42	International
1 Apr 1979	Pukekohe (NZ)	Steve Millen	B42	New Zealand Pacific
28 May 1979	Mallory Park	Jim Crawford	B45-Nicholson	Hitachi Atlantic
24 Jun 1979	Mallory Park	Jim Crawford	B45-Nicholson	Hitachi Atlantic
30 Jun 1979	Oulton Park	Jim Crawford	B45-Swindon	Hitachi Atlantic
8 Jul 1979	Mondello Park (IRL)	Derek Daly	B42-Smith	Irish Atlantic
15 Jul 1979	Donington	Jim Crawford	B45-Swindon	Hitachi Atlantic
29 Jul 1979	Mallory Park	Jim Crawford	B45-Swindon	Hitachi Atlantic

CHEVRON

| 8 Sep 1979 | Oulton Park | Jim Crawford | B45-Swindon | Hitachi Atlantic |
| 29 Oct 1979 | Mondello Park (IRL) | David Lambe | B25/27 | Irish Atlantic |

Formula 2

7 Feb 1971	Bogota (CO)	Jo Siffert	B18	Colombian Temporada
7 May 1972	Pau (F)	Peter Gethin	B20	European Championship
7 Nov 1976	Suzuka (J)	Jacques Laffite	B35-BMW	
24 Jul 1977	Enna (I)	Keke Rosberg	B40-Hart	European Championship
7 Aug 1977	Misano (I)	Lamberto Leoni	B40-Ferrari	European Championship
6 Nov 1977	Suzuka (J)	Riccardo Patrese	B40-BMW	Japanese GP
28 May 1978	Mugello (I)	Derek Daly	B42-Hart	European Championship
4 Jun 1978	Vallelunga (I)	Derek Daly	B42-Hart	European Championship
25 Jun 1978	Donington	Keke Rosberg	B42-Hart	European Championship

Formula 5000

29 May 1972	Oulton Park	Brian Redman	B24	Rothmans European
24 Sep 1972	Riverside (USA)	Brian Redman	B24	L & M North American
21 Oct 1972	Brands Hatch	Brian Redman	B24	Rothmans European
11 Feb 1973	Warwick Farm (AUS)	Steve Thompson	B24	Tasman Chesterfield 100
17 Mar 1973	Brands Hatch	Peter Gethin	B24	Rothmans European
23 Apr 1973	Brands Hatch	Steve Thompson	B24	Rothmans European
13 May 1973	Oulton Park	Teddy Pilette	B24	Rothmans European
27 Aug 1973	Oulton Park	Teddy Pilette	B24	Rothmans European
9 Sep 1973	Oulton Park	Peter Gethin	B24	Gold Cup, Rothmans European
12 Jan 1974	Pukekohe (NZ)	Peter Gethin	B24	Tasman Series
10 Feb 1974	Surfers Paradise (AUS)	Teddy Pilette	B24	Tasman Series
17 Feb 1974	Sandown Park (AUS)	Peter Gethin	B24	Tasman Series
16 Mar 1974	Brands Hatch	Peter Gethin	B28	Rothmans European
28 Apr 1974	Zolder (B)	Peter Gethin	B28	Rothmans European
3 Jun 1974	Zandvoort (NL)	Peter Gethin	B28	Rothmans European
30 Jun 1974	Monza (I)	Peter Gethin	B28	Rothmans European
26 Aug 1974	Brands Hatch	Tony Dean	B24	Rothmans European
20 Oct 1974	Brands Hatch	Vern Schuppan	B24	Rothmans European
31 Mar 1975	Brands Hatch	David Purley	B30	ShellSport 5000 Gp8
6 Sep 1975	Oulton Park	David Purley	B30	Gold Cup, ShellSport 5000 Gp8
21 Mar 1976	Mallory Park	David Purley	B30	ShellSport 5000 Gp8
31 May 1976	Thruxton	David Purley	B30	ShellSport 5000 Gp8
20 Jun 1976	Brands Hatch	David Purley	B30	ShellSport 5000 Gp8
27 Jun 1976	Mallory Park	David Purley	B30	ShellSport 5000 Gp8
30 Aug 1976	Brands Hatch	David Purley	B30	ShellSport 5000 Gp8
7 Nov 1976	Brands Hatch	David Purley	B30	ShellSport 5000 Gp8

Formula 1

| 18 Mar 1973 | Brands Hatch | Peter Gethin | B24 | 1st overall, Race of Champions |
| 20 Sep 1980 | Oulton Park | Jim Crawford | B45-BDX | 1st overall, Aurora British F1 |

Championship Titles

1967	BRSCC National Clubmans	Howard Heerey	B2
1967	*Motoring News* Special GT	John Lepp	B3
1968	Lombank Formula 3	Tim Schenken	[1]B9
1969	RAC British Sports Car	John Lepp	B8
1970	European 2-litre Sports Car	Chevron Cars	B16/B16-Spyder

SUCCESSES

Year	Series	Driver	Car
1970	South African Springbok Trophy Series	Brian Redman	B16-Spyder
1970	U.S. Formula B Championship	Mike Eyerly	B17B
1970	BOC Formule Libre	Steve Thompson	B17C
1970	RAC British Sports Car	Trevor Twaites	B8
1971	RAC British Sports Car	John Miles	B19
1972	South African Springbok Trophy Series	Gerry Birrell	B21/23
1972	Canadian Formula B	Brian Robertson	B20
1972	Formula 4 Championship	Nick Crossley	B15/17
1973	Rothmans European Formula 5000 Championship	Teddy Pilette	B24
1973	Angolan Sports Car Series	José Uriarte	B21
1973	Formula 4 Championship	Fergus Tait	B15/17
1974	Tasman Formula 5000 Series	Peter Gethin	B24
1974	Southern Organs Formula Atlantic Championship	Jim Crawford	[2]B27
1975	Player's Canadian Atlantic	Bill Brack	B29
1976	ShellSport 5000 Gp8	David Purley	B30
1976	European Formula 3	Riccardo Patrese	B34
1976	BP British Formula 3	Rupert Keegan	[3]B34
1976	Italian Formula 3	Riccardo Patrese	B34
1977	Stuyvesant New Zealand Atlantic Championship	Keke Rosberg	B34
1977	Ulster Texaco Formula Atlantic	Patsy McGarrity[4]	B39
1977	BP British Formula 3	Derek Daly	B38
1977	Italian Formula 3	Elio de Angelis	B38
1977	AMHEC Formula 4	Alex Lowe	B20
1978	Stuyvesant New Zealand Formula Pacific Championship	Keke Rosberg	B39
1978	Irish Formula Atlantic	Eddie Jordan	B29
1980	Varley Batteries Monoposto	Alex Lowe	B20
1986	Formula 4 Championship	Rob Moores	B38

[1] Includes points from one race win in a Titan
[2] Includes points scored with a March 73B
[3] Includes points scores with a March 743
[4] Includes points scored with a Ralt RT1

267

Index

Page numbers in italics refer to illustrations.

Abarth engine 123
Abbott, Jimmy 28
Abrahamsson, Kent 251
Adelaide 169
Aeromodeller 22
Agnew and Clarke 51, 108
Agostini, Giacomo 227, 258
Aintree 46, 80, 99, 123, 174, 175
Albi 161
Alderson, Derek 32, 33, 37–41, *42*, 43, 44, 216, 220
Alliot, Frederic 247
Allison, Bruce *195*, 196
'Amphicar' 255
Anderstorp 92, 107, 128
Andreason, Roger 245
Anglo-American Racing 159
Angolan Sports Car Championship 261, 262, 267
'Apache' 262
Arab-Israeli War 164
Arch Motors 75
Ardmore Racing 203, 205, 228
Arundel, Edward 248, 263
Ashbourne Grove 215
Ashcroft, Peter 31
Ashcroft, Robert 39, 44–47, 50, 52–54, 58, 62, 63, 73, 75, 223
ATS 189, 199, 233, 242
Attwood, Richard 118, 122, 250, 260
Aurora 266
Austrian GP 213
Autosport 10, 61, 152
Avus 262

Bailey, Neil 249
Baird, Gil 77
Baker, Clive 114
Balcarce 147, 261
Bamford, John 121, 260
Bancroft, Wink 256, 258
Barcelona 90, 125, 148, 163, 254, 255, 260
Barrios, Rafael 179, 262
Basche, Dieter 113
Baty, Team 172, 173, 183
Bay Park 199, 265
Beasley, John 249
Beatty, Bob 95, 259
Belcher, Tony 255
Belfast 52, 53
Belgium Racing 113
Bell, Derek 137, 146, 179, 194
Belle Vue 28, 30, 31
Bellm, Ray 248, 263

Beltoise, Jean-Pierre 13, 183
Bennett Specials
 –750 Formula 33, *34*
 –1172 Formula 34, *35*, *36*, 38
 –Formula Junior 38, 39, *40*, *42*, 44
Bennett workshops
 –Broad Street 31, 32, 38
 –Frederick Road 26, 29–31, 33
 –School Street 38, *40*, 44, 48, 49, 54, 55
Bennett, Arthur 17, 18, 20, 21, 24, 25, 37, 215
Bennett, Ethel 17, *18*, 19, 20, *21*, *24*, 25, 215, 239
Bennett, June 11, 17, *18*, 19, 21, 29, 51, 131, 152, 225, 239, 244
Bennett, Wendy see Smith, Wendy
Bennetts, Dick 206
Bilstein 99
Binder, Hans 183, 187–189, 191, 256
Birchenhough, Tony 125, 260
Birrell, Gerry 16, *114*, 116, 117, 148–151, *155*–157, 160, 163, 175, 178, 218, 260, 261
Birrell, Graham 119, 120, 260, 267
Blades, John 79, *81*
Blanckley, John 197, 263
Blancpain, Paul 262
Bleekemolen, Michael *236*, 238, 258, 264
'Blood, Bruce' 29
Bloor, Rodney 44, 46, 53, 60, 65, 71, 83, 84, 135, 249
Blundell Arms 174
BMW engines 64, 65, *75*, 76, 98, 113, 139, 147, 148, 183, 184, 187, 188, 202, 205, 207, 209, 232
BOAC 1,000km 114, 116, 119
BOAC 500 66, 76, 89, 259
Bogota 132, 133, 138, 255, 266
Bolton Royal Infirmary 222
Bonnier, Jo 106
Bosch, Niki 146
BP Superman of the Year 177
Bracey, Ian 247
Brack, Bill 182, 192, 198, 256, 257, 264, 265, 267
Bradford 33
'Bramen' 196, 262
Brands Hatch 13, 15, 16, 35,

36, 43, 61, 63, 66, 68–72, 76, 77, 84, 86, 88, 89, 92, 93, 95, 116, 119, 125, 134, 135, 143–145, 151, 153, 154, 157–160, 169–171, 176, 177, 179, 181, 190, 193, 196, 212, 213, 247, 248, 254–256, 259–266
Bridges, Charles 65, 79, *118*
Bridges, David 7, 65, 70, 80, 99
Bridges, John 66, 77, 79, 80, *81*, 83, 84, 87, 88, 99, 102, 106, *118*, 119–121, 126, 138, 139, 146–148, 161, 163, 177, 216, 218, 239, 244, 249, 254, 255, 261, 262
Briedenbach, Don 236, 258
Briggs, John David 236, 258
British Air Ferries 190
British Airways 1,000km 179, 262
British Automobile Racing Club 152
British GP 84, 94, 181, 213, 263
British Racing Drivers' Club 212
Brno 116, 263
Brown, Albert 28, 33
Brown, Bobby 16, 159, *192*, 255, 257
Brown, Creighton 203
Brown, Paul 242–244
Budge, Richard 248, 251, 252, 263
Budweiser Spyder 244
Buenos Aires 147, 261
Bulawayo 7, 119, 124, 260, 261
Buller–Sinfield, Derek 154
Bullman, Philip 238
Burke, Reverend Charles 17
Burton, John 89, 106, 107, 120–122, 146, 148, 161, 162, 260–262

Cadwell Park 79, 93, 116, 151, 254, 256
Campbell-Bowling, Michael 250
Can-Am *195*, 236, 243, 244, 248
Canary Isles 223, 224
Candy, Vivian 265
Canon Cameras 122, 146
Cape Town 7, 119, 124, 149, 166, 191, 201, 256, 257, 260
Capuano, Ignazio 255
Carden, John 54, 56, *60*
Cardwell, John 50, 66
Casale 264

Castle Combe 96, 135, 255, 259, 264
Castrol 136, 151
Champion 136, 151
Chapman, Colin 39, 43, 59, 61, 68
Charlton, Dave 124, 149, 150
Charnell, Tony 197, 246, *247*, 262, 263
Charnock, Jim 56
Cheetham 17, 30
Cheli, V. 263
Chester Royal Infirmary 36
Chevrolet Vega engine 123, 124, 146–148
Chevron factory 9, 16, 56, 57, *62*, 64, 71, *73*, *76*, 99, *100*, 107, 125, 164, 174, 177, 201, 206, 215, *217*, 220, *221*, 223, 224, *240*, *242*, *243*, 246
Chevron GT 9, 56, 57, *58*
Chevron type numbers
 –introduction of 79, 80
 –B1 49–*52*, 53, 56, 79, 125, 253
 –B2 54, 56, *60*, 69, 70, 80, 84, 125, 253, 267
 –B3 9, 56–*58*, 59, *60*, 63, 66, *67*–69, 80, 253, 259, 267
 –B4 61, *62*, 63, 80, 253
 –B5 7, 65, *66*, 70, 80, 253, 259
 –B6 62, 66–*68*, 69, 70, 78, 80, 125, 212, 253, 259, 260
 –B7 70, *71*, 72, 80, 94, 253
 –B8 7, 10, *73*, 76–*81*, 84, 88, *89*, 90, 95–98, 115, 116, 125, 239, 249, *250*–252, 254, 259, 260, 267
 –B9 83–*85*, 86, 94, 126, 196, 252, 254, 263, 267
 –B9B 86, 254, 263
 –B10 126, *127*, 134, 136, 254
 –B12 *81*, 82, 254
 –B14 94, 254
 –B15 88, 90, *91*, 92–*94*, 95, 116, 128, 239, 254, 263, 267
 –B15B 254
 –B15C 254
 –B16 7, 10, 96, *97*–99, *100*–103, *104*, *105*–109, *110*, 113–118, 121, 124, 129, 130, 137, 141, 218, 249–251, 253, 254, 259–261, 267
 –B16-Spyder 7, *108*–110, *112*, 118, 119, 123, 131, 254, 260, 267
 –B17 116, *117*, 255, 263
 –B17B 133, *134*, 255, 267
 –B17C *128*, 255, 267

268

INDEX

–B18 129, *130*, 131, *132*–136, 255, 266
–B18C 255, 264
–B19 7, 119, *120*, *121*–124, *125*, 126, 133, 136, 146–148, 161, 198, 248, 250, 252, 253, 255, 260, 261, 263, 267
–B20 136, *138*, 139, 144, *145*, 146, 151, 153, 156, 184, 252, 255, 264, 266–268
–B21 138, *139*, 146–*149*, 150, 162, 249, 253, 255, 261, 262, 267
–B23 16, 154, 161, *162*, 163, 164, 166, 172, 178, 196, 197, 239, 255, 262
–B24 8, 13, *14*–16, 139, *140*, 142–144, 146, *154*–159, *160*, 169–*171*, 193, 218, 248, 256, 266, 267
–B25 15, 16, 150, 151, 153–*155*, 160, 161, 164, 168, 174, *175*, 256, 264, 266
–B26 164, *165*, 166, 177–*179*, 197, 248, 256, 262, 263
–B27 168, 172, *173*, 176, 177, 183, 186, 256, 264, 267
–B28 168, *169*, 170, 193, 194, 256, 266
–B29 171, 179–*182*, 183, 186, 191–193, 238, 256, 264, 265, 267, 268
–B30 *193*, *194*, 256, 266, 267
–B31 183, 186, *197*, 246, *247*, 256, 262, 263
–B32 256, *257*
–B34 184, *185*, 186, 189, *190*, 191, *192*, 198–200, 252, 257, 263–265, 267
–B35 184, 186–189, 198, 199, 202–*204*, 205, 207, 210, 211, 257, 265, 266
–B36 196, 197, 238, 247, *248*, 257, 262, 263
–B37 *195*, 196, 258
–B38 210, *212*, 213, *214*, 236, *237*, 238, *251*, 252, 258, 264, 267, 268
–B39 198–*200*, 207, 226, 238, 257, 258, 265, 267, 268
–B40 201–*208*, 209–*211*, 214, 228, *229*, 235, 258, 266
–B41 *221*, 245, *246*, 258
–B42 211, 226–228, *230*, 232, *233*, *234*–236, 240, 241, *246*, 258, 265, 266
–B43 *236*–238, 252, 258, 264
–B45 227, 233, 235, 246, 258, 265, 266
–B46 258
–B47 242
–B48 *241*, 242
–B50 242
–B51 *243*, 244
–B52 245
Chorley Old Road 54, 174, 223
Chorley 218

Choularton, Stephen 174–177, 180, 191
Chrysler 183, 197
Cicale, Anthony 197
Cinotti 258
Clark, Jim, racing driver 39, 46, 126, 127, 159, 169
Clark, Jim, stylist 98, 103, 184, 218
Classick, Brian 47–49, 53, 54, 56, *76*, 77
Clubmans Formula 47, 48
Cochesa, Juan 186, 257
Colmore Depot 25–27, 38
Cosworth 39, 65, 98, 123, 124, 147, 148, 178
Craft, Chris 77, 78, 95, 99, 111, 119, 121–124, 126, 133, 162, 260
Crawford, Jim 173–*175*, 176, 177, 180–183, 220, 221, 238, 246, 264–267
Croft 70, 78, 79, 81, 90, 95, 99, 125, 126, 154, 164, 170, 175, 176, 255, 261, 264
Croix-en-Ternois 213, 264
Croker, Terry 96
Crossley, Nick 252, 267
Crossley, Peter *60*, *81*
Crystal Palace 61, 65, 66, 70, 79, 91, 92, 135, 139, 141, 253, 259
Cullingworth 18, 19
Curl, Bob 114
Cussins, John 257
Cuthbertson, Les 245

Daily Mail 14
Daily Mirror 43
Daly, Derek *212*–214, 226–228, *230*, 232, 235, 241, 251, 252, 258, 264, 266, 267
DART 119–125, 218, 239
Daytona 63, 77, 81, 95, 259
de Angelis, Elio 209, 210, 211, 214, 232, 235–*237*, 258, 264, 267
Dean, Tony 16, 70, 79, 159, 160, 170, 171, 193, 266
Demon Tweeks 56
Deprez, Yves 114
Derek Bennett Engineering 20, 55, 79, 153
Devaney, Bernard 242
Dickson, Nigel 239, 242–244
Dijon 146, 147, 196, 197, 258, 262, 263
Dobbie, Denys 119, 218
Docking, Alan 238, 241
Dolhem, José 186, 189, 257, 261
Domecq 179
Donington 180, 211, 213, 214, 227, 232–234, 236, 238, 241, 242, 249, 252, 264, 266
Donnybrook, Rhodesia 258, 265
Donnybrooke, Minnesota 142

Doodson, Mike 144
Dowsett, Phil 191, 265
Driver, Paddy 124, 261
Dubler, Jürg 87, 116, 239, 255, 263
Duckworth, Keith 39, 98
Dufresne, Albert 239, 262
Dunboyne 53
Dunes Trophy 120
Dunlop 122, 123
Dupont, Michel 261, 262
Durex 245

Earle, Mike 194
Eaton Bray 22
Eccles 28
Ecurie RCS 43, 44
Eden, Graham 134, 245, 246, 254
Edwards, Guy 95, 147, 160, 162, 205, 227, 232, 260
Edwards, Neil 174, 175, 221
Elf 228
Elford, Vic 109, *110*, 111, 119–121, 123, 136, 137, 139, 185, 260
Elgh, Eje 213, *214*, 228, 233, 235, 258, 264
Elkhart Lake 142
Ellice, Bob 134
Enna 109, 148, 172, 173, 187, 196, 207–210, 235, 238, 256, 258, 260, 262–264, 266
Ertl, Harald 173, 183, 187
Estoril 164, 183, 188, 262
Ethuin, Christian 183
Eyerly, Mike 133, *134*, 255, 267

F & S Properties 236
Falkenberg 92
Fangio, Juan Manuel 147
Faulkner, Bob 20, 22, 26, 34, 42, 48, 56, 74, 218
Faulkner, Derek 20, 74, 222, *243*
Fausel, Jutta 137
Fearnall, Robert 212
Felday 91
Fenning, John 89
Ferrari Dino V6 engine 201, 202, 207, 209, 210, 227, 232, 236
Ferrari, Enzo 202
Ferrari, Piero Lardi 202, 209
Ferrier, Laurent 258, 263
Fiorano 201, 202, 207, 209
Firestone 122, 137, 157, 173
Fisons 196
Fittipaldi, Wilson 116, 125
Fletcher, Andrew 119, 260, 261
Flixton Cottage Hospital 17
Ford GP 78, 95, 259
Ford 148, 149, 151, 218
Forge Mill Racing 179
Forghieri, Mauro 202, 209
Formula 1

–British Championship 232, 245, 246, 258, 266
–Chevron project 218–*221*, 245, *246*
–South African Championship 122, 131, 150
Formula 2
–Chevron début in 126
–European Championship 16, 130, 136, 138, 139, 151, 153, 155, 172, 183, 185, 186, 201, 202, 205, 211, 226–236, 246, 266
–John Player British Championship 146
Formula 3
–BP British Championship 181, 189–191, 211–214, 238, 252, 263, 267
–Chevron début in 70
–European Championship 191, 210, 213, 236, 238, 263, 264, 267
–German Championship 185
–Italian Championship 191, 214, 263, 267
–Lombank Championship 83, 85, 94, 116, 263, 267
–*Motor Sport* Shell Championship 116
–ShellSport Championship 191, 264
–Swedish Championship 92
–Vandervell Championship 238
Formula 4 British Championship, 252, 267, 268
Formula 5000
–Chevron début in 139
–North American Championship 143, 157, 158, 195, 266
–Rothmans Australian Championship 195
–Rothmans European Championship 13, 16, 139, 143, 158–160, 170, 266
Formula Atlantic
–Canadian Championship 182, 192, 207, 235, 265, 267
–Hitachi British Championship 246, 265, 266
–Indylantic Championship 265
–Irish Championship 238, 264–267
–John Player British Championship 176, 177, 180, 181, 264, 265
–Labatt's North American Championship 227, 235, 265
–Players American Championship 192, 264, 265

269

CHEVRON

–South African Championship 191, 198, 199, 265
–Southern Organs/MCD Championship 177, 182, 264, 265, 267
–Stuyvesant New Zealand Championship 199, 265, 267
–Ulster Texaco Championship 267
–Yellow Pages Championship 134, 153, 264
Formula B 94, 95, 133, 134, 177, 192, 267
Formula Pacific, Stuyvesant New Zealand Championship 226, 265, 267
Formula Super Vee 242
Formule Libre
–Bob Gerard Championship 51, 53
–BOC Championship 128, 267
Foulds, Norman 255
Francia, Giorgio 186
Francisci, Claudio 262
Franey, Mike 260
Fray, Joe 33, 34
Freeman, Bill 243, 244
Freeman, Geoff 167, 168
Frey, Walter 147
Fuji, Mount 172

Gabbiani, Beppe 213, 214, 227, 236, 258, 264
Gagliardi, G. 196, 262
Gaillard, Patrick *236–238*, 241, 264
Galland, Tony 163
Gama, Paul Perez 261
Ganley, Howden 13, 90, 93, 148, 261
Garton, Mike 260
General Motors 124
Gethin, Peter 13, *14, 15*, 16, 60, 63, 68, *71*, 72, 83, 86, 88, 126, 127, 136–*138*, 142, 144, 146, 150–*154*, 155–161, 163, 164, 168, *169*–171, 178, *179*, 193–195, 198, 218, 225, 236, 248, 253–256, 258, 261–263, 266, 267
Gitanes 186, 187, 189, 192
Goetz, Rolf 263
Gold Cup, Oulton Park 9, 61, 78, 116, 117, 142, 159, 193, 248, 263, 266
Goodwin Racing 94
Goodwin, Tony 125, 260
Goodwood 53, 249
Goodyear 137, 157, 158, 173, 206, 208
Gordon, Robin 9, 54, 67
Gordon, Tony 250
Gough, Peter 260

Grace Hill Motor Works 53
Green, Willie 96
Greenhalgh, Colin 54
Gregg, Peter 244
Grob, Ian 166, 196, 256, 262
Grob, Jim 255
Gropa *114*, 260
Group 8 194, 196
Grovewood Awards 65, 85, 153, 172, 177, 180, 189, 196, 198
Guerra, Miguel Angel 236
Gunn, John 95, 259
Gunston, Team 122, 148–151, 165

Hailwood, Mike 13, 80, 118, 124, 131, 144, 156, 161, 261
Halifax, Nova Scotia 256, 264, 265
Hameenlinna 107, 116, 260, 263
Hamilton 235, 265
Hanson, Peter 90, 93, 116, 148, 263
Harper, Bob 172, 211
Harper, Team 176
Hart 420 engine 178
Hart 420R engine 187, 203, 209, 232, 248
Hart, Brian 37, 38, 99, 123, 124, 148, 149, 151, 157, 177–180, 187, 203, 209, 219, 220, 228, 230, 232
Harvey, Alan 70, 78
Haslam's Mill 57, *76*
Hawthorne, Bert 116, 117, 144, 168, 255, 263
Hayje, Boy 258
Heath, Edward 166
Heaton Park 19, 20
Heavens, Roger 150, 260–262
Heerey, Howard 56, *69*, 70, 86, 267
Hemming, Peter 243
Henry, Jacques 239, 262, 263
Herd, Robin 151, 152
Hesnault 247, 263
Heys Road Secondary School 19, 24
Hezemans, Toine 99–101, 119, *121*–123, 147, 261
Hill, Don 56
Hill, Graham *125*, 133, 181, 182
Hine, John 89, 95, 100–103, 114, 118, 120–122, 124–126, 138, *139*, 146–150, 166, 196, 256, 259–262
Hire, Roger 163, 177
Historic Sports Car Club 249
Hobson, Graham 222–224
Hockenheim 16, 94, 107, 113, 123, 126, 144, 154, 168, 177, 178, 183, 186, 189, 196, 203, 204, 227, 254, 257, 261–263

Holland, Keith 143, 160
Holme, Jack 260
Holmes, Howdy 192, 235
Horrocks, Jimmy 33, 56, 79, 216
Horrocks, Maria 216
Hoskins, Johnny 28
Howlings, Bob 153, 245
Hudson, John 223
Hughes, Derek 167
Humphreys, Tommy 38, 55, 222
Hunt, James 13, 93, 116, 135, 146, 172, 173, 192

ICI 205, 207, 214, 226–228, 230, 232, 233, 235
Imola 100–103, 144, 237, 264
International Trophy 83, 88, 107, 226, 236
Isle de Notre Dame circuit 235
Isle of Man 257

Jackson, David 64
Jackson, Peter 64
Jacobsen, Laurence 245
Jarama 90, 136, 146
Jarier, Jean-Pierre 154, 155, 160, 161, 186, 187, 189
Jaussaud, Jean-Pierre 186, 197, 257, 258, 262, 263
Jim's Snack Bar 32, 33, 37, 40, 216
Johannesburg 7, 80, 118
Johansson, Stefan 242
Jones, Alan 135, 170, *171*, 177, 192, 196, 205, 211
Jones, Richard 247, 263
Jordan, Eddie 238, 242, 265, 268
Joscelyne, Brian 125, 260
Joubert, Denis 81, 260
JPS Victory Race 143
Juncadella, José 125, 146–148, 261
Justice, C. 263
Jyllandsring 78, 95, 159, 259

Kallay, Jack 235
Karlskoga 116, 160, 172, 173, 256, 263
Kassel Kalden 264
Kazato, Hiroshi 172
Keegan, Mike 190
Keegan, Rupert 189, *190*, 191, 264, 267
'Kelly, Paul' 66
Kendal's 215
Kessler, Freddy 238, 246
Killarney, Cape Town 124, 166, 191, 260–262
King, James 256
Kinnane, Gerry 52, 53
Kirkistown 51, 52, 252, 253, 264, 265
Kleinpeter, Hugh 95, 255, 259

Kloden, Ugo 184
Knight, Mike 125, 260
Knight, Richard 125, 260
Koepchen, Peter 113
Kozarowitsky, Mikko 199
KVG Racing 166, 196
Kyalami 80, 102, 118, 122, 124, 131, 146, 148, 149, 165, 166, 179, 200, 256, 258, 260–262

Labatt's 207, 227, 235, 265
Laffite, Jacques 172, 183, 186, 187, 189, 198, 205, 206, 257, 266
Lafosse, Jean-Louis 147, 197, 258, 262
Laguna Seca 157
Lake District 217
Lambe, David 266
Lapeyre, Xavier 183
Lauda, Niki 13, 116, 119, *120*, 146, 148, 260
Laurent, Y. 248, 263
Lawler, Alo 181, 256
'Le Mans', film 114
Le Mans 82, 113–115, 155, 239, 246, 247, 262, 263
Lec 194
Lees, Geoff 189–191, 198, 207, 213, 214, 235, 244, 258, 264
Leinster Trophy 53, 264, 265
Leoni, Lamberto 209–*211*, 211, 266
Lepp, John 9, 10, 59–61, 66, 67–69, 78–80, 90, 95, 96, 101, 102, 116, 121, 122, 153, 154, 161, *162*–164, 177–179, 197, 249, 255, 256, 259, 261, 262, 264, 267
Leslie, David 245
Lewis, John 222, *243*
Lexington, Team 179
Ligonnet, René 254
Lime Rock 143, 233
Linton, Doug 11, 32, *35*, 38, 39, 43, 49, 55, 72, 73, 79, 153, 239
Liverpool 27, 51
Lobden Moor 222, 224
Lourenco Marques 80, 119, 124, 149, 150, 260, 261
Lovato, Willi 257
Love, John 119, 124, 256, 260
Lowe, Alex 252, 268
Lower Broughton 38
Lowry, L.S. 26
Luanda 262
Lucas 91
Lucas, Charles 103
Lucky Strike 122, 148, 149
Lythgoe, Frank 83, 126, 127
Macau GP 211, 265
MacDonald, John 170
Mackey, Pat 232
Magione 191, 264
Mahle 75

270

INDEX

Malkie, Vin 248, 249, 252, 263
Mallock, Ray 203, 205, 245, 246, 258
Mallory Park 16, 41, 45, 51, 53, 67, 68, 84, 86, 94, 95, 127, 132, 135, 153, 159, 174, 180, 181, 194, 197, 213, 246, 256, 259, 262–266
Manchester Ship Canal 17
Manchester 17, 19, 21, 27, 44, 48, 54, 75, 153, 245
Manfeild 191, 199, 265
Mansell, Nigel 232, *233*
Mantorp Park 128, 130, 144, 160, 168, 255
Maranello 201, 202
Marathon Oil 15
Marazzi, Roberto 186, 257
Marlboro 199
Marshall, Chris 172
Martin, Tony 191, 200, 257, 258, 265
Martini International 121, 147, 259, 261
Martland, Digby 9, 57, *60–63*, 65–*68*, 69, 70, 75, *76*, 77, 80, 82, 83, *102*, 103, 114, 115, 212, 253, 259, 260
Maskell, Barrie *94*, 116, *117*, 135, 255, 263
Mason, Nick 250
Mass, Jochen 137, 148, *149*, 150, 189, 204, 205, 227, 228, 258, 261
Matchett, Steve 116
Mather, Kim 245, 257
Mazda rotary engine 113
Mazet, François 133
'McBoden, Frank' 262
McGarrity, Harold 265
McGarrity, Patsy 161, 238, 264, 265, 267
McLaren, Bruce 169
McLaren, Iain 197, 262
McMahon, Derek 212, 227, 230, 242
McQueen, Steve 114
Mead, Chip 256
Meek, Chris 77
Merton Road 17, 19, 20, 29, 74
Merzario, Arturo 109, 110, 120, 138, 146, 149, 162, 210, 235
Metropolitan Vickers 25
Mid-Cheshire Motor Club 35
Midget Racing 28–31, 33
Miles, John 59–61, 68, 69, 72, 83, 85, 119, 121, 123, 124, 260, 261, 267
Millen, Steve 199, 211, 265
Minshaw, Alan 56, 57
Misano 209–211, 235, 237, 258, 264, 266
Monaco 85, 90, 91, 172, 190, 210, 237, 264
Mondello Park 159, 264–266

Monoposto Formula 252, 267
Monti, Paulo 262
Montjuich Park 90, 116, 125, 146, 162, 261, 263
Montlhéry 62, 63, 80, 85, 86, 91, 93, 102, 148, 263
Montreal 235
Monza 47, 76, 170, 171, 196, 197, 210, 257, 262, 263, 266
Moore, Arthur 66
Moore, Ted 181
Moores, Nigel 66
Moores, Rob *251*, 252, 268
Morelli, G. 261
Moreschi, Luigi 262
Morgan, Dave 16, 117, 153, 173, 174, 264
Morgan, Richard 180, 238, 256, 264
Mosport 197
Moss, Stirling 159, 249, *250*, 251
Motoring News GT Championship 9, 66, 67, 69, 78, 96, 259, 267
Motoring News 9, 10, 152
Mountbatten, Earl 84
Mugello 109, 173, 188, 196, 207, 227, 230, 232, 235, 256, 258, 262, 266
Muir, Bob 188
Muir, Brian 66
Mylius, Andy 114, 260
Nash, Ray 125, 260
National Geographic 217
Needell, Tiff 245, *246*, 248, 258, 263
Neerpasch, Jochen 139
Nellemann, Jac 242
Nesti, Mauro 261
Newman, Paul 243, 244
Newsweek 205
Nilsson, Gunnar 181, *182*, 265
Nogaro 176, 189, 207, 233, 235, 261
Norisring 126, 261
North Manchester Hospital 225
Novamotor 91, 238
Nunn, Mo 77, 84, 93, 235
Nürburgring 65, 66, 75, 77, 78, 95, 99–103, 110, 114, 123, 125, 137, 139, 141, 147, 148, 163, 178, 183–185, 196, 204, 205, 207, 227, 228, 237, 254, 255, 259–264
O'Donnell, Hugh 24
O'Donnell, John 19, 22–24
O'Donnell, Michael 24
Obermoser, Jorg 188, 203
Odsal Stadium 33
OPEC 165
Opert, Fred 63, 64, 94, 95, 128, 133, 134, 167, 168, 172, 177, 182, 186–189, 191, 192,

199, 203, 205–209, *219*, 220, 226–229, 233–235, 242, 246
Oran Park 258
Osterreichring 163, 179, 196, 213, 236, 261, 262, 264
Oulton Park 7–10, 16, 34, 35, 41, 42, 44–47, 50, 51, 53, 56, 59–61, 63, 65, 67, 68, 70, 72, 77, 78, 83–85, 94, 95, 100, 102, 108–110, 116–118, 128, 139–143, 146, 158–160, 164, 171, 175, 177, 180, 182, 184, 190, 193, 194, 214, 227, 232, 238, 246, 248, 253, 255, 256, 259, 260, 263–266
Owens, Paul 7, 10, 11, 30, 34, *35*, 37, 39, 40, 42, 44, 47, *49*, 51–55, *62*, 65, 66, *75*, *76*, 95, 102, 103, 109, 111, 124, 130–132, 136–138, 141, 144, 145, 150, *154*, 156, 163, 169, 185, 187, 195, 200–202, 205–207, 209, 211, 216, 222–228, 230, 231, 239–*241*, 242
Oxford University 152
Oxton, David 265

Parker, Bob 28
Parker, Don 9
Patrese, Mario 184
Patrese, Riccardo 184, *185*, 189, 191, 201–*204*, 205–211, 214, 219, 227, *241*, 247, 257, 263–267
Pau 90, 133, 137, 138, 144, 186–188, 198, 205, 228–230, 235, 255, 263, 266
Pendleton Racing Motors 28, *29*, 31
Pennine Hang Gliding Club 223, 224
Pennines 18, 19, 217
Perrot, Xavier 132, 133
Peterson, Ronnie 90–93, 121, 122, 125, 144, 146, 151, 213
Phoenix Park 53, 166, 174, 250, 264, 265
Piaccadori, G. 262
Piazzi 258
Pietermaritzburg 7, 103, 119, 124, 150, 199, 258, 260, 261
Pignard, Michael 239, 262, 263
Pike, Roy 63, 64, 72, 84, 86, 93
Pilette, Teddy 16, 89, 158–*160*, 168, 169, 171, 193, 195, 266, 267
Piper, Richard 248, 263
Pironi, Didier 189, 207, 210, 237
Pitt, George 50
Plastic Padding 213
Plygrange Racing 246
Pocono 258
Prestwich 17, 19

Prince Charles 84
Prost, Alain 228, *229*, 232, 238
Pryce, Tom 172, *173*, 186–188, 205
Publicator Racing 128
Pukekohe 169, 191, 199, 265, 266
Purley, David 96, 135, 172, 174–176, *193*, *194*, 256, 266, 267
Pygmee 91

Quebec City 235, 265
Quester, Dieter 107, 113, 138, 147, 148, 172, 176, 255, 261

Race Engine Services 123, 175
Race of Champions 13, 16, 151, 154, 156–159, 218, 266
Race Organisation Course 183, 197, 239, 247
Racing Car Show 73
Rahal, Bobby 192, 226, 235, 241, 242, 265
Ralph, John 254
Rapid Movements 181
Raymond, Martin 162, 196, *197*, 247, 262, 263
Read, Phil 257
Rebaque, Hector 177, 182, 183, 186, 256
Red Rose Motors 79, 83
Red Rose Racing 56, 85–87, 102, 119, 122, 125, 138, 146–149, 154, 161–164, 177, 218, 239, 249
Redex-RPA 125, 260
Redman, Brian 7, 8, 10, 12, 56, 63, 65, *66*, 70, 77, 80, 89, 99–102, *104*, 106–*108*, 109–*112*, 113, *118*, 119, 122–124, 131, 132, 136, 138–*140*, 141–144, 157, 158, 167, 170, 172, *179*, 183, 185, 191, 195, 249, 252–254, 256, *257*, 259, 260, 262, 266, 267
Rees, Dave 84, 125
Reeves, Ed 153
Regazzoni, Clay 138, 149, 205, 235
Regout, Hervé *246*
Restivo 262
Reynard racing cars 132
Reynard, Adrian 190
Ricard, Circuit Paul 7, 16, 106, 107, 119, 122, 147, 161, 162, 233, 255, 258, 260, 262–264
Rice, Paul 167
Richter, Franz 118
Riverside 143, 255, 266
Rivet Supply Six Hours 247
Rivington Pike 233
Road America 160
Road Atlanta 143, 192
Road car project 218
Robarts, Richard 196

271

Robertson, Brian 267
Robinson, Bill 55
Robinson, Brian 124, 150, 261
Rochdale Caravan Services 43
Rochdale Olympic 41, 42
Rochdale 44, 225
Roe, Michael 242
Rogerson, Roy 54
Rollinson, Alan 53, 54, 77, 83–86, 88, 91, 94, 140, 141, 248, 263
Roos, Bertil 168, 172
Rosberg, Keke 133, 188, 189, 199, 203, 204, 206–*208*, 209–211, 227, 228, 232–*234*, 235, 236, 242, 243, 246, 258, 265-268
Rosche, Paul 207
Rossiaud, Lucien 263
Rothengatter, Huub 241
Rothmans 50,000 144, 145
Rouen 155, 157, 173, 186, 187, 207, 209, 232, 256

Salford Technical College 38
Salford 11, 26, 28, 31, 33, 38, 44, 54, 72, 79
Salzburgring 107, 119, 120, 138, 139, 172, 173, 255, 256, 260, 261
Sandown Park 169, 195, 266
Santos, Carlos 261
Scheckter, Ian 165, 166, 200, 201, 256, 262
Scheckter, Jody 124, 135, 139, 148-150, 155, 157, 158, 261
Schenken, Tim 80, 82–*85*, 86–95, *102*, 103, 131, 142, 163, 196, 254, 263, 267
Schickentanz, Clemens 261
Schleizer-Dreieck 86, 263
Schlesser, Jean-Louis 237
Schnitzer 172, 173, 183
Schuppan, Vern 13, 134, 135, 154, 170, 193, 266
Scott, Richard 94, 179, 262
SDC Racing 180
Seattle 158
Sebring 94, 95, 128, 255
Servanin, François 258
Sheldon, Steve 132, 133, 249
Shell 50, 116
ShellSport 5000 Championship 193, 194, 266, 267
Shierson, Doug 15, 155, 157, 158, 161, 235
Shorthouse, Peter 31, 32, 38, 39
Siffert, Jo 89, 106, 111, 114, *132*, 133, 138, 218, 255, 266
Silverston, Phil 254, 259
Silverstone 66, 67, 70, 82, 83, 88, 94, 107, 121, 147, 159, 176, 178, 181, 183, 189, 191,

198, 201–203, 213, 226, 236, 242-244, 246, 249, 254, 255, 258-264
Silverwood, George 116, 154
Simca engine 183, 247
Simister 215
Skailes, Ian 106, 107, 114
Skeaping, Chris 78, 117, 252, 255, 259
Smiley, Gordon 192
Smith, Alan 137, 149
Smith, Barrie 78, 95, 96, 106, 259
Smith, Geoff 30, 55, 220, 239
Smith, Pete 196, 262
Smith, Robin 196, 245, *247*, 263
Smith, Wendy 11, 18, *21*, 23, 24, 30, 132, 216, 225, 239
Smothers, Dick 95
Snetterton 78, 88, 106, 131, 135, 160, 176, 177, 195, 250, 254, 255, 259, 260, 263, 264
Solar Productions 114
Soria, A. 262
Sotty, Bruno. 247, 263
Southgate, Tony 239–*241*
Spa 80, 111-114, 125, 138, 140, 147, 196, 252, 254, 260-262
Spanish GP 90
Specialised Mouldings 64, 75, 98

Spitzley, Matt 181
Sports 2000 242, 243, 245
Sports cars
 -RAC British Championship 78, 88, 89, 95, 106, 115, 124, 260-262, 267
 -European 2-litre Championship 7, 16, 103-107, 109, 115, 119–122, 139, 146-148, 154, 161, 162, 177, 196, 254, 260-262, 267
 -Interserie 118, 126, 197, 261, 262
 -Springbok Series 7, 80, 81, 102, 103, 117, 118, 122-124, 131, 146-151, 164, 166, 260-262, 267
 -Thundersports 248, 263
 -World Championship 62-64, 66, 76, 77, 82, 89, 95, 114-116, 118, 119, 125, 138, 139, 147, 148, 163, 178, 179, 196, 197, 238, 247, 256-263
Sports Motors 44, 45, 54, 60, 71, 83, 84, 87, 90
Spreafico, Fernando 264
St Felicien 235
St Margaret's Parish School 17, 19
Stalder, Fred 183
Steele, Chris 67

Stewart, Jackie 127, 151, 159, 169, 225
Stiller, Harry 84, 86, 170
Stohr, Siegfried 237, 241, 258, 264
Stoke Mandeville Hospital 148
Stommelen, Rolf 89, 131, 133, 189, 261
Suez Crisis 31, 32
Super Sports 250, 251
Surfers Paradise 169, 258, 266
Sutherland, Richard 197
Suzuka 198, 211, 241, 257, 266
Swart, Ed 122, 124, 261

Taggart, Peter 253
Tait, Fergus 252, 267
Tambay, Patrick 176, 183, 187, 192, 205-207, *219*, 228
Targa Florio 125, 260, 262
Tasman Series 158, 169, 191, 194, 266, 267
Taylor, Clarrie 260
Taylor, Murray *108*
Taylor, Sid 70, 122, 131, 136, 139, 142, 143, 158, 159, 170, 193
TechSpeed 77, 78
Temple, Geoff 125
Teretonga 265
Tergal 138, 146, 147, 161, 249
Thompson, Steve 127, 128, 158-160, 248, 255, 266, 267
Thruxton 89, 96, 106, 117, 128, 154-156, 171, 174, 183, 190, 191, 197, 203, 204, 212, 213, 226, 227, 238, 248, 255, 256, 258, 260-266
Time 217
Times, The 92
Tondelli, Eris 161, 262
Tourist Trophy 95, 259
Toyota Formula 3 251, 252
Trafford Park 18, 25
Trivellato Racing 184, 186, 191, 197, 201-204, 210, 211, 213, 214, 218, 219, 227, 236, 237
Trivellato, Pino 184, 202, 205, 207, 241
Trois Rivières 186, 192
Tuckett, Bill 119, 260
Tunmer, Guy 150, 179, 262
Turner, John 196, 262
Twaites, Trevor *81*, 115, 116, 267

Uriarte, José 267
USAC racing 243, 244

Vallelunga 147, 191, 205, 214, 232, 236, 255, 261, 266
Valvoline 63, 234
van der Straten, Count Rudi 16, 158, 167-169, 194, 195,

244
van Rooyen, Basil 200
VDS, Team 89, 158, 169, 170, 193, 195, 244
Vernaeve, Julien 114
Vestey, Paul 89
Vicenza 184
Vila Real 163, 178, 260
Villeneuve, Gilles 192, 198–*200*, 201, 235, 257, 258
VIP Petrol 47

Walker, Dave 116, 117, 135, 163, 193
Walker, George 223
Warsteiner 188, 199
Warwick Farm 266
Warwick, Derek 198, 212–*214*, 238, 258
Watkins Glen 142, 157, 188, 261
Watson, John 53, 128, 144, *145*, 146, 160, 161, 165, 166, 168, 178, 256, 262
Weaste 30
Weaver, James 248, 263
Webb, Martin 256
Welkom 119, 200, 260, 261
Weslake 98
West Palm Beach 180, 257
Westwood 207, 227, 258, 265
Wheatcroft, Tom 180, 232, 249
White City 27
White, Grahame 152, *154*, 219
Whitefield Model Aircraft Club 19, 22
Whitefield 215, 216
Wilds, Mike 170, 246, *248*, 263
Willars, Dave 20, 26, 45–48, 51, 55, 216, 217, 222, 224
Williams, Cyd 83, 84, *94*, 134, 135, 255, 264
Williams, Ian 188
Williams, Chris 58, 79, 80, 83, 86, 87, 254
Wilson, Dave 87, 88, 95, 119, *125*, 167, 168, 202, 218, 220, 236, 239, 240–244
Winchester 245
Winter Hill 221-223
Wisell, Reine 84, 86–89, 90, *91*, 92-95, 106, 109, 116, 128-131, 133, 254, 255, 259, 263
Wollek, Bob 155, 261
Woolfe, John *81*, 82, 254
Wrigley, Alan 22, *24*
Wunstorf 259, 261
Wylie, Adam 47, 53

Zandvoort 116, 120, 122, 123, 159, 170, 185, 246, 257, 261, 263, 266
Zolder 127, 170, 183, 197, 245, 246, 256, 258, 262, 266